METAGILITY

Managing Agile Development for Competitive Advantage

David A. Bishop

ISBN-13: 978-1-60427-155-3

Printed and bound in the U.S.A. Printed on acid-free paper.

10 9 8 7 6 5 4 3 2 1

Library of Congress Cataloging-in-Publication Data
Names: Bishop, David A., 1970- author.
Title: Metagility : managing agile development for competitive advantage /
David Bishop.
Description: Plantation : J. Ross Publishing, 2018. | Includes
bibliographical references and index.
Identifiers: LCCN 2018044684 (print) | LCCN 2018060229 (ebook) | ISBN
9781604278040 (e-book) | ISBN 9781604271553 (hardback)
Subjects: LCSH: Agile software development. | Competition. | BISAC: BUSINESS
& ECONOMICS / Project Management. | BUSINESS & ECONOMICS / Management.
Classification: LCC QA76.76.D47 (ebook) | LCC QA76.76.D47 .B573 2018 (print)

| DDC 005.1--dc23
LC record available at https://lccn.loc.gov/2018044684

Phone: (954) 727-9333
Fax: (561) 892-0700
Web: www.jrosspub.com

CONTENTS

FOREWORD

JUST IN TIME!

Just in Time. In the movies, it's the firemen arriving just in time to save the home; it's the posse arriving just in time to capture the bad guys; it's the hero arriving just in time to rescue the child. In manufacturing, it's the parts arriving on the assembly line just in time to keep the product rolling. In logistics, it's product arriving just in time to go straight onto shop shelves and bypass the stockrooms.

Like many other information systems professors, I am fascinated by *just in time*. Innovations seem to diffuse in a way that is driven by new technology. But it isn't just tech. My research has shown how it is driven by a rising problem: a demand for new solutions that is resolved by the availability of new technology *just in time*. Only then does the technology diffuse. For example, the aging population is triggering a falling rate of labor participation, placing new demands for workforce productivity. Along comes a wonderful new range of robotics, *just in time*.

In digitalization, *just in time* is the arrival of digitalization right at the moment we need it. Just when urban travel becomes too expensive, along comes ride-sharing (e.g., Uber). Just when medical clinics become too crowded, along comes telemedicine (e.g., MDLive). Just when socializing becomes too risky, along comes social networking (e.g., Facebook).

Just when digitalization becomes too big, too fast, and too furious, Dr. Bishop's Metagility arrives. It's *just in time*.

The success of companies everywhere now depends on their software development skills. It doesn't matter whether software development is outsourced or insourced. It doesn't matter whether the company is manufacturing cars or brokering real estate. Digitalization infects both the product and the production process. Oh, and markets not only demand these large-scale digital innovations, they also demand them right now, *just in time*. It's like a perfect storm forming on the horizon.

So how do companies manage software development projects that can keep pace with this fast-paced, large-scale change unfolding in all walks of human existence? Everywhere, digitalized systems are in development and redevelopment. Everywhere, this development needs to be both really fast and really scalable. In this book, Dr. Bishop shows us how to cope and succeed. His basic idea is simple: harness the inertia. The inertia created by this digitalization is strong; its presence is boundless. If we can make this inertia work for us, instead of against us, we can prevail in profiting from this rushing stream of digitalization.

It takes someone with the background of David Bishop to discover how to do this. He is practiced at this problem. He spent many years managing embedded software development projects in coordination with new product design and manufacturing. He knows the ropes. He has the scars. He also knows how to theorize this problem.

Metagility is as simple as it is brilliant. Use agility not only in software development and manufacturing processes, but also in management processes. Using metagility, management agility can integrate agility into the underlying parallel processes of complex new product development. This integrated agility (which Dr. Bishop calls a hybrid approach) provides a means by which to align difficult-to-coordinate parallel processes, such as iterative software development and large-scale hardware manufacturing. Metagility minds the inertia in each process, channeling each into a vortex that curves slower processes around faster processes until they align. Slow and fast processes meet, without breaking their inertia, *just in time*. It's like a project management wormhole that will look like magic if you haven't read about Bishop's vortex.

Few doctoral students will get through my seminar in evidence-based management without hearing me quote Kurt Lewin, "there is nothing as practical as a good theory." The book you are about to read delivers both aspects of Lewin's Maxim: a theory with practical how-to guidance. Metagility provides a means by which managers can channel the inertia created by digitalization. Smart management of this inertia channel can be used to direct the digitalization into a vortex that can deliver large-scale products, well-coordinated speed, and the quality that those of your customers who are going digital will deserve to get, *just in time*.

Richard Baskerville, Regents' Professor
Georgia State University

PREFACE

In my 25 years of experience as an executive, technical leader, and researcher in technology management, achieving product development deadlines on time and under budget while still meeting market needs is and always has been a perennial struggle for most organizations. This problem is compounded by the fact that the rate of market change and technological innovation have increased exponentially in recent years. The well-known computer scientist and futurist Ray Kurzweil put it best:

> "We're entering an age of acceleration. The models underlying society at every level, which are largely based on a linear model of change, are going to have to be redefined. Because of the explosive power of exponential growth, the 21st century will be equivalent to 20,000 years of progress at today's rate of progress; organizations have to be able to redefine themselves at a faster and faster pace."
> —Ray Kurzweil in *Perspectives on Business Innovation*

In a rush to match the pace that Kurzweil has described, companies and organizations have sought out solutions to get innovative products to market faster and faster. Some of the first of these were lean manufacturing techniques that were first brought forth as part of the widely acclaimed Toyota Production System in the 1970s. Among other attributes, this system resulted in fewer defects and greater customer satisfaction, which led to significant growth in market shares for Japanese auto companies that were once considered incapable of threatening the Big Three. When the original *Agile Manifesto* was developed in 2001, it was very much an outgrowth of these same lean manufacturing and development ideas. Since then, it has become almost ubiquitous in the software industry. Agile concepts are used in some form or another in virtually all software development performed today. One problem, of course, is just that—agile is largely a set of concepts, not a well-defined process, and as such it has often been interpreted and implemented differently across the world. Despite this, there's no doubt of its benefits, and there is no mistaking that agile concepts are here to stay.

However, in keeping with Kurzweil's statement, much has changed since 2001. First, there is more software than ever in our society. In fact, it's in virtually everything. Brick-and-mortar businesses are being supplanted by virtual ones, and from our dishwashers to our homes and cars, they each have far more software in them today than they did in 2001.

Second, we live in a world of hyperconnectivity. Social media platforms, smartphones, and cloud storage allow for an almost immediate exchange of ideas and opinions resulting in much higher degrees of customer empowerment. Customers have a huge virtual megaphone today that lets providers know right away if things are going well or badly for their product(s). When customers are happy, sales can soar into the stratosphere seemingly overnight, but when they are not, the results can be devastating.

Third, development is more complex today with a plethora of devices, platforms, libraries, frameworks, and languages available—many of which may be open source. Technology companies today tend to have larger and more diverse product portfolios than in 2001. Back then, Google was nothing more than a search engine and Amazon was a great place to buy books. Now, both behemoths are much more.

Fourth, agile has worked well for software developers, but other stakeholders within most businesses have faced challenges with it, including business analysts, project managers, and executives. Although iterative development of working software increases productivity, such stakeholders still have a great desire for more certainty around budgets, timing, and what the end product will ultimately be. As agile concepts suggest, interactions are certainly of paramount importance over processes or tools, but all too often decisions and conversations go undocumented. Communication is more challenging than ever due to globalization and geographically dispersed teams. The timing to get technology products to market seems to be getting tighter and tighter every day. To many such stakeholders experiencing these frustrations, much of the promised benefits of agile remain elusive with many companies achieving only incremental gains.

Finally, it's not just about software anymore. Technology development has become somewhat less focused on software or websites and much more so on smart devices. Smart cars, home automation, smart meters, and smartphones are creating the *Internet of Things* that has become the basis for some of today's most innovative advances. Development of these devices is more complex in nature because they are more than just software; they blend in hardware and firmware as well.

These issues present an entirely new set of challenges. How can a single product composed of software, firmware, and hardware that were developed on different tracks be delivered in an agile way? How do you find out just how agile you really are, if at all? How can agile concepts be leveraged to maximize the capabilities of your organization? Most important, can agile help your company become number one in its market?

Over the past several years I have researched these questions in earnest. Out of this work, I found that stakeholders can manage both market and process agility within challenging environments, such as embedded systems, via a hybrid agility implementation and product genesis to achieve the desired result. This is referred to as the notion of *agile vorticity*, the point at which market and process agility collides to produce *business momentum* at a specific point of innovation within the *agile business vortex*.

To put that in plain English, agile has indeed changed since its 2001 inception, and it is being adapted to maximize innovation and time to market in today's most challenging and complex product development. *Metagility* provides a unique playbook and system of measures based on our most successful case studies that can put your organization into hyperdrive and help your company become number one in its market.

ABOUT THE AUTHOR

Dr. David A. Bishop is a technology consultant, enterprise architect, researcher, and instructor with over 25 years of experience working for clients such as AT&T, Bell-South, EDS, Delta Airlines, Toshiba, and government agencies. In addition to this experience, David holds an ABET accredited Bachelor of Computer Engineering degree from the Georgia Institute of Technology, an MBA from DeVry University with a concentration in IT management, and a Doctorate in Business Administration from Georgia State University. David is CEO and Founder of Agile Worx, LLC (http://www.agile-worx.com), a software development firm that provides program and project management tools based on his research. He is a member and committee chair for the International Electrotechnical Commission (IEC) based in Geneva, Switzerland, a member of ANSI, and a Senior Member of the Institute of Electrical and Electronics Engineers (IEEE) and the Association for Computing Machinery. David is also founding chairman for the Atlanta IEEE Technology and Engineering Management Society. Dr. Bishop is the creator of the agile vortex theory, which is the result of years of intensive practitioner research in some of the world's most successful organizations in their respective industries. Its focus was to study how these organizations managed both agile and waterfall techniques to outperform their competition in industries with very high technological change, turbulent markets, and innovation.

David resides in Woodstock, Georgia, U.S.A.

At J. Ross Publishing we are committed to providing today's professional with practical, hands-on tools that enhance the learning experience and give readers an opportunity to apply what they have learned. That is why we offer free ancillary materials available for download on this book and all participating Web Added Value™ publications. These online resources may include interactive versions of material that appears in the book or supplemental templates, worksheets, models, plans, case studies, proposals, spreadsheets and assessment tools, among other things. Whenever you see the WAV™ symbol in any of our publications, it means bonus materials accompany the book and are available from the Web Added Value Download Resource Center at www.jrosspub.com.

Downloads for *Metagility: Managing Agile Development for Competitive Advantage* include:

1. An agile artifact template: Provides a detailed format for creating requirements and user stories with guidance on how to fill in the blanks.
2. A user story workflow infographic: Provides users with a detailed workflow of how user stories move through the development process. It can be used as a training tool and poster.
3. A requirements workflow infographic: Provides a workflow specific to requirements artifacts and could be used in the same way as the user story infographic.
4. An agile metrics calculator: This spreadsheet provides important metrics-calculating tools for project managers or other team leaders.

Part 1

The Need for Metagility

Establishing a New Direction for Your Organization

1

AGILE METHODS TODAY: WHAT HAS CHANGED AND WHY

INTRODUCTION

Agile methodologies have become a popular and widely respected method for managing software development. Since the inception of the *Agile Manifesto*, agile development methodologies have superseded waterfall methodology in many, if not most, software development organizations. Despite its apparent success, however, many organizations have struggled with the adoption and implementation of agile and exactly what level of adoption provides the most agility. Agility is commonly held in the literature to be constructed of elements external to a company or project but, in fact, may be composed of both external and internal elements. The exact relationship of the *adoption* of agile development techniques to a company or organization's *true agility* remains unclear. Crucially, there are no measurements available for each of these factors in an embedded software development context nor is there a method to determine the impact of one against the other. A major reason for the lack of measurements is due to the somewhat amorphous definition of agile itself. In academic literature, the concept is still relatively young and poorly defined. In practice, organizations have largely opted for a hybrid approach to agile, mixing its concepts and method with existing stage-gate or waterfall methodologies. This has made the management of agile even more complex. These issues beg the following questions:

- How do organizations orchestrate and assess agility?
- How is agile best managed in difficult or complex situations?
- How can some of the commonly known shortcomings of agile be mitigated?

- Most important, given the apparent efficiency and performance gains of agile, how can it be leveraged to maximize organizational performance and product success?

Metagility answers these questions by examining multiple dimensions of the issue (agile definition, history, adoption, implementations, hybrid solutions, project/program management) to determine how agility processes are orchestrated (*meta-agility*) in a number of companies *that were successful in leveraging and maximizing agility to become number one in their respective market(s)*. Throughout this book, we highlight one of these case studies in particular. A study of an embedded systems development organization was conducted with twelve managers from hardware, firmware, and software development groups within the company. These managers included product, project, people, and technology managers with direct responsibility for managing agility processes. An innovative form of research, referred to as grounded theory, was utilized to perform data analysis and determine a *central phenomenon* or theory at the crux of the agile question. This research revealed the central phenomenon to be *agile vorticity*—the point at which maximum agility is achieved. This point is reached through the management (meta-agility) of two main subcategories: process and market agility. The relationships of these categories are illustrated with a thought experiment of a whirlpool vortex. Included is an empirical account of how agility can be managed and tweaked for optimum results. In the chapters that follow, we examine market and process agility to determine the success factors for achieving agile vorticity and becoming number one in your market!

We begin by establishing a historical perspective of agility—its evolution and its current state as compared to when it was first developed.

THE *AGILE MANIFESTO* TODAY

The *Agile Manifesto* as it was originally written in 2001 is a set of four now very well-known tenets:

- Individuals and interactions *over* processes and tools
- Working software *over* comprehensive documentation
- Customer collaboration *over* contract negotiation
- Responding to change *over* following a plan

The idea being that while all elements in the previous statements have value, the ones on the left side are valued even more. In this section, we will explore each of these four tenets and how today's environment is influencing them to change.

Individuals and Interactions over Processes and Tools

In 2001, people worked more independently as waterfall processes tended to limit interactions and focus on well-defined goals. Agilists hoped to break this lack of interaction by emphasizing teamwork, but much of this was predicated on colocated teams. As Table 1.1 illustrates, teams today and the communication channels they use are more complex. Many development organizations are distributed all over the world and use a variety of communication methods and tools. With that in mind, tools themselves have become much more sophisticated and user friendly. Many such tools are easily customizable and have agile concepts built in.

Table 1.1 Globalization and technology: illustrates how the agile tenet of *individuals and interactions* has changed since 2001

2001		
Individuals and interactions	OVER	Processes and tools
Today		
Individuals and interactions	PLUS	Processes and tools
Globalization has led to more complex teams and interactions		Today's tools have matured: they facilitate interactions and drive processes
Results of interactions must be documented		Agile is a process

Waterfall was extremely *heavy* with a plethora of burdensome steps and operating procedures designed for CYA (cover your ass!) rather than focusing on creating a great product. On the other hand, some aspects of agile, such as team collaboration, have proven challenging to implement at scale. Although interactions are certainly very important, the lack of process around documenting the outcomes and decisions of these interactions can result in a great deal of *churn*. Churn in this context means burning resources and losing time due to repetitive meetings and rework.

Many organizations have found that today's tools can facilitate conversations and can be used to drive, not inhibit, development. Additionally, they have also discovered that implementing agile itself is a process, even if it is much smaller in scope than waterfall was. The right combination of process and tools can be decisive in the success of your business.

Working Software over Comprehensive Documentation

Older waterfall processes often resulted in cumbersome and exhaustive *word documents* which included requirements documentation, design documents, standard operating procedures, maintenance documents, support documents, and much more. Emphasis was placed on writing many of these documents up front before attempting to build anything. This *comprehensive documentation* tended to inhibit response to change and resulted in a slow-down of innovation and productivity. Documentation is still needed for today's development, but it takes a different form. It is no longer a series of heavy *word documents*, rather it comes in the form of features, epics, user stories, and other artifacts that may be documented within collaboration tools or other applications. Table 1.2 illustrates these differences. As mentioned previously, outcomes of key interactions need to be documented, just not in a process heavy or cumbersome document, but within a lean and easily managed set of tools.

Table 1.2   Products and documentation redefined: illustrates the changing tenets of *working software* and *documentation* today as compared to earlier this century

2001		
Working software	OVER	Comprehensive documentation
Today		
Working product	WITH	Documentation
Products are more complex and are not just software anymore		Artifacts such as epics, user stories, and decision outcomes are documented with tools as opposed to long-form comprehensive documents

The need for documentation is even more critical with today's complex products such as smart devices or Internet of Things (IoT) applications that are created using multiple teams, development tracks, and sub-products.

Customer Collaboration over Contract Negotiation

Contracts are a fact of business life. They aren't going away. Regulatory requirements, idiosyncrasies of specific industries, or the nature of certain products require them. In today's world, contracts and collaboration are not mutually exclusive; in fact, they are anything but. When we discuss contract negotiation, that negotiation within itself is a form of collaboration with the customer. The difference is that this collaboration is not necessarily a one-time thing where all items are discussed and documented up front in a contract, rather it is an ongoing process of communication and alignment.

Collaboration has become more than just talking directly to the customer. Often, the customer may not be able to articulate exactly what they need, and it may require a variety of stakeholders on both the customer side and internal to the development organization to glean succinct requirements and break those down into increments that can be developed into a working product. Table 1.3 illustrates this change.

Table 1.3   Collaboration *is* negotiation: negotiating with the customer, including the contract, is a form of customer collaboration

2001		
Customer collaboration	OVER	Contract negotiation
Today		
Customer collaboration	INCLUDES	Contracts and negotiation
Collaboration happens faster via a variety of internal and external stakeholders		Collaboration and negotiation are one and the same

Responding to Change over Following a Plan

In 2001, *plans* were synonymous with *rigid*. A plan was often considered to be a representation of the final work. Making changes midstream once the plan was finalized was discouraged, and if changes were implemented, it often resulted in a painful approval process and reevaluation of delivery timelines, costs, and performance expectations. A great deal of work was performed up front to ensure that the plan, and the requirements it entailed, were as complete as possible so that developers knew exactly what they needed to do down to the finest detail. Different interpretations of the plan, unanticipated engineering challenges, and inability to accommodate changing customer needs often resulted in failure. Today, markets are simply moving too fast to adhere to this kind of rigid approach. At the same time, there must be some kind of plan to ensure that the company is getting the business value out of the development work that not only makes the customer happy but also satisfies their strategic goals. This means that the definition of a plan has changed. As Table 1.4 illustrates, no longer is it a long, exhaustive document that is full of requirements and design specifications, rather it is more of a vision for the organization. Change is inevitable, but every change must be evaluated against the values and needs of the business.

Table 1.4   Vision versus plan: accelerated market pressures have caused rigid, short-term project plans to be replaced by more flexible, long-term visions

2001		
Responding to change	OVER	Following a plan
Today		
Responding to change	WHILE	Following a vision
Change must always be evaluated for business value and adherence to strategic goals		Plans have been replaced by visions

Now that we understand how the *Agile Manifesto* has changed from a practitioner standpoint, let's take a look at what the business research says about the topic.

AGILE MANAGEMENT TODAY: A RESEARCH PERSPECTIVE

The management of agile methodologies can be a challenge to organizations on many levels. The first issue is the concept of agile itself. The current research literature on agility is sparse, particularly in relation to information systems development (ISD). This is largely due to the fact that agile is a relatively new concept in an ISD context and is therefore not entirely solidified. It is, in essence, a set of concepts or ideas, not necessarily a methodology or framework of its own. The second challenge is the management of agility. Most agile-based frameworks available today are operational in nature, focusing on project management indicators such as velocity, release frequency, sprint completion, and so forth (Highsmith, 2010). Still, other methods focus entirely on the outcome of agile adoption in relation to environmental turbulence (Yauch, 2011). This type of study, however, does not allow for the evaluation of the adoption of agile principles, such as people over processes and tools, against quality and customer responsiveness. Giachetti holds that the assessment and management of agile should not only consider performance, but agile characteristics that have been assimilated into the organization (Giachetti et al., 2003). Although there have been methods describing agile adoption, none of these has related the level of adoption to agility outcomes. As a result, these existing methods do not completely address all dimensions of agility. These challenges are compounded by the fact that recent research has revealed that most organizations have not adopted agile in its entirety, but instead have assimilated a variety of agile concepts and methods into existing traditional methods. Such *hybrid agile* implementations have only added to the complexity of agility management.

Orchestration of agility within any organization is often poorly defined, due to its fluid, quickly changing, and somewhat amorphous concepts, processes, and methodologies. Hybrid implementations, environment specific assessments, and varying degrees of market turbulence are just a few dimensions of agility that should be considered within a management context. In short, the management of agile methods requires their own brand of agility. Our goal from a research perspective was to examine our case studies against the various dimensions of this agility to determine how agile processes are typically managed and orchestrated.

WHY ARE AGILE METHODS AND AGILITY CONCEPTS SO CRITICAL TO BUSINESS SUCCESS NOW?

The short answer to that question is that it is becoming increasingly difficult to stay ahead. Technology today is changing at an ever-accelerating rate. In his essay "The Law of Accelerating Returns," futurist Ray Kurzweil said that this rate of acceleration is occurring exponentially and could eventually result in "technological change so rapid and profound it represents a rupture in the fabric of human history." We see evidence of this change in our everyday lives, not just in technology. Companies must work harder and harder to keep up, tweaking ever more agility out of their processes and teams.

Hyper-Accelerated Markets

Many case studies in our research experienced *hyper-accelerated markets*, which created some very unique conditions. One of these conditions is what is referred to as an *agile vortex* or *whirlpool*. Agile vortices are created when extreme levels of market pressure are torqued by high innovation or quickly evolving technology. This provided an excellent laboratory under which it was possible to observe how a company achieved *optimum* performance, or essentially *agile nirvana* in today's most challenging markets. This phenomenon is referred to as reaching the point of *agile vorticity*, which will be explained in a later chapter.

How these hyper-accelerated markets take shape can be illustrated by close examination of one of our cases studies. In this case, the technology developers were in the smart grid market, developing smart meters for power utilities that wanted to upgrade their grids to the latest *green technologies*. These are the same kind of meters that you may find on the side of your house or business; the difference is they are automated, more accurate, and in most cases communicate wirelessly without the need to send out technicians to read them. Not only do smart meters save money and protect the environment, they provide greater security as well. The subject of our case study faced several challenges which could be summarized in the following ways.

Extreme Innovation

1. *Carrier and networking technology was rapidly changing*: From low power radio frequency (RF) signals to cellular to power line carrier, there are a host of communication methods that could be used to transport meter data from the field to the utility. Adopting the best technology could make or break a company. Our case study had invested deeply into RF mesh networking technology and was constantly faced with new threats.

2. *Meter capabilities dramatically increasing*: Originally fairly dumb devices, electric, gas, and water meters were acquiring the ability to manage smart devices throughout the home, communicate pricing to customers, and gather detailed event and power data. In many ways, the growing capabilities of the available technologies were outpacing the company's ability to get them tested and implemented—not to mention the fact that competitors were in the same race. The same thing was happening, and in fact still is happening, with other IoT solutions. Our case study was rushing to create the most intelligent smart meters of all!

Extreme Market Pressure

The customers for the subject of this case study were power utilities. In many cases, governments in many parts of the world provided these utilities with incentives to switch to smart meters. At the same time, these smart meters had a long life span of 10 to 20 years, thus, once a utility selected a vendor, that customer would be out of the market for quite a long time. There were several start-up smart metering vendors and only a fixed number of *big utilities*. This created a *land grab* situation where each vendor was rushing to capture as many big utilities as they could. Whoever managed to garner the largest chunk of early market shares would dominate the market for a LONG time. This combination of incentives, long-term contracts, and limited customer base resulted in extremely high market pressure.

Combined, these extremes of market pressure and innovation created a hyper-accelerated market. One in which innovation and market pressure are so great that they result in a virtual hurricane for vendors to navigate.

What Is the Solution?

Transitioning to, adopting, and implementing agile methodologies in a software organization is a costly and time-consuming proposition. Companies and organizations need to know where they stand in terms of adoption/assimilation and its impact to the external agility of the business. They also need a framework to manage their performance so that strategic adjustments can be made. We set out to conduct studies that would provide greater understanding with regard to how agility can be managed and the impact of assimilation and adoption on these management processes. As we will see in a review of the latest research literature, most embedded systems environments, such as the one mentioned previously, with larger, more mature organizations, have taken a hybridized approach to agile adoption by combining agile with existing stage-gate methodologies. The orchestration of the processes required to support agile principles in such an environment and the way those principles are affected can reveal new insights into agility in new and different contexts. Such contexts include:

- Large teams,
- Geographically distributed teams,
- Hybrid agility evolution, and
- Embedded systems (environments which include the synchronization of firmware, software, and hardware development).

APPROACH FOR BUILDING A NEW DIRECTION

The experience of practitioners such as project managers, developers, testers, program managers, engineering managers, and executives is of the utmost importance. The challenge is gleaning out this knowledge and experience, analyzing it, and producing new knowledge and insights that can be applied in useful ways by other practitioners repeatedly in the same situations. All too often, consultants or other practitioners try to create methodologies or frameworks based on trial and error or completely in a vacuum, relying on their own limited experiences to determine the best path forward. In many such cases, such experts will create an approach that simply matches what they think the client wants, thereby producing a work that makes the customer happy in the short run but produces lackluster long-term results. The best way to approach business problems today is through what we call engaged scholarship. In a nutshell, engaged scholarship is the concept of applying scientifically valid research techniques to solve business problems and develop innovative business solutions.

This technique produces work that is not only scientifically valid, but also appli-cable to a variety of situations and contexts in a repeatable fashion. It does not rely solely on the limited experiences of a few, or on the specific opinions or methods of a small number of consultants. Instead, it takes a holistic view of what is going on in a particular market and produces a solution that, in short, is of much higher quality than approaches that do not make use of business research. In this work, a scientific approach has been taken to ensure that the results have the highest integrity and validity, therefore providing the highest value possible to practitioners in the field. In this section, the approach to devel-oping the theoretical aspects of this work is described.

This research consists of an interpretive case study using a grounded theory analysis. Grounded theory is an innovative form of qualitative analysis that is particularly well suited to studying information systems, technological develop-ment, and innovation in a business context.

The grounded theory approach makes use of the Straussian brand of grounded theory outlined in Strauss and Corbin's *Basics of Qualitative Research: Grounded Theory Procedures and Techniques* (Strauss and Corbin, 1990). Such studies can provide theories arising from the research effort itself, and therefore do not generally employ theoretical frameworks as a lens to examine a prob-lem. However, such studies can use other research to inform the study at hand (Strauss and Corbin, 1990). This case study uses the four basic agile principles mentioned previously, as stated in the *Agile Manifesto*, for this purpose.

This is a participative study that includes perspectives on agile from a vari-ety of stakeholders within the various case study subjects. It examines the nor-mative questions dealing with the management, design, and evaluation of agile assimilation that is specific to embedded systems development. These traits are characteristic of an engaged scholarship effort using design and evaluation research (Van de Ven, 2007). Contributions of the study include:

- An empirical account of how agility principles and methods are orches-trated in embedded software development, and hence, the orchestration of hybrid agility,
- A method or framework for orchestrating agility over time in context, while constantly adapting and fine-tuning it, and
- Greater insights into the drivers of agile process innovation.

Any good study begins with a review of the current research literature in the subject area at hand. In the following sections, important works in the fields of software, technology, and agile development are brought forth for the reader's benefit. This is part of the process of ensuring the validity of what is being done here. In addition, it is also an interesting review of the history of agile and the forces that brought it about. Having a greater understanding of what brought agile development to its current state will enhance our ability to develop future solutions. We begin with an exploration of engineering and software traditions, followed by agility, embedded systems, and the current state of research on each.

THE EVOLUTION OF AGILITY: ENGINEERING AND SOFTWARE TRADITIONS

In the past, there has been much debate as to whether software development is considered to be science or engineering. In the literature, most researchers believe it to be the latter. This perception is due in large part to the difference between the tools that scientists and engineers use. While a scientist may use experimentation; the engineer develops prototypes or demonstrations. In his study on the traditions of computing, Tedre stated that *computer science is an empirical science not based on traditional scientific experimentation* (Tedre and Sutinen, 2008). Over time, software development became more regarded as an engineering discipline as the size and scale of computing projects required larger teams (Tedre and Sutinen, 2008). As a result, the guiding mantra for software engineers and computer scientists is more often considered to be *demo or die,* as opposed to the traditional *publish or perish* employed by so many traditional researchers. These precepts have had a significant influence on the management of large software development efforts. This section seeks to explore the evolution of software development management and how this evolution has been influenced by engineering, science, and innovation.

Although larger teams and more complex development projects have led to software development becoming more of an engineering discipline, this has also led to a need for a more efficient means of management. Early software engineering managers and developers were faced with challenges in design, development, communication, and production. Arguably, the earliest form of software development management is traditionally referred to as the software development life cycle or *waterfall* method. It is also often referred to as a stage-gate method due to its rigid process orientation and the use of *gates* to pass from one phase to another. The creation of this method is most often attributed to Winston Royce—dating back to 1970 when he documented the process he used to develop software packages for spacecraft mission planning (Royce, 1970).

Although not originally intended to be a comprehensive roadmap, Royce's work proliferated throughout other government agencies and became widely adopted within the software development industry. According to Christiane Floyd in her 1992 publication of "Software Development and Reality

Construction," this software development tradition is based on the following precepts (Floyd, 1992):

- Software engineering is produced based on a series of fixed requirements.
- These requirements are provided via an analysis process that is performed before design begins.
- Developers are only responsible for producing a solution that meets these specific requirements.
- Software development is independent of individuals. Developers are considered to be interchangeable resources.
- Communication should be managed and regulated through fixed interfaces.

Floyd argues that while this existing methodology has brought about impressive advances in programming methods and allows for a greater understanding of software development before coding begins, it does not support the subsequent emergence of insights into functionality, implementation, and usability (Floyd, 1992). The need to provide such insights gave rise to a greater usage of the engineering concept of prototyping.

The concept of prototyping, or even rapid prototyping, is not new. Rather, it is a tradition that has been a part of electrical and mechanical engineering for many years. One reason for its success is that it allows for more teleological requirement definitions based on outputs and constraints (Orr, 2004). Back in 1985, many authors believed that prototyping would replace traditional life-cycle methods of systems development (Janson and Smith, 1985). However, a study from this time period does not recommend that. Instead, it performed a comparison of prototyping based on existing engineering practices against proposals to use the same technique in information systems design. This comparison suggested that prototyping should be integrated within existing waterfall processes in order to:

- Verify user requirements,
- Verify design specifications,
- Aid in selecting the best design,
- Assist with various stages of testing and development, and
- Gain approval for new product concepts (Janson and Smith, 1985).

This need for prototyping in software has given rise to iterative software development in which regular demonstrations of incremental components are critical to developing an entire product line.

Manufacturing concepts have also had a significant impact on software development. The concept of lean or *just-in-time* manufacturing became prominent in the 1970s as part of the highly regarded Toyota Production System. Lean development is based on removing any aspect of a process that does not add customer value. At Toyota factories, inventory was kept to a minimum by only manufacturing the necessary products, at the necessary time, in the necessary quantities. In addition, the system included a *respect-for-human* system that allowed workers the latitude to display their capabilities by improving their own work processes (Sugimori et al., 1977). Lean techniques improved the flow of information and materials across the business, focused on market pressure created by the customer, and required an organizational commitment toward continuous improvement. Although lean manufacturing was driven in large part by Japan's need to compete with Europe and America with fewer resources, the concepts became widely adopted in the automotive industry all over the world.

The production control of the Toyota system was referred to as the *Kanban* system, which consisted of a series of order cards instead of computers to manage production (Sugimori et al., 1977). Kanban is yet another outgrowth of the Toyota Production System which has made its way into software development management. Using Kanban, software development organizations have been found to reduce the amount of work in progress. Such lean concepts of value and waste elimination have been found to provide *target and route* for continuous software development improvement, particularly with agile development (Wang, Conboy, and Cawley, 2012). Organizations that employ Kanban techniques have moved away from the time-boxed iteration to more of a *continuous flow*. This has been shown to be especially true in organizations with mature adoption of agile development techniques (Wang, Conboy, and Cawley, 2012).

Agility

Agility originated—in a manufacturing context—primarily as an output of lean or flexible manufacturing (Mathiassen and Pries-Heje, 2006; Kidd, 1995; Dove, 2002). It concerns the economy of scope, as opposed to scale (Dove, 2002). It has been defined as the ability to manage and apply knowledge effectively, to adapt to change (Arteta and Giachetti, 2004; Dove, 2002), and it has been summarized as the capability to quickly respond to market requirements (Ramesh and Devadasan, 2007). The concept of agility was first introduced in a report from the Iacocca Institute (Nagel and Dove, 1991). Other notable research articles include:

- A Hewlett-Packard (HP) agility assessment expands on agility as comprising three factors of speed, range, and ease to assess an organization's ability to respond to change (HP, 2005).

- Agility was defined by Goldman, Nagel, and Preiss (1995) as the ability to prosper in a competitive environment characterized by constant and unpredictable change. This concept was further broken down into four dimensions of agility, which include:
  - Enriching the customer,
  - Cooperating to increase competitiveness,
  - Organizing to control change and uncertainty, and
  - Leveraging the impact of people and information.

Haeckel expands on these dimensions in a different way by enumerating the organizational characteristics that are required to achieve agility as described in Goldman's dimensions.

The speed with which an organization can respond to customer requests, market dynamics, and emerging technical change is seen as a key element. This includes:

- Time to sense relevant events,
- Time to interpret what is happening and assess the consequences for the organization,
- Time to explore options and decide which actions to take, and
- Time to implement the appropriate responses (Haeckel, 1999).

Organizational capabilities, both tangible and intangible, that provide the basis for conducting business and creating change are also considered to be a prerequisite to achieve agility. These include people, technology, processes, and knowledge (Haeckel, 1999).

Adaptability is also essential. How well organizations respond to changing demands, threats, or opportunities depends on their ability to learn and to use flexible processes and products that can be reconfigured without extensive additional costs (Haeckel, 1999; Dove, 2002; Mathiassen and Pries-Heje, 2006).

Agility has perhaps been best described as a solution for maintaining competitive advantage during times of uncertainty and turbulence in the business environment (Sharifi and Zhang, 2001). Further research into the literature reveals that agility is more than a method or an organizational capability. Rather, it is a business philosophy (Highsmith, 2010). As agile concepts champion people over processes, focus should be on the organizations and the individuals that comprise them. Agile *minds* should be quick, resourceful, and adaptable in character. Agile *organizations* should respond quickly, be resourceful, and be able to adapt to their environment (Mathiassen and Pries-Heje, 2006).

Indeed, organizations are complex adaptive systems. Such systems have been defined as being comprised of decentralized independent individuals interacting in self-organizing ways, guided by a set of simple, generative rules, to create innovative emergent results (Highsmith and Cockburn, 2001). Highsmith and Cockburn emphasize creativity over written rules as the way to manage complex software development problems and diverse situations (Highsmith and Cockburn, 2001). It is this style of management from which *organizational* agility is said to have arisen. Additionally, organizations do not think objectively about software development agility (Sheffield and Lemétayer, 2013). Adoptions of agile practices are typically subject to the organizational structure and context. In one study, it was found that developmental organizations—those which focus on adaptation and creativity—were much more conducive to the adoption of agile practices than a hierarchical culture that focused more on command and control (Iivari and Iivari, 2011).

Although the concept of agility has been available in manufacturing for some time, it was not adapted to ISD until the advent of the *Agile Manifesto*. Information systems have brought about a new context and application for agility. The ability of an ISD to support agility has been defined as the continual readiness to rapidly or inherently create change, embrace change, and learn from such change while contributing to perceived customer value. Such value is often characterized as additions to economy, quality, and simplicity. This is accomplished via the collective components of the ISD and its relationships with its environment (Baskerville, Pries-Heje, and Madsen, 2011).

Based on the literature that has been discussed, it can be noted that agile is somewhat conceptually weak from a research point of view due to the number and variation of definitions. In practice, however, it is considered to be defined well enough for *practitioners*—particularly with respect to how they use and combine agile with plan-driven methods (Baskerville, Pries-Heje, and Madsen, 2011).

Agile Software Development Methodologies

Agile is an iterative software development methodology based on self-organizing and cross-functional teams. Although mentioned at the beginning of the chapter, it is reiterated here with reference as interpreted by the research. It is based on the following key concepts derived from the highly popularized *Agile Manifesto* (Alliance, 2001; Vinekar, Slinkman, and Nerur, 2006) that argues:

- Individuals and their interactions are more important than processes and tools
- Working software is more important than documentation
- Customer collaboration is more important than contract negotiation
- Responding to change is more important than following a plan

Using Ward's method, Dingsøyr et al. (2012) identify the seminal works in agile research and many of the key underlying themes. Most of the early research focused on understanding agile concepts. Other key topics included adoption or adaptation, reconciliation between agile and plan-driven methods, and evaluation of adoption issues in environments not conducive to agile. Prior to our study, more research is needed to better define what the core of agile is and its role in architecture and knowledge management (Dingsøyr et al., 2012). Additional research was also found to be needed with respect to examining agile across various contexts such as different projects and organizations.

One such context that demands study includes methods for ISD. An ISD method can be defined as one that *encompasses the complete range of practices involved in the process of designing, building, implementing, and maintaining an information system; how these activities are accomplished and managed; the sequence and frequency of these activities; as well as the values and goals of all of the above* (Conboy, 2009). Such a method is not a set of rules, but an ideal in the sense that it is not expected to be followed literally.

Conboy finds that an agile ISD method should meet the criteria of:

- Flexibility—the ability to create change (proactively, reactively, or inherently)
- Ability to embrace change in a timely manner through its internal components and relationships with its environment
- Leanness—the ability to contribute to perceived customer value through economy, quality, and simplicity from the *customer's perspective*

Agility is the combination of flexibility and leanness with continual readiness. Qumer adds speed, learning, and responsiveness to these criteria (Qumer and Henderson-Sellers, 2008). One problem with current agile method thinking is that some practices are now commonly referred to as agile even though the connection to the concept may be tenuous at best, and even if this link is clear, it may be too simplistic to be considered agile in every context or circumstance (Conboy, 2009). Conboy states that the following steps should be taken to evaluate such practices based on the aforementioned criteria:

1. Evaluate whether certain practices or procedures are agile with respect to long-term sustainability and implementation.
2. Examine the *behaviors* and *outcomes* that contribute to agility.

This idea could be extended by developing assessments to evaluate performance outcomes (Conboy, 2009). Applying such assessments across methods, method variants, organizations, and projects could not only reveal interesting insights, but improve orchestration of agile processes. As we shall see in a later chapter, there are several *agile frameworks* in the market today that would not pass a critical agile assessment.

The integration of agility concepts into ISD has created a number of variations on a theme. These include adaptive systems development, dynamic systems development, test-driven development, and feature-driven development to name a few. By far the most popular of these methods used in the industry today are XP and Scrum (Baskerville, Pries-Heje, and Madsen, 2011). A more recent addition to this list of commonly used methodologies is Kanban.

Scrum, XP, and Kanban

Scrum is more of an agile management methodology with a greater focus on projects, while XP is more of an engineering philosophy concentrated on code management and quality (Wang, Conboy, and Cawley, 2012). Both methods can be, and often are, used in tandem. Weaknesses with XP have been cited with medium- to large-sized projects because of inadequate testing, architectural planning, and documentation—all of which are often required with large complex systems in which the cost of change can be high (Qureshi, 2012). Studies have shown that some shortcomings such as defect rates can be mitigated by extending XP to include more analysis and architectural design—characteristics which look similar to waterfall-based methods (Qureshi, 2012). For the purposes of this study, we are primarily focused on the management aspects of agile and, therefore, the focus will be on Scrum. Another reason for this emphasis is that Scrum is commonly used in hybrid implementations of agile methods. This is mostly because Scrum acts as a wrapper around existing development methodologies and can be used with virtually any existing method (Schatz and Abdelshafi, 2005).

Despite its success, Scrum has been found to present challenges with resource allocation. This has led to a noticeable shift in the industry from agile to lean software development practices (Wang, Conboy, and Cawley, 2012). Kanban is one such process, and it is a less-structured method than Scrum, which focuses on minimizing the amount of work in progress. Instead of using time-boxed iterations, Kanban employs more of a flow by allocating time and resources as they are needed. Software development organizations that have challenges with work estimation and interruptions have been shown to display improvements over lead time and defect rates by using Kanban over the time-boxed method of Scrum (Sjøberg, Johnsen, and Solberg, 2012). A significant area for further research is operational guidance on mapping such lean and agile processes to their current roles and a roadmap for implementing them (Wang, Conboy, and Cawley, 2012).

Successful implementation of an agile methodology has been found to rely heavily on the establishment of many cultural and procedural changes within an organization. The first of these is building a continuous feedback loop to allow for constant replanning (Vidgen, 2009). Shared responsibility by empowering Scrum team members to manage day-to-day work is also important (Vidgen, 2009). A key enabler for self-managed teams is fostering high communication and collaboration on a daily basis. Spontaneous interactions should be supported by structured interconnected practices such as Scrum meetings and pair programming (Vidgen, 2009). A willingness to adapt the process to the development context is crucial, and the development iterations themselves should work toward a sustainable rhythm (Vidgen, 2009). Agile implementation is not limited to the development organization. Product management should also integrate agile methods into their work. This can be accomplished by establishing sprints that alternate with the development teams. Implementing agile in product management as well as in development provides for structured detailing of complex requirements, early collaboration, and disciplined backlog administration (Vlaanderen et al., 2011).

For requirements prioritization, it was found that a mix of agile and plan-based methods proved to outperform either agile or plan-based methods alone in which volatility is not very high or low (Port and Bui, 2009). Since volatility is rarely at the extreme and often unknown, it was inferred that mixed strategies should be the most widely used. However, it should be noted that very turbulent markets or *gold rush* situations could accelerate the volatility or *pull* rapidly. The adoption of such mixed practices has been found to allow for change, driven by close customer interaction, continuous requirements gathering, and frequent iterative delivery (Vidgen, 2009).

Although agile has been noted to increase productivity, foster shared learning, and create job satisfaction among developers (Vinekar, Slinkman, and Nerur, 2006), it may not be the best choice for all environments. The literature as well as practitioner experience shows that successful adoption of agile in its purest form may depend on the following factors:

- Size of the project and team,
- Consequences of failure or criticality of the project,
- Volatility of the environment,
- Skill level of the development team(s), and
- Company culture (Vinekar, Slinkman, and Nerur, 2006).

One example of such an environment—embedded systems development—is impacted by these factors on many levels. Firmware and hardware development teams tend to be much smaller than their software counterparts with a much higher degree of specialization. While there are many software developers in the organization with skills that are easily transferable from one project to another (such as C#, Java, or .NET programming), their firmware counterparts do not share the same level of transferability. Firmware professionals often have very focused knowledge of the embedded systems stacks for home area networking, RF network communication, or metering metrology that inhibits them from being easily inter-changeable. Embedded systems are often *mission critical* systems with high conse-quences for failure. As a result, organizations developing such systems tend to be less comfortable with the higher rates of change that often come with the iterative and potentially chaotic agile development than their software counterparts.

HOW HAVE MOST COMPANIES DEALT WITH THESE ISSUES?

Simply put, technology products are developed using a *process*, and companies usually deal with the issues mentioned in the previous section by implementing a process that is tailored to their organizational needs and market. As we stated earlier in the chapter, processes are here to stay, and agile development is a pro-cess. As we have shown, such processes have changed over the years, beginning with the stage-gate process that came from the space program in the 1960s, to the famed Toyota production system of the late '70s that touted *lean manufac-turing* techniques and the concept of *continuous improvement*. At the dawn of the new millennium, lean manufacturing concepts began making their way into software development in the form of *agile methods*. Today, virtually every ven-dor of technology products—from cell phones to software—utilizes some form of agile to create and bring their products to market. Some of the challenges encountered with technology development processes include:

1. *Productizing innovation*: Technology is constantly changing and ven-dors are always seeking out ways to tweak their process so that they can get new innovative technologies to market quicker.
2. *Responding to market pressure*: Customers want the latest technologies and there are always competitors out there that are working just as fast as you are to get those new technologies to market. Often, the first out of the gate will have the best chance at capturing the largest market share.
3. *Overcoming organizational resistance*: Vendors must make the neces-sary changes within their organizations in order for the *improved pro-cess* to work. This is often easier said than done.
4. *Maintaining quality*: Customers don't want an inferior product. Period. Quality is defined as giving the customer what they want. Steve Jobs was successful because he had an intuitive sense of what customers wanted—and provided it.

Achieving *Agile Vorticity*

So what have the companies in our best case studies done in this situation? The short answer is that they made specific changes in their process, which allowed them to become #1 in their market. Through a series of organizational and product management changes, they managed themselves into a *sweet spot* which we refer to as *agile vorticity*. As we shall elaborate on in a later chapter, agile vorticity is defined as the point at which a company has achieved maximum agility in its market.

This is important because hyper-accelerated markets are becoming increasingly common and the method of responding to them may become the operational standard for technology developers. Just as our own weather is slowly becoming more turbulent with greater occurrences of hurricanes and tornados, so are markets becoming more volatile.

In the next chapter, we take a deeper look at what the current body of research says about the performance of agile methodologies since its 2001 inception.

2

THE PROBLEM: PERFORMANCE AND LIMITATIONS OF AGILE METHODS

UNDERSTANDING THE PERFORMANCE OF AGILE METHODS IN CHALLENGING SITUATIONS

Pure agile implementations are not always the best option for many organizations. Due to the nature of specific technologies, and their size or complexity, an agile strategy may need to be augmented significantly to work. On the other hand, agile implementation issues may come down to simple organizational resistance. For the agile purist, making these kinds of changes is not necessarily forbidden, but is typically avoided to maximize agility. However, in many situations the roadblocks have proven too significant to overcome by mere dogmatic determination, and compromises have resulted. Before any sort of process improvement or change in methodology can be put into place, it is important to understand how similar concepts have adapted and performed in the past under varying circumstances. Whether we're talking about a pure agile/Scrum implementation in a software context, or a mix of sorts with other approaches in a manufacturing context, it is important to gain an understanding of how agile has worked out in these situations.

The purpose of this chapter is to thoroughly explore what the current body of research has to say about the performance of agile in some of the most interesting situations encountered, including embedded systems development, distributed teams, continuous development, and large, complex development environments. This is followed by an exploration of agile adoption and an argument for advocating a hybrid agile approach. The chapter ends with a discussion on the limitations of the current body of research as it relates to these topics, thereby establishing the need for the approach discussed in this book.

To begin, the following two sections outline the positive contributions of agile methods to information systems development (ISD), and the challenges those methods face during their implementation and management. Understanding the literature with respect to how these facets of agile are managed is important in developing agility measures, controls, and assimilation.

Agile's Positive Contributions

There is almost no question as to the positive contributions of agile development methods. While at times controversial, they are being adopted in one form or another worldwide across a variety of contexts. Agile methods are here to stay, and the perception of the impact of agile methods is predominantly positive (Laanti, Salo, and Abrahamsson, 2011). Much of this successful adoption has been due to the impact agile has had on project performance. Agile has been proven to reduce defect density by a factor of seven and allows projects of six to 12 months in duration to be delivered ahead of schedule with high quality (Fitzgerald, Hartnett, and Conboy, 2006). These improvements in cycle time and quality are the most significant characteristics of agile development that have allowed it to capture the attention of the industry and over the past ten years become standard practice.

The literature has shown that many negative perceptions of agile do not hold up under scrutiny. Contrary to popular belief, agile is not an undisciplined approach. In fact, it has been found to require just as much discipline as traditional methods (Fitzgerald, Hartnett, and Conboy, 2006). Agile coaching has become of bit of a cottage industry with many companies hiring agile managers, trainers, and consultants just to keep them on track with their agile strategy. Setting up regular Scrum meetings, collaborating with customers, and inculcating a system of continuous improvement are anything but undisciplined.

Agility's contributions are not limited to project management and software development improvements. It has also been shown to create improved job satisfaction, productivity, and increased customer satisfaction (Dybå and Dingsøyr, 2008). The practices of sprint planning, daily standups, and retrospectives have been shown to help people function better as teams (McHugh, Conboy, and Lang, 2012). Agile greatly increases the visibility and input for both software developers and customers, and testimonials have shown that they like it. Developers working in an agile environment are not always bound to processes, standards, or predesigned architectures that they do not agree with. This extra latitude encourages creativity and makes even entry-level developers feel like a vital part of the team. Customers get a chance to see the product unfold and provide regular input on their preferences. This process of collaboration often brings forth bugs, design problems, or previously unknown requirements before production, thereby resulting in a higher quality end product.

Additionally, agile methods have been found to positively influence quality, especially in highly turbulent markets where requirements often change. This has been especially true in situations where high outcome controls are used, such as established standards for evaluating project performance. It has also been found to lower software complexity in rapidly changing environments (Maruping, Venkatesh, and Agarwal, 2009).

Agile's Challenges

Despite all of its contributions, agile methodology is not a panacea. Agile can be difficult to introduce into large, complex projects, and having continuous customer input can be unsustainable for long periods (Dybå and Dingsøyr, 2008). Agile can also generate obstacles with decision making, such as commitment, conflicting priorities, unstable resource availability, ownership, implementation, and empowerment. These can result in the absence of strategic roadmaps, lack of team engagement, and an ever-growing backlog of delayed work from previous iterations. This backlog is often referred to as technical debt (Drury, Conboy, and Power, 2012). The high level of empowerment that an agile team often has can result in groupthink or Abilene paradox (Abrahamsson, Conboy, and Wang, 2009). Determining solutions to these obstacles is critical to agile project and team success (Drury, Conboy, and Power, 2012).

For the individual developer, agile presents another set of challenges. Gold plating, or adding features that the customer never asked for, can be a common issue because programmers like to be creative and the autonomy provided by agile gives them this latitude (Baskerville and Pries-Heje, 2004). Agile techniques such as Scrum can put developers *on the spot* and cause them to fear exposure of their weaknesses. Placing two developers to code together, referred to as pair programming, can be one technique to guard against such shortcomings. Also, agile developers must wear many hats, often playing the roles of coder, tester, architect, customer, QA expert, etc. It can be difficult to find people with such a broad skill set, particularly when it comes to the interpersonal or business skills necessary to function in these roles. Taking on such responsibilities often makes it difficult for developers to hone the specific skills required for their job, which may inhibit promotion. Mitigating these issues requires agile-specific policies across the organization. Agile values and principles need to be integrated throughout, and periodic assessments of a team's agility should be conducted using an assessment framework that is based on agile goals as opposed to practices

(Conboy et al., 2011). This is yet another example of a need for an agile-based measure at the organizational level.

Agile methods derive much of their agility by relying on the tacit knowledge embodied in the team instead of formal documentation. As a result, unapparent shortfalls in this knowledge can lead to significant mistakes. This may be exacerbated if the teams are large. Agile has been found to become unwieldy with teams beyond fifteen to twenty developers (Boehm, 2002). Distributed development teams can have their own unique set of conflicts related to agile, including lack of team cohesion, people versus process controls, communication, and formal versus informal agreements. However, studies have shown that much of this can be mitigated through knowledge sharing, intensive communication, trust, and a practice of continual improvement (Ramesh et al., 2006). Such issues can further be resolved with the establishment of contextual ambidexterity through the balancing of formal structures with flexibility, trust with verification, and process assimilation with quick delivery (Ramesh, Mohan, and Lan, 2012).

Iterative agile development can often cause too much focus on short-term deliverables, which can create situations in which the resulting end product is unshippable. Dedicated sprints must often be created to fix bugs due to the time-boxed nature of sprint planning. Lack of focus on non-functional requirements—such as scalability or long-term maintainability—has always been a challenge for the agile organization. Burndown charts do not sufficiently communicate remaining work for a release because of the changing nature of requirements. Accurate reporting requires a greater level of discipline within the teams to provide regular and accurate feedback (Schatz and Abdelshafi, 2005). It has also been noted that there is a tendency to underestimate tasks in agile because even for experienced developers, estimating the unknown can be difficult (McHugh, Conboy, and Lang, 2012).

Finally, agile increases the risk of overemphasizing functional requirements, incomplete or inadequate requirements, and inadequate design (Ramesh, Cao, and Baskerville, 2010). This makes the management of agile particularly challenging at the organizational level where requirements are emergent rather than specified up front (Boehm, 2002). Misunderstanding user requirements has been cited as a major cause for software quality problems in agile as well as other methods of development. Studies have shown that such quality problems can be better solved by improving communication, rather than testing (Kong, Kendall, and Kendall, 2012). Ensuring that such communication occurs can be a challenge in an environment with no stage-gate process to provide checks and balances.

MANAGING AGILITY WITH EMBEDDED AND REAL-TIME SYSTEMS

An embedded system can be defined as having at least one central processor even though it may not provide computing services to end users. It is typically a system that consists of a combination of software, firmware, and hardware components that must be developed and tested in tandem (Douglass, 2004). Embedded systems are becoming more prevalent in today's technology. Virtually any kind of smart device—such as cell phones, smart meters, and *Internet of Things* (IoT) devices—include embedded systems in their design. The exact nature of an embedded system may vary according to the application, but it typically consists of the following key characteristics:

- *Embedded systems are real time*: A real-time embedded system is one where the predictability and schedulability of the system affects the correctness of the application. For example, if a purchase is made on a website, it may appear as though the transaction is immediate or *real time*, but in fact, it is being queued on a server and is being processed accordingly. If it takes a few extra minutes to process a credit card or order, the functionality of the application is not affected. However, in the context of a complex avionics system on a fighter jet or heart pacemaker, if a signal is not sent correctly at a specific instance in time, disastrous consequences could result—meaning that the application has failed. This also applies to smart metering devices. If meter readings are not calculated and sent at a specific instance in time, incorrect billing could result. If the meter fails to respond to a load shedding event or power interruption, this could cause problems on the electric power grid.

- *More stringent reliability and safety requirements*: Such requirements call for extensive reliability and safety testing to ensure that the equipment in question is safe for workers to manage and that the public interest is protected. In the case of smart metering, much of the equipment may have thousands of volts flowing through it at any given time. Safety guidelines must be determined through extensive testing. Utilities that purchase this equipment must answer to the public service commissions of their respective states, which often have questions regarding accuracy and reliability.

- *Complex change management*: Information technology (IT) systems are often-maintained systems. In other words, the software work they entail consists of small incremental efforts to add features and repair defects.

This work is easily conducive to an iterative approach. By contrast, an embedded system contains software, hardware, and firmware that are intertwined. A small change in one component could result in a cascade of changes in other parts of the solution. Affected components may be part of an entirely different development track. For example, when a hardware change requires a firmware change to support it, and then a software change is also required—managing this across all requisite tracks can be a challenge. The impact may be even greater for an embedded device if production has already started. Making a change to a smart meter, particularly once a few thousand circuit boards have already rolled off the assembly line, could be a monumental undertaking—both technically and financially. Additionally, such organizations are usually not built on a limited set of monolithic technologies, but are often a combination of different solutions and systems that may be the result of corporate acquisitions. These situations can add even more complexity when it comes to making a change. One product manager described the situation as follows:

> "A lot of our complexity is driven by the fact that we are an amalgamation of various communication technologies; be it PLC, be it RF, be it cellular communication technologies and several different variants of RF communication technology as far as firmware goes. There are several different head-end [software] systems."

- *More device-driver-level software required*: As implicated in earlier statements, embedded systems often have custom hardware that require custom software drivers to operate them. A smart meter is a good example. It consists of a radio, metrology, and home area network hardware components—all of which are operated by custom software applications. If one component changes, many of the others may be impacted as well.
- *More restrictive optimization requirements due to highly resourced constrained platforms*: A smart meter or a heart pacemaker only has a very limited amount of memory and CPU to operate on. This can be true of IoT devices in general. Much of the processing takes place on the devices themselves. Fitting complex features into a device with limited processing power is an art form unto itself. Unlike typical agile-based software development, features cannot simply be added as time and resources permit. New feature functionality must be balanced with upcoming changes in the hardware and the current abilities of the device. For example, if additional processing power is a must-have to support a certain feature set, then the developer may have to wait on the latest chip

set from their vendor. Development from other tracks that are impacted by this will have to be planned accordingly.

- *Specialized target environments*: Finally, there is a significant difference in target environments between embedded systems and traditional software applications. A typical software application is developed on a PC and can be installed, tested, and run in the same or very similar environment. An embedded system, however, must be developed on a different environment from its target. For example, a smart metering application may be developed on a laptop computer, but it must be tested and run on a smart meter or radio frequency (RF) network environment. The characteristics of these environments are difficult to simulate, and so they must be tested as much as possible with real equipment. Due to size and cost restrictions, full-scale testing can be exponentially more complicated than traditional software applications.

Despite these barriers, embedded systems development organizations have successfully integrated XP and Scrum-based agile practices with positive results. One such successful example provided for acceptance testing that drove a high level of prototyping beyond what standard XP development would provide (Smith et al., 2009). As one may expect from such examples, the literature shows that the integration of specific practices and their adaptation varies from company to company and from project to project (Salo and Abrahamsson, 2008; Kong, Kendall, and Kendall, 2012). Most critically, a study of process model selection in embedded systems development found that for large, complex projects no single method applied most of the time, rather, a *hybrid model blending and balancing the features of different models is often the choice* (Kettunen and Laanti, 2005).

Why Are Embedded Systems so Important?

All of the aforementioned characteristics—combined—significantly differentiate embedded systems from the traditional software application development effort. Cellular, smart meter, smart grid, smart cars, smart cities, IoT, and related technologies are all embedded systems. Considering that most technological innovation happening today is occurring in these fields, embedded systems are arguably the most important and innovative context in today's market.

CONTINUOUS DEVELOPMENT AND MANAGING COMPLEX CHANGE

The concept of continuous software releases consists of providing for a series of smaller, sequential releases, as opposed to one large monolithic production.

Such concepts have been long known to provide better time-to-delivery for software products. More specifically, continuous development has been found to have the following benefits (Greer and Ruhe, 2004):

- Requirements can be prioritized so that a working, beneficial system can be produced sooner
- It allows customers to receive at least a piece of a working system earlier and provide feedback
- It allows for the integration of customer or user feedback at incremental stages
- It simplifies scheduling and estimation due to working with *smaller chunks* instead of larger products
- It makes adapting to change easier

The key components of continuous development have been found in the literature to be release planning, iteration pacing, and continuous integration of change.

Release planning or roadmapping is important when it comes to directing iterative releases. In one study, a systematic review of 24 release planning models was performed, and sixteen of these belonged to the EVOLVE family of models. EVOLVE employs a genetic algorithm to determine an optimal requirements set for each iteration (Greer and Ruhe, 2004). It can be used to build a release plan within certain technical constraints once requirements have been categorized and estimated. Most planning methods found in the literature focus on a small set of requirements selection factors and emphasized constraints such as budget, technology, and schedule. About 58% of these methods included soft factors such as customer or company value, risk, stakeholder influence, or resources. Although most of these models were validated with case studies, very few were tested in full-scale industry projects. Additionally, all such models were intended for market-driven development (Svahnberg et al., 2010). In essence, Svahnberg's study revealed that there are few real choices for practitioners who are wishing to adapt a release planning model—and most of those in existence are very interrelated. Finding a model that suits a company's unique needs, which at the same time has enough empirical evidence from industry to prove that it works, is challenging (Svahnberg et al., 2010).

Continuous releases typically require the creation of successive development iterations. Iterations can be used from the product development level down to the organization of individual coding tasks. Companies that compete in very fast-paced markets have found that proactively setting a time-boxed pace for new product development, based on an established *rhythm*, allows them to keep one step ahead of the competition (Eisenhardt and Brown, 1998). It does this by combining flexibility and control in turbulent environments (Vidgen, 2009). This is in contrast to *event pacing*, which is more reactionary. Although every market will have its surprises that require companies to be reactionary at some point, making proactive commitments to innovation in this way has been shown to have a direct impact to the timeliness and effectiveness of new product introduction (Eisenhardt and Brown, 1998). A key in making time pacing successful is the use of time-based performance metrics such as speed, rate, and elapsed time, in addition to costs or profit margins.

Another component of continuous development is the practice of continuous integration of development changes. Continuous integration has been found to increase quality by up to 30% because it eliminates the integration periods required by the delivery milestones of a traditional systems development life cycle (Karlstrom and Runeson, 2005; Schatz and Abdelshafi, 2005). Although often considered an important contributor to the success of extreme programming methods, a recent study concluded that the concept is *not homogeneous and has many contextual variations* (Ståhl and Bosch, 2014). The study identified a need for a model that described these variants and their effects. Industry stakeholders could then decide which variant they should seek out based on their respective goals. As with time pacing, more advanced tools or reporting systems are needed to allow for greater user input into this continuous integration flow (Muthitacharoen and Saeed, 2009).

MANAGING DISTRIBUTED TEAMS

Distributed development teams can have their own unique set of conflicts related to agile, including lack of team cohesion, people versus process controls, communication, and formal versus informal agreements. One software product manager characterized this challenge as follows:

> "We have a lot of offshore resources and those teams do not work as well in an autonomous, self-directed mode; they require a more structured deliverable to be given to them to build to a spec or to a highly granular detail level of user story that can then be measured and more repeatedly checked for quality, so to speak, against the original requirements."

However, studies have shown that much of this can be mitigated through knowledge sharing, intensive communication, trust, and a practice of continual improvement (Ramesh et al., 2006). Communication is the key word here because any time you have large distributed teams, or even smaller teams of largely remote workers, you need to communicate much more than if the team was all colocated. This means going far above and beyond the typical daily Scrum meetings and into regular information communication between team members. Video communication has proven to be particularly effective in creating a sense of team unity, solidarity, and cohesion so critical in this context. In subsequent chapters, we will discuss in detail the various types of interconnections that make for the most successful distributed teams.

ADOPTION OF AGILITY: THE NEED FOR AGILE TRANSFORMATION

Agile Has Become the Industry Standard for Managing ISD Efforts

It is important to understand how agile methods are commonly being adopted and implemented before an accurate measure of their success and impact on agility can be determined. Even more important, the motivations for organizations and their stakeholders to take on an agile transformation effort and what they hope to gain from it should also be understood.

Many companies are feeling the need to move to more *internet speed* development methods to stay competitive. This has become so pervasive that even the government has taken notice. In a recent study, the Department of Defense cited insufficient progress/performance with traditional methods and an inability to provide urgent responses to evolving mission needs as key reasons for adopting agile methods (Broadus, 2013). Many companies have felt the need to adopt agile methods simply to maintain their competitive edge. In our case studies, many respondents stated that being able to tell potential clients that they were an agile organization was critical in helping them *win business*. Other respondents stated that the push to adopt agile was driven by complex projects that were becoming increasingly longer to complete and were consistently over budget. Even still, as the industry evolved, so did the workforce; and the addition of *new blood* into our case studies had its own hand in influencing adoption. As one firmware product manager in our studies stated:

> "We had just a different project management style that was adopted. We had experienced folks come in from different software industries that wanted to bring in agile."

Finally, it is improvements in quality that organizations often hope to gain by going agile. As another product manager stated:

> "It wasn't just time to market; it was quality that was one of the major factors in us trying to go agile."

As we discuss quality in the context of an agile environment, we find that what quality is depends very much on the eye of the beholder. As the following interview excerpt illustrates, quality may depend on an internal or external perception, and may differ according to who you ask. In subsequent chapters, we discuss the different types of quality, and the impacts that agile methods have on each. More important, we nail down how these different perceptions can be translated into one holistic view of quality.

> **Interviewer:** How do you think quality is defined here? How do we define quality? Is it how well we fit with the customer requirements and the customer needs? Or is it more or less based on what we think quality is?

> **Firmware Architect:** "I would say it's based on what we think quality is."

Despite Its Apparent Success, Complete Acceptance of All Aspects of Agile Practices Have Not Been Realized

Adoption or assimilation of agile methodologies into new organizations entrenched in traditional waterfall methodology is often faced with significant resistance. Many stakeholders are uncomfortable with the key tenets of the *Agile Manifesto* and fear that loosely defined requirements and iterative development will cause significant disruption in complex projects (Barlow et al., 2011).

Organizational, process, and procedural barriers to agile adoption are numerous. Some of the most commonly cited are management of non-functional requirements, documentation, contractual issues, resource management, and cost estimation (Boehm and Turner, 2005). Depending on the industry, conflicts with critical design review processes, regulatory requirements, and HR policies can also be difficult to overcome. More important, in relation to this study, maturity assessments and traditional engineering measurements can become issues (Boehm and Turner, 2005). Critics often doubt whether the benefits of agile outweigh the costs of adoption. Many cite the lack of needed documentation, too much focus on coding as opposed to implementation/planning, and implementation failures in large, complex projects (Barlow et al., 2011).

All of these issues are valid, but for the most part, they boil down to management discomfort around having a flexible scope for a release as opposed to a fixed one and managing this expectation with the customer(s). In the beginning stages of agile adoption, it takes a great deal of effort to get this right. In the short term, more burden is placed on upper management to negotiate and manage this flexibility and level of collaboration with customers. Managers must strike the right balance that suits their organizational capabilities and needs of their clients.

Agile Adoption in Large, Complex Environments: Leveraging a Hybrid Approach

An organization or company need not be concerned with complete adoption of all agile practices. Some of the latest research has shown that many adopters, particularly larger organizations, are taking a hybrid approach, stating that an *a la carte* selection of agile practices can work very well (Fitzgerald, Hartnett, and Conboy, 2006). Combining agile with other approaches has proved promising. Mixed strategy for requirements prioritization outperform either agile or plan-based methods (Abrahamsson, Conboy, and Wang, 2009). Hybrid approaches are further strengthened by the fact that they build on the strength of plan-based and agile methods while mitigating the weaknesses of both (Barlow et al., 2011). Additionally, much research has shown that agile is often not the best choice in different contexts—such as larger organizations—and combining it with stage-gate models has proven best (Dybå and Dingsøyr, 2008). Those contexts that are facing high uncertainty and reciprocal interdependencies in their software projects should implement a hybrid method that combines the strengths of their current software life cycle with complementary agile practices (Barlow et al., 2011).

Most important, this trend of hybridization is expected to continue and proliferate, perhaps to the extent of changing the face of the agile method itself. The *agile development process is a cyclical evolution that continues to this day and will ultimately combine agile and plan-driven techniques* (Baskerville, Pries-Heje, and Madsen, 2011).

Success of the Hybrid Approach Depends on Cross-Organizational Implementation, Not Just Development Methods

Agile is as much a business philosophy as it is a software development methodology. With its adoption comes an entire change in the way a company does business. Design reviews are handled differently, product delivery is iterative, and management of expectations relating to acceptance and decision making have to change (Broadus, 2013). In fact, adapting to agile often requires moving away from the iron triangle of cost, scope, and schedule into an entirely new project management paradigm (Highsmith, 2010; Baskerville et al., 2003)

Successful agile adoption depends not only on agile teams, but agile organizations. Particularly in large or relatively mature companies, it is necessary to focus on human/social interaction in order to succeed (Dybå and Dingsøyr, 2008). In such organizations, the high levels of *individual* autonomy provided by agile must be balanced with high *team* autonomy and corporate responsibility (Dybå and Dingsøyr, 2008). This requires teams with highly functioning employees who are capable of trust, strong communication skills, interpersonal skills, and confidence in their own abilities (Dybå and Dingsøyr, 2008).

Integration of agile at the organizational level requires an understanding of the adopters, understanding the risks, and time to allow change to work (Broadus, 2013).

Determining the Best Mix for a Hybrid Approach Is Not Trivial, but Methods to Discover It Have Been Developed

Barlow provides a framework to evaluate what kind of approach is best for a given situation based on the examination of project interdependencies and volatility. It was found that large, mature organizations often require a hybrid approach to agile due to complexity, IT governance processes, and the size of the teams (Barlow et al., 2011). Additional studies came to similar conclusions. It has been found that environments can dictate practices, and that some combinations work better in different environments based on project size (Baskerville et al., 2003).

Using adaptive structuration as a lens, one study concluded the following points regarding successful agile adoption (Baskerville et al., 2003):

1. Successful adoption requires top management buy-in and support
2. Methods should be tailored to the team
3. Developers need to understand the impact of their autonomy

A key factor to making all three of the points above happen is *communication*. Indeed, an organization's support of formal and informal communication affects the outcome of the type of hybrid approach used (Barlow et al., 2011).

The ultimate point here is that successful integration of agile practices requires doing so at the organizational level, not just the team level. As a result, management of and metrics for measuring organizational performance also need to be modified, just as they are for project or team performance.

Prior to Metagility, There Has Been No Way to Measure the Success or Contribution of These Hybrid Approaches with Respect to Agility

Despite the extensive monetary and organizational commitment required to adopt agile practices, it is rare to have any comparable date to explain the impact of agile before and after adoption (Laanti, Salo, and Abrahamsson, 2011). In one study, it was difficult to assess whether the hybrid method that Intel eventually developed was superior to either XP/Scrum or traditional methods. There was no clear way to measure success (Fitzgerald, Hartnett, and Conboy, 2006).

Barlow maintains that the success of an agile team could be measured as a function of the density of the project team's advice network, moderated by the cost of maintaining informal relationships (Barlow et al., 2011). However, this metric is only at the team level as opposed to the organization and does not provide a link to agility in the marketplace.

From a research perspective, links between social interaction and project outcomes (budget, schedule, and quality) are subjects of ongoing research (Cao, Mohan, Peng, and Ramesh, 2009).

Key takeaways with regard to adoption include:

1. Agile assimilation or hybridization with traditional methods is fast becoming the leading method of adoption, particularly with larger, more mature organizations

2. Prior to the development of the research we will discuss in the next few chapters, there was no clear method of evaluating or assessing the effectiveness of differing levels of adoption and juxtaposing them with its impact on a company's true agility in the marketplace

PROBLEMS WITH THE CURRENT LITERATURE: LIMITATIONS OF AGILE RESEARCH

A good agile strategy should be grounded in scientific research. All too often strategies are based on best practices derived from the limited experiences of a few people. Research helps ensure that the ideas we implement have been proven out—not only at the practitioner level but at the research level as well. At the same time, we need to understand the limitations of this research—what it can tell us and what it cannot. In the previous sections, we explored what this body of research is telling us about agility, but in this section, we outline the limitations of that research, thereby building the case for Metagility and its results.

What Is Agile, Really?

Agile software development methods have only been around a little over 15 years, since the inception of the *Agile Manifesto*. As a relatively new concept in software development, much of the current literature lacks clarity, theoretical glue, and parsimony. In addition, much of it has limited applicability to various contexts (Conboy, 2009). Additionally, the current body of research lacks clarity with regard to what agility is, its adaptability, and how it is deployed in practice (Abrahamsson, Conboy, and Wang, 2009). Even though agile has become fairly well disseminated—at least in a software development context—questions are always arising as to exactly what agile is and what processes it constitutes. Many project managers, developers, and related professionals still maintain that agility lacks clear definition and is still somewhat blurry to them.

An Apparent Lack of Rigor

The literature reveals that there is an overall need to improve the rigor of agile research (Abrahamsson, Conboy, and Wang, 2009). In many such studies, research methods were not well defined and weaknessess regarding bias, validity, and reliability were not addressed. Employment of applicable theoretical frameworks is rare or nonexistent. Adaptive structuration and innovation diffusion are two examples of applicable theoretical frameworks that are virtually absent in the literature. Data collection and analysis processes are often poorly defined and the *current contribution of agile research remains low and uncertain* (Abrahamsson, Conboy, and Wang, 2009).

No Research in Differing Contexts

The current literature lacks agile research in a variety of contexts. Agile methods, especially in the early years of the *Agile Manifesto*, have been used primarily in small teams at newer companies. As a result, there have been few studies in mature teams or teams in larger organizations (Dybå and Dingsøyr, 2008). Research studies framed in known general contexts—such as embedded development—are lacking (Abrahamsson, Conboy, and Wang, 2009). This is compounded by a dearth of research in post-adoption contexts and innovation (Abrahamsson, Conboy, and Wang, 2009). More case studies are needed to evaluate control patterns in different contexts. For example, it has been found that multiple categories of control, including both formal and informal, are needed in large distributed development contexts (Persson, Mathiassen, and Aaen, 2012).

Most of the time when agile research is referenced, it is referring to team organization and operation. Very little research has been performed at the enterprise level.

Lack of Research at the Organizational Level or Across Business Units

Although there is a significant and growing body of research on agile, many aspects are yet to be explored, particularly outside systems development at the organizational level (Conboy 2009). The extent to which various stakeholders inside and outside of the organization contribute to agility and agile teams is yet to be investigated (Conboy and Morgan, 2011). This is largely due to the fact that agile has traditionally been championed from the bottom up, being implemented at the development team level with little or no agile concepts or methodologies being adopted upstream (Abrahamsson, Conboy, and Wang, 2009).

As one software project manager in our study was quoted as saying with regard to previous adoption efforts:

"It was very much a bottom-up approach, which I would disagree with. I think, in any organization, if you're making a large change like that, it should come from the top down."

Barlow cites that team culture, top management support, and alignment with organizational strategy were not included in determining an approach to agile adoption (Barlow et al., 2011). However, Highsmith maintains that agile is a management philosophy, not just a development method, and that true agility requires assimilation of agile concepts into all aspects of the business—including how success is measured (Highsmith, 2010). *Agile is not just a development method, it is an entirely new way of doing business.*

Abrahamsson tells us that "there is a poignant need to identify rigorous ways *in* which agility can be assessed" (Abrahamsson, Conboy, and Wang, 2009). Examples cited included determining the decline of agility over time, across projects, and at the organizational level in order to identify improvements. Most important, there needs to be a way to bridge the understanding of agility to system development success (Abrahamsson, Conboy, and Wang, 2009).

To bolster these claims further, Conboy asserts that "mechanisms for scanning the project landscape should be incorporated into project management practices in agile organizations." The same study further asserts that "project managers need to be aware that an information system project is no longer a local matter that can be treated as a closed innovation isolated from the rest of the organization. Such projects should be seen in light of other projects within an organization" (Conboy and Morgan, 2011). Similar studies have drawn a clear distinction between *doing* agile and *being* agile. True agility requires significant cultural and procedural changes within an organization as well as a new thought process. A prerequisite for ISD agility has been stated as the practice of *mindfulness routines* as *organizational routines*. Mindfulness routines have been described as the practice of "gathering new information from multiple perspectives via self-assessment and reflection to promote continuous creation and refinements of organizational routine performance" (McAvoy, Nagle, and Sammon, 2013).

A practice perceived as new by its adopters, such as agility, can be considered an innovation (Rogers, 2003). Agile methods are often viewed as process innovations of an ISD organization (Wang, Conboy, and Pikkarainen, 2012). The assimilation of agile has been conceptualized using innovation diffusion as a lens, concentrating on the stages of acceptance, routinization, and infusion (Wang, Conboy, and Pikkarainen, 2012).

In a software context, agility is affected by the extent of innovation in base technologies as well as process innovations in complementary assets (Lyytinen and Rose, 2005). Software organizations organize themselves differently during different innovation periods while they decide to explore fast or deliver fast. They control their focus on agility on how good they want to become in managing technologies in different innovation phases (Lyytinen and Rose, 2005).

Current research needs more careful constructs for agility and other process features. Variances have been found in process features, across phases, and between companies due to varying focus on exploration or exploitation. There is a poignant need to explore other factors than just an organization's learning focus to establish causal explanations of agility in organizational contexts (Lyytinen and Rose, 2005). In summary, systematic and insightful understanding of agile methods in use is yet to be achieved (Wang, Conboy, and Pikkarainen, 2012).

In the next chapter, we explore how all of the situations we discussed are influencing change in the agile landscape, including how these factors—and more—are creating a need for a more flexible agile approach hybridized with traditional methods. Additionally, we explore how these hybridized approaches take shape both from a technical and organizational perspective.

3

HYBRID AGILITY: DETERMINING AND IMPLEMENTING THE RIGHT APPROACH

WHY ORGANIZATIONS ADOPT SOME ASPECTS OF AGILITY AND NOT OTHERS, AND HOW THIS IS CHANGING AGILE METHODS

"There are specific things that we rejected. One is the concept that only the teams doing the work shall estimate the work, and it was abandoned relatively quickly due to the sheer scale and number of agile teams that we are using."

—Software Product Manager

The push to adopt agile development methodologies within the technology sector is strong. Many companies have been made to feel that adoption of agile is critical to staying competitive. However, as the previous chapter illustrated, there have been many *bumps* or concerns along the path to adoption. The most serious concern is that some agile environments development methods were found to skip procedures or processes when the company was under tight deadlines, causing the process to proceed in an ad hoc, shortsighted way (Karlstrom and Runeson, 2005). Such concerns tend to be more pervasive with complex development contexts such as embedded systems development.

Some studies found, not long after the advent of the *Agile Manifesto*, that although agile methods were designed to solve many of the same problems that faced embedded development, existing methods were not well suited to the task

(Ronkainen and Abrahamsson, 2003). As one software manager in our case studies explained:

> ". . . and that flew right in the face of agile's emphasis on lighter documentation and less overhead work, the only work that matters is coded, tested software. Well, we were investing a lot of spikes in the agile cycle to do documents that the hardware team needed to be able to produce the widget to a spec and that undermined some of the benefits and the quick turnaround time that you could otherwise get on the system as a whole."

Embedded systems often place the following constraints on agile assimilation (Ronkainen and Abrahamsson, 2003):

- Up-front architecture design cannot be avoided and must be provided for
- Refactoring must include configuration management for both software and hardware—supported by system level analysis
- Transitioning prototypes to well-documented production code requires techniques for increasing code maturity
- More formalized communication and coordination methods are needed between teams
- A method is needed for throttling changing requirements gradually as the product gets closer to release
- Techniques are needed for building and optimizing test cases

Integration of agile with stage-gate methodologies addresses many of these constraints, such as resolution of communication problems (Karlstrom and Runeson, 2005). Although more prevalent, such dependencies are not limited to an embedded systems environment. In a study of agile integration with software product line engineering, it was found that although collaboration between teams is encouraged, project managers should also manage the boundaries between teams. Additionally, project managers should manage the scope based on market, organizational, and technological factors (Mohan, Ramesh, and Sugumaran, 2010). Software product line engineering is similar in complexity to embedded systems development in that it involves the development of one comprehensive solution that may span multiple domains.

An organization need not be concerned with complete adoption of all commonly accepted agile practices. Environments dictate practices as opposed to principles and some combinations of practices may be better suited for specialized environments (Baskerville et al., 2003). Some of the latest research has shown that many adopters, particularly larger organizations, are taking a hybrid approach, stating that an a la carte selection of agile practices can work very well (Fitzgerald, Hartnett, and Conboy, 2006). Other studies have shown that combining agile with other approaches has proved promising and that practitioners should not be afraid to adopt hybrid methods that are tailored to their needs (Sheffield and Lemétayer, 2013). In fact, a one-size-fits-all solution for software agility has been found to be inappropriate because it is often contextual and organizationally dependent (Kong, Kendall, and Kendall, 2012; Sheffield and Lemétayer, 2013). Mixed strategies for development work, such as requirements prioritization, have been found to outperform either agile or plan-based methods alone (Abrahamsson, Conboy, and Wang, 2009).

Hybrid approaches are further strengthened by the fact that they build on the strengths of both plan-based and agile methods while mitigating their weaknesses (Barlow et al., 2011). For example, agile methods have been shown to provide the stage-gate model with tools for planning small iterations, day-to-day work management, and reporting. In turn, the stage-gate model can provide agile methods a means to coordinate with other development teams and communicate with marketing and upper management (Karlstrom and Runeson, 2005). Most critically, much research has shown that agile is often not the best choice in certain contexts, such as larger organizations, and combining it with stage-gate models has proven the best approach (Dybå and Dingsøyr, 2008). Such contexts need development approaches that balance flexibility and disciplined methodology (Baskerville et al., 2003). The causal factors for such a hybrid approach have been stated to include:

- A desperate need to rush to market
- A new and unique software market environment
- A lack of experience of developing software under the conditions imposed by the environment (Baskerville et al., 2003; Lyytinen and Rose, 2005)

Indeed, those facing high uncertainty and reciprocal interdependencies in their projects should implement a hybrid method combining strengths of current software life-cycle development with complementary agile practices (Barlow et al., 2011).

Finally, this trend of hybridization is expected to continue and proliferate, perhaps to the extent of changing the face of agile development methods themselves. The proliferation and assimilation of agile development methods is a cyclical evolution that continues to this day and will ultimately combine agile and plan-driven techniques (Baskerville, Pries-Heje, and Madsen, 2011).

AGILE IS NOT JUST A DEVELOPMENT PROCESS ANYMORE, IT'S A NEW WAY OF DOING BUSINESS

The need for certainty leads to an assumption that we must know what we are building so we can determine the effort it will take to build, the resources required, and ultimately the cost. Accomplishing this in itself requires tremendous effort and negotiation because the time and cost estimates are typically much larger than the organization is willing to invest. The business usually knows in advance when the product needs to go to market and how much they are willing to spend to get there—it's more a question of how much feature functionality can be built and whether or not that functionality will be worth the investment.

The *Agile Triangle* Replacing the *Iron Triangle*

The iron triangle that is depicted in Figure 3.1 focuses on three points: scope, cost, and schedule. It is referred to as the iron triangle because it was long assumed that an increase in one of the three points would require a trade-off or compromise within one or more of the other two. This model for project success has proven inefficient on a number of levels, not the least of which was the lack of ability to account for customer satisfaction. Agile dispenses with the notion of scope-driven projects and focuses instead on value.

The agile triangle, first proposed by Jim Highsmith, replaces scope, cost, and schedule with value, quality, and constraints (Highsmith, 2010):

1. *Value*: The value of a project should be measured by the stakeholders and their expectations.
2. *Quality*: Quality means delivering what the customer needs. As we will discuss, there are two perspectives on quality—intrinsic or internal

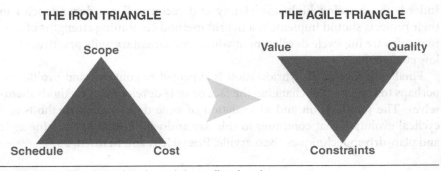

Figure 3.1   The *iron triangle* and the *agile triangle*

perceptions by developers and architects; and extrinsic quality, which is the quality of the project from a customer's perspective. Both are critical, but the extrinsic quality from the customer's point of view is based on feature functionality and ease of use, whereas intrinsic quality could be more architectural or technological.

3. *Constraints*: The three elements of the iron triangle are grouped within this category—project scope, schedule, and cost.

Using the agile triangle, flexibility is increased by focusing on delivering as much value and quality as possible within a set of constraints as opposed to concentrating only on hard limitations with little deference to customer satisfaction and business value.

This is accomplished by leveraging the Scrum process to contain the two variables that most organizations are primarily concerned about—time and cost. The schedule is fixed by the duration of the sprint or the release; cost is fixed by the size of the team. Most of the practices introduced by agile methods provide the means which allow the organization to maximize the number of features built within predetermined time and cost constraints. The business can always decide to invest more time and more money after the initial investment is spent.

OBTAINING EXECUTIVE INVOLVEMENT AND BUY-IN

Agile transformation is a potentially expensive and time-consuming proposition. Such a transformation pushes organizations to the limits of their comfort zones—requiring extensive training, coaching, and cultural change. Doing this successfully requires support and buy-in from all levels of management—especially at the executive level. As mentioned previously, one of the biggest mistakes made in such a transformation is starting from the bottom up, instead of from the top down. Executives and other organizational leaders must not only understand the potential benefits, but the challenges that lay ahead to achieve those benefits. This step should be taken first, before any transformation is attempted. Obtaining this buy-in is best approached as follows:

1. Explain the benefits of achieving agile transformation to the organization:
   a. *Faster time to market*: More companies are looking to get innovative products to market faster. The typical 18-month release cycles can be reduced to six months or less using the proper agile approach.

b. *Early return on investment* (ROI): Iterative development allows for early feature creation and collaborative feedback from the customer.

c. *Feedback from real customers*: Customer collaboration ensures that most of the feature functionality that is being built will actually be used, thereby making the most efficient use of time and resources.

d. *Building the right products*: Iterative development allows customers to see the emerging product, and to evaluate and tweak it as necessary.

e. *Early risk reduction*: Agile reduces the risk of building the wrong product, reduces the risk of not delivering within the allotted period and budget, and reduces the chance of severe defects negatively impacting your customers' business.

f. *Improved quality*: Agile allows the organization to vary the business and technical scope of the solution while maximizing value and quality.

g. *Culture and morale*: Agile empowers individuals, such as developers and testers, to provide input into solutions as opposed to building strictly to a spec; it provides a shared sense of purpose.

h. *Efficient use of resources and people*: Through scrums and pair programming, agile increases communication and knowledge transfer and reduces wasted time and churn.

i. *Better customer satisfaction*: Quite simply, building what the customer wants at the level of quality they need makes them happy. Customer collaboration makes them feel like they have a hand in the process. Customers can hardly criticize something that they had a part in evaluating and testing. This is especially true in new innovative markets.

j. *Emergent outcomes*: Many organizations are building products for markets that don't exist yet—using technologies that are brand new and innovative. Agile promotes innovation and a *learn-as-you-go* mindset that is conducive to promoting innovation.

k. *Predictable results*: Estimation is difficult and many organizations are not good at it. Agile allows for teams to make and meet commitments to a higher degree of predictability.

2. Explain the benefits of agile transformation to the executives personally:
    a. The biggest challenge that executives have with agile is understanding what is going on within their organization at any given point in time. What is the status of development? What is the status of project x or y? Are we on target, on budget? Are we developing what the customer wants? Are we going to meet our contractual commitments? The key here is providing executives with an agile dashboard that gives them the gauges to see what is going on, and the dials and knobs to adjust or make changes. Being able to provide detailed and precise program and project portfolio management solutions with the right metrics and monitoring tools is critical. We will provide examples of the most effective of these solutions in a later chapter. At this point, executives need to be given the necessary comfort level to know that they have the visibility and control into the process that they need.
3. Explain the short-term pain points that may be encountered during this activity, along with a plan to mitigate them. Changes in processes, project reporting, and communication will need to occur, which may encounter some cultural resistance. Broad-based training on agile will be needed to mitigate these issues. What that means is first providing training to all resources within the organization on agile basics, followed by more specialized training targeted to specific roles, such as a Scrum Master, project managers, program managers, product managers, and product owners.

Failure to properly explain and mitigate these issues, along with the inability to flex or tailor the solution to the organization, can have catastrophic results as it did for one software product manager in our case studies:

"A third step, which was more significant and transformative, was that a different director for software process and software quality was hired and he brought in a (what I would call) more idealistic view of how agile should be implemented—frankly, the exit of the director that came in to make the changes. He was summarily fired because of the more or less heavy political pain and pressure that it brought on his boss for trying to follow those kinds of agile methods to the letter."

When it comes to obtaining executive buy-in and achieving all three of the aforementioned points, typically an outside resource, such as an agile consultant and/or coaching team, will be needed. Although it is possible for internal experts to achieve buy-in, outside experts typically have an easier time convincing stakeholders due to the fact that they specialize in agile training and transformation as opposed to only having some knowledge or familiarity in it. As many stakeholders in our case studies explained:

> "(We) brought in a stronger outside consultant who was able to influence both director and senior leader levels more and it was really that ability; it was the agile charmer, so to speak, that was able to be that kind of voice to all the layers of the organization."

> "So those folks did the initial groundwork with an outside consultant who brought in some external credibility and gave them some entries to the senior leadership in ways that they hadn't considered with case studies, examples, contacts who could staff qualified agile people, and so forth."

Our most successful case studies in agile transformation were those who had an internal champion, such as a development or engineering director, coupled with external consultants who could provide the expertise needed to convince executive management of the benefits of transition and ease any concerns they may have.

OLD HABITS DIE HARD: CONVINCING OTHERS TO BREAK AWAY FROM WATERFALL

Approaching other stakeholders besides executives, such as project managers, program and product managers, and development managers, about breaking away from waterfall and embracing agile is very much a selling activity. On the one hand you will need to address common fears and discomforts, and on the other you must be able to answer the question, "What's in it for me?" It is important to position the argument for agile such that it makes people's jobs easier and/or provides opportunity for greater input and visibility. Some common concerns are as follows (Sliger and Broderick, 2009).

Agile Requires Too Many Meetings

Many people are put off by the number of meetings that agile requires. As we have discussed, face-to-face communication and interactions are a key tenet of the *Agile Manifesto*. Such meetings include demos, retrospectives, stand-ups, release planning, and backlog reviews. This negative view of meetings is usually based on people's experience with traditional corporate meetings that tend to start late and go on for too long, lack an agenda or the ability to follow the agenda that has been set, and result in the meeting eventually ending with little or no objectives being accomplished. People often leave such meetings feeling as though their time has been totally wasted. It is important to stress that agile meetings are run very differently. There are clear agendas, the meetings are time-boxed, and there is no need to repeat or produce complex documentation because all attendees are actively participating in the decision making.

Probably the most controversial meeting in agile is the daily stand-up. Many developers and testers feel that this is an attempt at micromanagement. Remind the team that this meeting is all about them so they can adapt their work in response to how the sprint is turning out and allow them to coordinate with their peers. After all, it's only fifteen minutes, and the work they accomplish in this meeting will keep them out of other meetings that can be a serious drain on time.

We Don't Want to Provide High-Level Estimates

Developers and engineers tend to resist giving high-level estimates for feature functionality because they've been pressured to give *perfect estimates* in a plan-driven environment. In many cases, providing low estimates resulted in working overtime in order to make up the mistake—or in other cases, management may have made promises based on these estimates that they could not keep.

The team should be reminded that these high-level estimates are a way to pull *time* out of the equation and focus on complexity. Teams should be coached to devise estimates based on level of effort—considering skill, technology, culture, team composition, and product complexity. Using time as a predictor rarely results in accurate estimates, but focusing on complexity has a better chance of doing so, and studies show that, over time, teams get better at doing estimates in this fashion. This method of estimating also allows for faster and more efficient decision making when evaluating new features and the possible ROI they could provide. Stakeholders can reprioritize efforts based on the complexity versus ROI equation.

Agile Does Not Provide for Sound Technical or Architectural Planning

As the product owners plan the vision for the product, systems engineers or architects should be able to plan on how to support it. This type of planning is emergent and typically performed in the prior sprint or iteration. As one sprint completes, the team is already planning the architectural design for the next.

This results in a platform of sorts that the teams build the solution on, which is refined as iterations progress toward the release point.

In traditionally managed projects, a large portion of features are never used because stakeholders are often forced to brainstorm for every conceivable option that may arise. Refinement or scope changes along the way are discouraged so this kind of up-front work is typically expected in fixed-price and fixed-scope situations. Unfortunately, by the time the product is released, the customer's business needs have often changed, making much of the developed solution obsolete. Agile allows for the products as well as the architecture to be built incrementally with an ever-present eye on the end goal of the release.

Agile Requires Colocation

This concern harkens back to the idea that agile was originally developed for small, colocated teams. As we will discuss in later chapters, geographically distributed teams have challenges—even with agile—when it comes to communication. Direct, real-time communication, whether via video, audio, or face-to-face, are critical and differences in time zones and distance coupled with language barriers can make this a serious challenge.

In short, agile does not require colocation. With effective use of technology and with a heavy emphasis on communication every day, teams can build a sense of cohesion and community.

Agile Does Not Allow for Long-Term Planning

High-level estimates are important for long-term planning. The backlog is reviewed regularly and items within it are assigned high-level estimates by the team. Once these items are estimated, the team uses the amount of work that a team can complete in a sprint—known as the *velocity*—to compute a monthly or quarterly forecast. Release planning meetings are conducted to take these items and place them into planned iterations or sprints until they are full. Budgets can be determined by calculating the cost per point. In many hybrid implementations, a point can be described as an ideal engineering day, which we will discuss in a later chapter. The loaded salaries of the teams for a given time divided by the number of points the team can complete in that time provides the cost per point. Budgets can then be calculated for a series of estimated features from the backlog.

As we will find, a visionary style of roadmapping can be employed in a hybrid agile environment that allows for a longer term view from a product perspective.

Our Product and/or Development Environment Is Too Complicated for Agile

Many organizations often think of themselves, their products, and their teams to be special in many ways—and typically more complex and difficult than *anything else out there*. Rarely have I come across a company that doesn't think they are elite—not only in terms of their human resources, but what they have produced and accomplished.

One way to get past this concern is to present case studies from similar companies that are developing similar products that show how they implemented agile. Agile has been used in government and private industry alike—developing products that run the gamut of complexity. At this point in time, agile has become so pervasive that this argument is much easier to dissuade than it used to be. However, it should be noted that at one time, it was a legitimate issue. As we will find, the emergence of hybrid agile implementation is one outgrowth of this concern. With the Metagility approach, the more complex the project is, the more likely it is to benefit from an iterative approach with cyclical feedback.

Unspoken Concerns

As with any kind of organizational change, there are fears and discomforts that people have based on personal insecurities. Fear of being exposed in some way, fear of not being able to adapt, and a general fear of failure are some of the reasons why people may push back. The best way around this problem is with extensive training and coaching from agile consultants and experts. This kind of support will need to be in place for some time—not only to train teams on the basics, but to enforce the training and provide a supportive and nurturing environment that reduces the fear of failure and the exposure of one's weaknesses.

ANALYZING YOUR ENVIRONMENT TO DETERMINE THE CORRECT HYBRID AGILE APPROACH

There are two types of analysis to perform when adopting an agile methodology. The first step is to determine the right kind of agile approach. Should you adopt agile in a hybrid way or a purely agile approach? Perhaps you are better off remaining with a plan-based method? As illustrated in Figure 3.2, some organizations are. Once the approach has been determined, then the current state of agile, if there have been any prior attempts at assimilation, needs to be

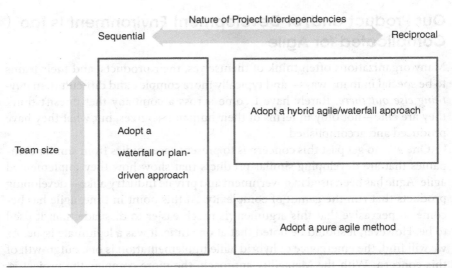

Figure 3.2 *Discovering the approach*: team size and the complexity of interdependencies are the key determinants for a methodological approach

determined. Barlow provides a framework to evaluate the first step based on the examination of project interdependencies and team size and volatility.

As per Figure 3.2, the decision as to whether an organization should be plan driven or agile depends on the complexity of its interdependencies. If they are sequential, a plan-driven approach is satisfactory; however, if there are a great number of reciprocal interdependencies then agile is preferred. As we discussed earlier, much of today's technological development includes reciprocal interdependencies, with embedded systems being one good example. As will be illustrated in later chapters, the idea of multi-track development and the intertwined nature of agile interconnections that it takes to manage them is exemplary of this idea of reciprocal interdependencies. The next factor to consider is team size. Agile was originally designed with smaller teams in mind. This does not mean that it cannot be scaled up though; it simply means that it has to be accomplished in a different way. Figure 3.2 illustrates that larger teams demand a more hybrid approach.

In most of our case studies, as in Barlow's recommendations, large, mature organizations often require a hybrid approach due to complexity, IT governance processes, and the size of the teams (Barlow et al., 2011). This is particularly important when considering multi-track development.

Once the approach has been determined based on an environmental assessment, the next step is to determine the level of agility or find out where the organization is with their agile strategy based on what they have accomplished thus far. Many organizations today have at least attempted agile methods in some form so it is important to determine what processes, if any, are still in place from those efforts. We assessed the agile capability of our case studies with a series of 25 points based on a scale of one to five as illustrated in Tables 3.1 and 3.2. The scale in Table 3.1 is used to assess the points in Table 3.2.

Analysis of case studies on all of these points revealed some common observations. These included:

1. *Too much work in progress*: This is a common challenge for many organizations. Restructuring the process while still delivering on commitments is required.
2. *Lack of product owner role*: While common in an agile environment, a well-defined product owner role is rarely pre-existing. Our case studies revealed that transformed business analysts who were assigned to decompose requirements into user stories were taking on this role.
3. *Technical debt that was out of control*: It is crucial to implement a process that allows for regular reviews and resolution of technical debt and defects.
4. *Too many releases running in parallel, creating stiff competition for resources*: This slows down work in-flight.
5. *Commitments made before teams have sufficient understanding of high-level requirements*: Premature commitments cause thrashing and constant descoping.

Table 3.1 General agile health assessment scale

1	Non-existent	No time devoted to agile assimilation
2	Starting phase	Agile transformation has just begun with little or no progress
3	Implementation phase	Agile transformation has occurred in some areas with limited practices being followed
4	Committed and stable	Agile transformation has occurred with practices being followed throughout the enterprise
5	Mature and sustained	Mature agile assimilation has taken place with decidedly measurable results, including reduced cycle time, improved quality, and greater customer satisfaction

Table 3.2 Agile health assessment criteria: agile assessment points for pre-existing implementations with corresponding success factors

Assessment Point	Success Factors
• Agile awareness	· Does the organization and its leadership know how agile they are?
• Executive engagement	· To what degree is the agile process supported by the executive level?
• Product vision and strategic planning	· Is the product vision well understood and communicated throughout the enterprise?
• Product roadmap	· Does the organization know where it is going with its products? Although roadmaps can change to some extent in an agile environment, this is no excuse not to have one.
• Requirement comprehension	· Is there a process and resources in place to decompose requirements into user stories? Do product owners have access to customers or product experts who can answer questions about detailed feature functionality?
• Estimation	· How accurate do the estimates turn out to be? Are estimates being performed by the right people?
• Acceptance criteria	· Every requirement should be decomposed into one or more user stories with defined acceptance criteria.
• Planning rhythm	· Planning for new releases should be regular and predictable.
• Requirement decomposition	· Requirements should be decomposed into user stories, acceptance criteria, and a series of tasks or activities that developers and testers must complete.
• Regular cycle times	· Delivery for new releases should be regular and predictable.
• Work in progress	· Work in progress should be limited and controlled.
• Organizational and contractual alignment	· Is the organization on point with achieving commitments? Is it regularly overcommitted?
• Business intelligence and analytics	· Is there a well-defined program and project portfolio management solution that provides agile-based metrics that can start at the program level, and be broken down into the project and team levels? Do the tools provide executives and managers alike with the visibility into what is going on from the programs down to the projects and even team levels?
• Velocity	· Is velocity predictable and regular?
• Continuous improvement	· Are retrospectives being regularly scheduled and input translated into action?
• Backlog grooming	· Is the release backlog regularly being reviewed and worked?

• Communication	• What interactions, both formal and informal, are occurring regularly between teams, leaders, and managers?
• Customer collaboration	• To what level are customers involved in defining solutions and testing?
• Empowerment	• Do teams and individuals feel empowered to offer solutions, exercise creativity, and actuate change?
• Trust	• Is there a *we vs. they* mentality between departments and teams inside the organization?
• Architecture	• Is the organization capable of defining detailed solutions?
• Execution	• Ability to build the solution that has been defined.
• Quality	• Is the organization able to properly test the solution? To what level?
• Technical debt	• Is there a program of regularly reviewing and resolving technical debt? Is it growing out of control?
• Deployment	• Are the defined, built, and tested solutions actually being deployed to customer sites?

The following organizational challenges were also often observed:

1. Is sufficient automation infrastructure in place?
2. Has a steady performance baseline been established?

Short-term items to focus on typically included:

1. Deciding which 20–30% of the backlog could be worked now
2. Establishing agile teams that can stay together
3. Aggressively managing the product backlog
4. Establishing a release cadence that only has one major release in flight at any given time
5. Focusing on cultural issues: communication, collaboration, empowerment, and trust

HOW WATERFALL IS COMMONLY BLENDED WITH AGILE METHODS

"We also need to keep in mind that there is another challenge to this, which is the tie-in to a different methodology on their hardware side. This gets to the embedded systems world more closely because when we say software, we're talking about one slice of the total hardware product,

which has a software component that then speaks to the larger software area which is our head end system and some of the advanced applications that reside on traditional IT-type server infrastructure. The problem we found in agile was morphing and meshing that set of work to the waterfall methodology for hardware development because those hardware projects will have 2- to 3-year life cycles instead of a 6- to 9-month software life cycle, so time differences of different intersection points and methods between hardware, which was waterfall, and software, which was following agile, caused us to have to document those intersection points where the hardware deliverable had to meet a spec."

—Software Project Manager

Notice how the aforementioned situation echoes the *reciprocal project inter-dependencies* that were mentioned by Barlow when building an agile or plan-based approach. The dilemma described by the respondent is a common one, and one that is best satisfied with a hybrid mix. Hybrid agile implementations commonly combine stage-gating with agile development practices. The purpose of the stage-gate process in this context is to provide program-level governance and incremental investment guidance for large enterprise-class initiatives. It serves as a sort of check and balance that provides the business with a higher degree of certainty and predictability with complex product development, such as embedded systems. This approach augments, enables, and enhances the agile/Scrum process by reducing sales and delivery issues in the long term.

Figure 3.3 references the phases and stage gates that are commonly used in hybrid implementations. These stages consist of discovery, scoping, feasibility, development, verification, and implementation:

- *Discovery stage*: This is where ideas are captured, prioritized, and scored according to their business value. The scoring helps prioritize the resources required to perform the more in-depth evaluation of subsequent stages.
- *Scoping stage*: This is a quick and inexpensive assessment of the market prospects and technical merits/risks of the project.

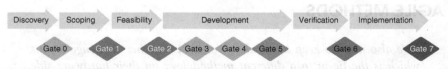

Figure 3.3 *Stages and gates*: illustrates the plan-based phases of a waterfall approach and the corresponding stage gates

- *Feasibility stage*: This is where the bulk of the vital homework is done and most of the market studies are carried out. These result in a business case that includes the product definition, the project justification, and a project plan.
- *Development stage*: This is where architecture is defined, development iterations are conducted, and prototypes are generated in order to verify performance.
- *Verification stage*: This is where the design is tested, debugged, and documented.
- *Implementation stage*: This is where the trial deployment, trial production, and market testing takes place.

These stages are considered flexible or *soft*; meaning that work in a subsequent stage can begin before work in a previous stage is complete—at the discretion of the program team or project manager. These phases are governed by a series of stage gates where progress and status are reviewed at various points within the process. With embedded systems, the process is fundamentally the same for all hardware, software, and firmware projects, but software and firmware projects tend to go through fewer stage gates. Gates that are common to all projects include the following:

- Stage 0: Project start
- Stage 1: High-level schedule, cost, and scope
- Stage 2: Committed schedule, cost, and scope
- Stage 5: Project ready for testing
- Stage 6: Project ready for user acceptance testing
- Stage 7: Project ready for production

Gates 3 and 4 serve as additional checkpoints for hardware projects that may or may not be used. In an embedded systems environment, systems releases introduce new software-only capabilities, expose capabilities developed in the firmware, and introduce support for new hardware products. Having many releases developed in parallel introduces a high degree of unnecessary complexity into the software development process. Concurrent releases end up competing for developer and testing time, are managed in different code branches that must be continuously merged, require fixes and defects to be ported to earlier release versions, and introduce management and planning dependencies that are difficult—if not impossible—to effectively manage.

The hybrid agile model requires that no more than one release be active in development at any one time. Releases are time-boxed and features are targeted for a specific release during release planning. If a feature misses one release, it can either be rescheduled for the subsequent release, or put onto the backlog for consideration in a future release. The hybrid agile concept applies the same fundamental iteration-based planning techniques at the release level that Scrum teams apply at the sprint level.

Stage-Gate Governed Release Train

To keep releases moving regularly, a pace needs to be established between teams and releases being developed. The hybrid agile model minimizes the number of concurrent releases by synchronizing the stage gates across neighboring releases as illustrated in Figure 3.4. Several policies around the timing of these gates are required:

1. The current in-flight release is always the most important release. Allocation of project resources to other releases should always be subordinated to the current release.
2. The release architecture team can begin work defining the upcoming release any time after the current release has passed Stage Gate 2.
3. The upcoming release cannot pass the date for Stage Gate 2 until the current release has passed Stage Gate 5. This policy effectively establishes the linkage in the model; Stage 5 of the current release is always tied to Stage 2 of the upcoming release.
4. We must exit Stage 7 of the current release before Stage 5 of the upcoming release. It is assumed that one or more agile teams will *stay behind* with the current release until it has passed the final Stage 7. After Stage 7, those teams will move to the upcoming (now current) release already in progress.

Hybrid Agile Stage-Gate Definitions

Taking an agile approach to software development implies a new way of thinking about estimating and planning. This has a direct impact on the stage gates and the conditions required in order to pass from one to the other. The following list includes summaries of typical pre- and post-conditions for passing between the various stage gates in a hybrid agile implementation.

- *Stage 0*: Pre-engineering or scoping—idea approved to move forward
  - *Pre-conditions*: Current release has passed Stage 2, product management has a preliminary scope statement based on an approved roadmap, and the release architecture team has sufficient capacity to begin planning the upcoming release.

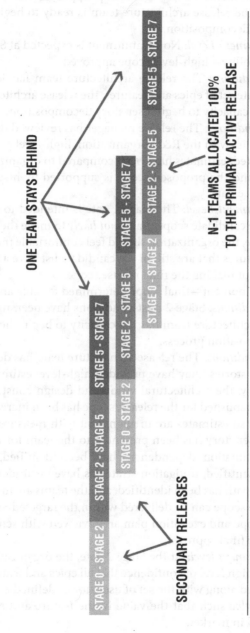

Figure 3.4 Stage-gate release train

□ *Post-conditions*: Senior leadership approves the preliminary scope; the release architecture team is ready to begin epic and feature decomposition.

□ *Commitment Level*: No commitment is expected at Stage 0.

- *Stage 1*: Feasibility—high-level scope approved
  - □ *Pre-conditions*: The release architecture team has identified a candidate set of epics and features; the release architecture team has the capacity to begin user story decomposition.
  - □ *Post-conditions*: The release manager has reviewed the epic and feature list with the R&D organization, high-level estimates are completed, estimates have been compared to organizational velocity, and the proposed scope is supported by historical performance data.
  - □ *Commitment Level*: The Stage 1 gate is intended to communicate the candidate scope that is *not likely* to make the release. At this gate, the organization should feel comfortable that the epics and features that are still in the candidate list have a reasonable chance of making the final release scope.
- *Stage 2*: Development—final scope determined feasible and approved
  - □ *Pre-conditions*: Stage 2 post-conditions have been met. The release architecture team has the capacity to begin the user story decomposition process.
  - □ *Post-conditions*: The release architecture team has decomposed all user stories, they have provided high-level estimates on every story, the architectural vision and design constraints have been established for the release, scope has been increased or decreased so estimates are in alignment with measured capacity, each user story has been presented to the team for review and final estimation, dependencies have been identified, risks have been identified, mitigation strategies have been identified, the critical path has been identified, and the teams are in agreement that the scope can be delivered within the targeted Stage 5 date. The scope and execution plan are reviewed with senior leadership for final approval.
  - □ *Commitment level*: At the Stage 2 gate, the organization should have a high level of confidence that all epics and features can be delivered along with the set of user stories defined as *minimally marketable* such that the value in the feature and epic can be realized in market.

- *Stage 5*: Feature complete
    - *Pre-conditions*: All Stage 2 post-conditions have been met. The current release has passed the final gate. Development teams are ready to begin work on the release.
    - *Post-conditions*: All in-scope epics and features are delivered; a sufficient number of user stories are complete, and the release is at least minimally marketable. Product management has accepted all epics, features, and user stories. There are no critical, high, or medium open defects associated with the development in the current release that have not been accepted by product management.
    - *Commitment level*: Project management should have confidence going toward Stage 6 and Stage 7 that the rest of the project is achievable with the remaining time and budget allocated to the current release.
- *Stage 6*: Verification complete
    - *Pre-conditions*: All Stage 5 post-conditions have been met. One or two agile teams can complete remaining testing and issue resolution.
    - *Post-conditions*: All critical, high, and medium issues have been resolved. The beta customers are satisfied and ready to take the release.
    - *Commitment level*: Project management should have confidence going toward the final gate that the rest of the project is achievable with the remaining time and budget allocated to the current release.
- *Stage 7*: Go to market or general availability
    - *Pre-conditions*: All Stage 6 post-conditions have been met.
    - *Post-conditions*: Customers are using the release in production. Sustaining engineering is ready to support the release.
    - *Commitment level*: The release is finished.

Hybrid Agile for Firmware Teams

So, do these stage gates apply only to the software teams or to all? When the firmware teams are operating directly in support of a front-end software release, the hybrid agile process and gate definitions are the same for the firmware teams as they are for the software teams.

When the firmware teams are operating directly in support of a hardware project release, the hybrid agile process does not apply and the gate definitions are the same as they are currently implemented. This will become even more clear when we discuss the different development tracks of software, firmware, and hardware in an embedded systems environment. Firmware is often a *shared resource* that alternates between supporting development from the software and hardware tracks.

Hybrid Agile for Hardware Teams

The hardware teams are not operating using an agile methodology, given that hardware development does not currently lend itself to iterative and incremental team-based delivery methods. However, as we will discuss, the hardware teams do use methods that allow them to flex and keep up with their more agile brethren. Since they are typically tied to the stage-gating methodology used by the entire organization, they are able to keep in sync.

This section provided a high-level framework for how hybrid agile implementations integrate certain waterfall components. In the next chapters, we dive into this concept even further, explaining the driving forces behind the process, the details that make it successful, and how all of these factors contribute to a successful system release and becoming as *agile as possible*.

Part 2

The Agile Business Vortex

Understanding and Managing This New Phenomenon

4

UNDERSTANDING AGILE VORTICES

All too often in business, questions regarding process improvement, organizational change, and the like are answered based on tacit or tribal knowledge, opinions of a few experts with limited experience, or the preferences and consensus of a few key stakeholders with little or no research or due diligence being performed. In the worst of circumstances, such decisions are made based on politics or the idiosyncrasies of a few influential leaders with little research conducted as to how such decisions will affect the business. For any kind of fundamental business change such as agile transformation to be successful, efforts must be concentrated on putting the needs of the business first beyond any other considerations—be they political, personal, cultural, or otherwise. The best way to begin doing this is to start with proper, objective, and scientific research. Business research is a science just like any other, and there is much to be learned by approaching common business problems in such a methodical way.

In this chapter, the science behind Metagility is discussed, including the design of the research and the theoretical approach by which it was developed. Agile development was once described by one of my colleagues as a *red sea*—meaning that there is a great deal of *noise* around agility. There are many purported methodologies and experts in this field, many of whom propagate ideas, frameworks, and methodologies with little to no research to support it. Although it is somewhat academic in nature, I believe it is important to review the research design and methodology at least at a high level in order to give the reader a frame of reference for how solid research is conducted and to instill confidence in the validity and applicability of the results. Finally, the results themselves are discussed in detail, including the theory of agile vorticity, business momentum, and the part they play in Metagility.

THE SCIENCE BEHIND THE THEORY

Basic Design of the Research

The purpose of our study was to answer the question of *how* agile processes are orchestrated in an embedded systems environment. The study did not require any behavioral controls and it focused on contemporary events. The assimilation of agile methodologies within embedded systems development is indeed a most contemporary phenomenon that requires in-depth analysis in a real-life context. The boundaries between these are not clearly evident and there are many more variables of interest than data points due to the complexity of agility measurement. These are all key characteristics of research conducive to a case study approach (Yin, 2009). In addition, this case study approach was conducted in the interpretive tradition of information technology studies (Klein and Myers, 1999). As a result, focus was placed on the participants' descriptions of software development practices and the work related to them. A grounded theory method of data analysis was employed. Grounded theory is a qualitative research methodology that does not begin with a theory; instead, it starts with an area of interest and allows the theory to emerge from the data. Strauss and Corbin (1990) define it as *a qualitative research method that uses a systematic set of procedures to develop an inductively derived grounded theory about a phenomenon*. Research results consist of grounded theories discovered inductively by collection and analysis of qualitative, empirical data (Baskerville, Pries-Heje, and Madsen, 2011). Grounded theory is most appropriate where research questions are descriptive and explanatory, and the field of phenomena is not well studied and lacks a substantive body of theory (Galliers, 1991).

Two variations on grounded theory can be found in the literature: Glaserian and Straussian (Pozzebon et al., 2011). While the Glaserian method advocates an unstructured approach for data analysis and theory construction, Straussian provides a well-defined set of procedures for applying the method (Pozzebon et al., 2011). Although both approaches to grounded theory can be found in information systems literature, the Straussian method is much more prevalent. Its structured design also better lends itself to a doctoral dissertation (Pozzebon et al., 2011). It is for these reasons that this study employs Straussian grounded theory as its research methodology. The methodology herein is based on Strauss and Corbin's seminal work *Basics of Qualitative Research: Grounded Theory Procedures and Techniques* published in 1990. Part of the research consisted of a singular case study. One of the often-cited limitations of using one case study is its lack of generalizability since the data collected is often specific to the particular situation at a particular point in time (Fitzgerald, Hartnett, and Conboy, 2006).

However, quality with interpretive case studies is defined by the plausibility of the story and the argument it presents, as opposed to validity and reliability found in positivist studies (Klein and Myers, 1999). More important, the rich detail provided by case studies is considered more valuable than generalizability (Yin, 2003).

How Data Was Collected

The cases that were chosen for this study were embedded systems development organizations in various technological industries, including telecommunications and the power utility industry. Beginning years ago, these organizations instituted mandates to integrate agile development methodologies enterprise-wide. Although the implementation and evolution of agile adoption is known to many of the participants and adds context to the study, this research is focused primarily on the post-adoption state that the businesses currently find themselves in.

Participant observation, interviews, and documentation were all used as data sources for this effort. Respondents were regular participants in several projects including the continuous development of the organization's primary product line. Participants were regular attendees for virtually all meetings and activities relating to these projects, and were intimately familiar with not only the development processes and procedures themselves, but also how they have evolved over time. Respondents participated in the organization's adoption, assimilation, and ultimate hybridization of agile methodologies.

The second source of data consisted of semi-structured interviews with managers and lead architects involved in managing agility. Roles were selected based on their knowledge of and impact of the orchestration of agile processes and product development. This selection method was based on the criteria for *key informants* as outlined in Klein and Meyers (1999). Four key roles were identified as those regularly involved in these activities. These included product managers, project managers, engineering managers, and technical architects. These four roles were found to have the most hands-on impact in managing agility for the products, processes, people, and technology in the organization. Embedded systems development in this company consisted of three primary domains: hardware, firmware, and software. Candidates for each of the four roles in all three domains were selected, resulting in a total of twelve interviews.

As previously mentioned, the interviews were semi-structured in format. Interview questions were informed by the literature using the Straussian approach to grounded theory development (Strauss and Corbin, 1990). The candidates who were interviewed were assured of anonymity. Interview sessions lasted, on average, about an hour in length. The interview data gathered was recorded, transcribed, and coded using Nvivo software. Researchers had unfettered access to select any candidates that were willing to participate. In addition, interviewees seemed comfortable and candid with an interviewer they knew as a technical expert.

Documentation served as the final source of data which included archival data of agile processes and procedures, meeting minutes, and project artifacts such as feasibility studies. These sources allowed researchers to better understand the issues and outcomes of management decisions during project life cycles and to fill in any gaps of understanding with respect to processes, procedures, and history.

Qualitative Grounded Theory Analysis

Data analysis was performed based on the three commonly used coding techniques in grounded theory research: open, axial, and selective coding (Strauss and Corbin, 1990; Baskerville, Pries-Heje, and Madsen, 2011). Open coding is a process of analysis that develops concepts in terms of their properties and dimensions. Key tasks involved are the asking of questions regarding data and then making comparisons. Similarities are grouped to form categories (Strauss and Corbin, 1990). Essentially, the text was broken down into segments which were compared for similarities and differences. They were then labeled and grouped to form codes. A single code could have multiple text segments. During coding, 542 codes were created. As an interpretive case study, the data primarily reflected the interpretations that the interview candidates formed about agile process orchestration within their organization and their work relating to it. As a result, the coding categories included both positive and negative views of agility in the organization and described actions taken by many of the interview respondents.

Once the data was broken down via the open coding, they were reconstructed in new and different ways using the axial coding method. Axial coding is a process of relating sub-categories to a category through a process of inductive and deductive thinking. Although it too involves the tasks of asking questions and making comparisons, categories that arise from this analytic method are developed in terms of causal conditions, context, consequences, and action/interactional strategies (Strauss and Corbin, 1990). Through axial coding, six larger categories were developed. The first three categories reflected the company's market agility. The fourth category identified process agility and the organizational context: hybridized agile methodology and embedded systems development. The final two categories described agile orchestration. Sample codes for these categories can be found in Table 4.1.

Table 4.1 Key constructs and major categories from qualitative analysis

Category	Sample of Sub-categories
Market Agility	
Market Pressure	Competition, Government Regulation
Product Genesis	Requirements Comprehension, Dynamic Priorities
Process Agility	
Hybrid Agility	Software, Firmware, and Hardware
Agile Orchestration	
Interconnections and Interactions	Dependencies, Interdependencies, Linkages, Decision Points, Status Points, Touch Points
Making Adjustments	Customer Negotiation, Resource Adjustment, Scope Adjustment, Constant Reassessment

The final step was selective coding. Selective coding is the process of selecting the core category, relating that category to others, validating the relationships, and completing those that need further development (Strauss and Corbin, 1990). Strauss and Corbin advocate continuing this grounded theory coding of data until one single category stands out (Baskerville and Pries-Heje, 2004). Selective coding was considered complete once saturation had taken place. Such saturation occurs once there is no additional data to inform a category and the relationships between the categories have adequate data to support them. The final result is a story line that correctly conceptualizes this core category or primary phenomenon. This story line is the heart of grounded theory. The next section accomplishes this task by presenting the empirical analysis, followed by the presentation of the final theory of the *agile business vortex*.

AGILE VORTICES: HOW AND WHY THEY OCCUR

In the following sections, we describe the results of the research in the context of one of our case studies. Then we describe the three main constructs: generation of *market agility*, the development of *process agility*, and the *orchestration of agility* within the embedded systems development. These constructs are then rolled up into the grounded theory of agile vorticity, which is conceptualized by a comprehensive illustration combining all the constructs into one end-to-end view. Table 4.1 provides an overview of these constructs, their major categories, and sub-category examples for each. Each section includes a table of elements for each category. Figure 4.1 illustrates a master diagram that details how all the elements of agile vorticity are linked and fit together. As we go through this book, each of the elements in Figure 4.1 will be discussed so it is a good diagram to refer back to while reading.

A Vignette of a Case Study

The institution in this study is a company in the business of developing embedded systems devices for use at power utilities. It is an international corporation employing over 5,000 individuals worldwide and has recently become a subsidiary of a major electronics firm. It is important to note that the company's contracts with its customers are largely based on the number of embedded devices that they sell. These devices have a long lifespan of between 10 and 20 years. As a result, once a customer is *taken*, it puts them out of the market for quite some time. The company has developed a strategic direction of establishing itself as a market leader by *grabbing up* market share before its competitors, and it has been largely successful in doing so. Although the firmware and software aspects of the embedded systems are critical to the overall functionality of its products, company profits are primarily driven by how much hardware can be manufactured and sold to a given client. Because of this, it was critical to include hardware as well as software and firmware domains in this study.

It should also be noted that the subject of this study was the result of several mergers over the years with a large number of disparate technologies, processes, and procedures that have slowly evolved and converged over time. As it was largely a hardware development firm in the beginning, the company's projects are grounded in a waterfall process, termed *new product introduction*, that it has inherited and largely maintained over the last seven years while agile methods have been integrated. As with many similar organizations, the company has gradually adopted and adapted agile methods into the enterprise with the highest degree of adoption in areas with the highest rates of change, such as software and firmware.

Three years prior to the study, the company embarked on an initiative to adopt agile and Scrum methods in earnest, which was the third iteration of the company's agile adoption process. This phase is now considered complete with the result being a hybrid agile implementation across the enterprise with varying degrees of absorption per domain. At this time, the company has no further plans to make any process improvements or changes with respect to agility or agile methodologies.

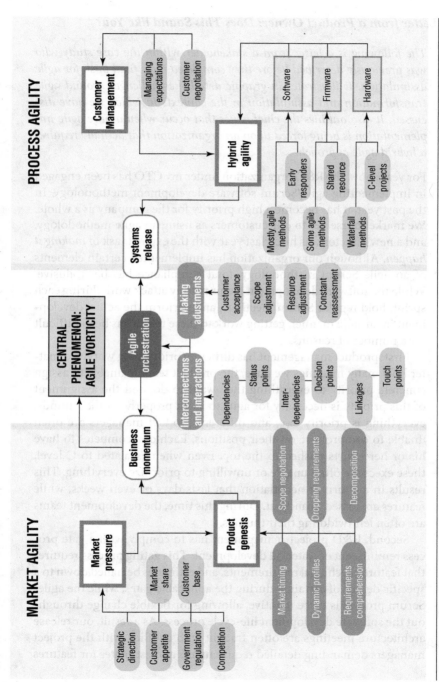

Figure 4.1 *Master vorticity diagram:* a master outline linking all of the components that comprise agile vorticity

A Letter from a Product Owner: Does This Sound like You?

The following is a letter from a stakeholder within the case study who was previously described before they completed their final push for agile assimilation. It illustrates in graphic detail the challenges around agile transformation and assimilation in the contexts in which we have discussed. It also outlines the chief issues that occur when a pure agile implementation is being forced upon an organization that actually requires a hybrid agile approach.

For years now, the R&D organization under my CTO has been engaged in implementing agile/Scrum software development methodology. In the past year, it has become a high priority for the company as a whole. We market ourselves to our customers as using an agile methodology, and a new director was hired last year with the explicit task of *making it happen*. Although our organization has implemented certain elements of an agile Scrum methodology, total compliance has been elusive. While the software development teams readily attack work during each sprint, hold regular Scrum meetings, and perform the actual development in an agile manner, getting work to these teams has been difficult for a number of reasons.

First, product management has difficulty prioritizing work. No matter how many meetings we have, the product team is unable to assign concrete priority to everything they want to do, and the assignment of this priority is necessary for agile to work properly. In their minds, everything is priority one, and different product managers are often unable to compromise on their positions. Each one competes to have his or her efforts pushed to the top. Even when escalated to C-level, these execs are often unable or unwilling to prioritize everything. This results in a churn of negotiation that lasts days or even weeks, while features are tossed in and out. During this time, the development teams are often left twiddling their thumbs.

Second, R&D project management has to comply with a gate process reminiscent of waterfall development. This gating process requires that features, technical requirements, and estimates be nailed down to a specific degree of certainty during the applicable gates, while the agile/Scrum process is more iterative, allowing for flexible change throughout the software development life-cycle process. As a result, our release architecture meetings are often fraught with conflict, with the project managers demanding detailed requirements and estimates for features that the product teams cannot prioritize, and our development managers waiting for work.

Third, our products include *embedded software development*, which means that our software is tied to firmware and hardware that is manufactured. Due to the nature of manufacturing, it is often difficult to coordinate the iterative nature of the agile software development, and the more static nature of firmware/hardware development. After all, it is easy to put out a hot fix or new release of software anytime, but once circuit boards start getting stamped at the plant, those are difficult, if not impossible, to change. Although the firmware/hardware team management participates in release architecture meetings and has Scrums of their own, their work is not as compliant to the agile process as the software development is. A few months ago, the new director hired an agile consultant to train the organization and enforce the agile process. Meeting after meeting was held. Training session after training session was taught. Each meeting seemed to digress into a gripe session. Project managers complained that upper management didn't know what was going on and that they were essentially *out to lunch*. R&D as a whole complained about the product team's indecisiveness. Development complained about the lack of definitive technical requirements and a list of prioritized features. It got so bad that at our last release architecture meeting, our consultant had a breakdown and informed the new director that this organization had more significant and broader issues than agile implementation. This resulted in an all-day off-site meeting at the director level. I don't have the details of this meeting, but was told that it was largely unpleasant and unproductive. Weeks later, the problem still remains, and we are still trying to stick to agile methodology for all current and future releases.

My role is to push the product teams to prioritize their features, get these features broken down into technical requirements to be consumed by the developers, and insure that the resulting work meets spec. Although I'm not sure agile is the right choice, the choice has been made so I have worked to enforce the process at my level. This has included bridging the gap between development and product management to broker compromises on feature priority and define the technical requirements as keenly as possible to increase the accuracy of our estimates.

My team is seen as the bridge between the business and R&D. In the seminar, I would like to discuss specific actions that myself and my

team could take to help solve this problem or at least reduce the severity of it. Perhaps develop a proposal for a modified version of agile/
Scrum strictly for our use? Or maybe even a position paper proposing
that we dump agile altogether for another process? Or maybe, given the
inferences above, there are other management problems at hand that
need to be addressed? Maybe it's not the process at all, but the people
or culture that are to blame?

Converging Forces

At the beginning of the chapter the process of research data collection and analysis was discussed. In grounded theory analysis, data is *coded* or analyzed using
a very specific approach. Through open, axial, and selective coding, grounded
theory methodology maintains that a central theory should be identified.
Strauss and Corbin define this phenomenon as the central problem that the subjects are trying to solve. Strauss and Corbin further hold that other categories
should be explained in terms of this central theory (Strauss and Corbin, 1990).
The previous sections illustrated the primary categories identified via axial and
open coding and the elements that compose them. These include market agility,
process agility, business momentum, and the systems release. In this section,
we explain these categories in terms of the central theory. Using concepts from
fluid dynamics, combined with the metaphor of a whirlpool, a succinct visualization is provided that describes how all of the categories are linked together
into one comprehensive model.

Figure 4.2 illustrates how the hybrid agile organization of software, firmware,
and hardware combine with the product genesis of the business as a result of
market pressure.

During selective coding, an analysis of the data indicated that both sides of
the business—the product management organization and development—are
constantly attempting to reach the same *point* throughout each product release
and will manage themselves into making this happen. According to the software
project manager:

> *"Usually we determine when the release is going to go out the door, and
> then from there we back into how much development can we squeeze in,
> and we really say how much quality are we willing to accept within this
> period and if it works out, then that period stays. If we need more quality,
> then we'll reduce capacity of the release and do less development."*

This point of convergence was identified as the central theory. The reason it is
identified as such is because it is the central problem that the subjects are trying

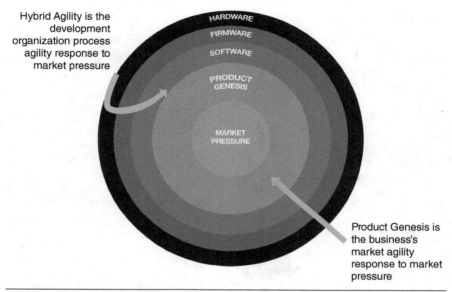

Hybrid Agility is the development organization process agility response to market pressure

HARDWARE
FIRMWARE
SOFTWARE
PRODUCT GENESIS
MARKET PRESSURE

Product Genesis is the business's market agility response to market pressure

Figure 4.2 *Product genesis and hybrid agility* into one view

to solve. Essentially it is the *gravity* that pulls all of the categories identified in axial coding together. Figure 4.3 illustrates this point of convergence. Product genesis is the business's *market agility* response to market pressure. Product genesis in turn *sets the tone* through its creation of business momentum. The development organization attempts to match this momentum through the creation of the systems release, which is created by the hybrid agile development organization. Hybrid agility is the development organization's *process agility* response to market pressures.

These linkages can best be explained using a metaphorical illustration as part of the selective coding process.

The Agile Vortex Thought Experiment

One of the best ways of visualizing complex concepts is through a thought experiment. Thought experiments are those that are carried out conceptually in the mind's eye. Einstein was famous for using this method. His theory of relativity was developed using his *elevator* thought experiment. To explain the theory of agile vorticity, we can use a vortex, or whirlpool of sorts. Try visualizing a whirlpool in your mind's eye. What does it look like? What does it do? How does it move? A whirlpool is a form of vortex that spins around a central axis.

Figure 4.3 *Business momentum and the systems release*

Based on what we know from fluid dynamics, the velocity of the rotation in a whirlpool becomes greater as you get closer to this axis. Next, visualize a tennis ball falling into the pool. What happens to it? The ball moves closer and closer to the center of the vortex. As the ball is drawn closer to the axis, it acquires a spin or rotation of its own and moves at a velocity and direction influenced by the vortex. As it does so, it gains *momentum*, based on its mass or size multiplied by its velocity. The movement of this ball illustrates the motion or circulation of the vortex. The circulation of the vortex at the position of the ball is its *vorticity*. Vorticity has been defined in fluid dynamics as the point in a vortex where the *curl is the strongest*. Another way to understand vorticity is to visualize a river with a vorticity meter. The water in the center of the river is moving the fastest, while water closer to the bank is moving slower due to friction. If you don't know what one looks like, a vorticity meter is much like an anemometer used to measure wind speed, except it does something similar for water instead. If a vorticity meter is dropped into a river, at first, it may not spin much or little at all because all of the water is moving at the same speed. At this point, there is little or no *vorticity* happening. As the meter moves further out from shore, something changes. At one point in the river, the vorticity meter will reach an area where the slower moving water close to the bank is on one side, while the faster moving water in the center is on its other side. This will cause the vorticity meter to spin, indicating that vorticity is indeed present. Taking this concept back to our thought experiment, the whirlpool serves as a metaphor for a complex embedded systems organization. Each band represents a different part of the organization, or the whirlpool, moving at a different speed, and this speed becomes faster as one moves inward. Vorticity can be used to explain the difference in speed between the bands. High vorticity means that some parts are moving much faster than others, while low vorticity between bands means that everyone is moving at about the same speed. One firmware manager character-ized how momentum is felt within his organization:

> "It (change) kicks off a whole chain of events that goes on, so I think there's always a lot of momentum going with project schedules. If you have something that changes midstream within a project, then it's very hard for us to change direction there, and it's got to be kind of planned into future releases."

Using this metaphor, we can easily map Figures 4.1 and 4.2 to the whirlpool. The central axis of the whirlpool illustrates the effect of market pressure. Market pressure is the center of the vortex that is driving the process. It is not always assumed that market pressure creates a vortex or whirlpool. However, under certain conditions, it can. The most typical examples are new markets, such as Internet of Things devices where there are many start-ups that are all vying for supremacy. Strong customer desire or drive to obtain the technology and a heavy competition with few or no dominant players are key drivers. Another important driver is survival since many small players in this new market strive for dominance. This is especially critical if the product or industry characteristics are such that capturing significant early market share has long-term ramifications for survival. The innermost ring of the pool is product development or product genesis, as we described earlier. This ring consists of requirements development based on customer input, as influenced by market pressure, and it is led largely by product management in conjunction with systems engineering. As the innermost ring, product genesis spins the fastest. The next innermost ring is the software development part of the organization. Software development can occur independently or in conjunction with other domains such as firmware and hardware. Because it runs on a fast release cycle of six months or less, it is the next innermost ring. Firmware and hardware domains make up the next two rings respectively with hardware furthest to the outside. Firmware is often managed within a software context but has linkages to both software and hardware within the organization. Hardware makes up the outermost ring because it operates on the slowest release cycle of all, which can be up to two to three years. Although all three domains can and do operate and release independently, during a full system release they must all be in complete alignment. This is a unique property of embedded systems and illustrates one of the key challenges present in this context. As in a whirlpool, although each ring is interconnected, they are all running independently at progressively slower velocities as the observer looks outward from inside the vortex at the observation point of the tennis ball, as illustrated in Figures 4.4 and 4.5. These domains and the management of them constitute our hybrid agility implementation.

The tennis ball in our metaphor falls between the first ring, *product genesis*, and the second ring, *software*. The position here represents the dividing line between *market agility* (the area between market pressure, product genesis, and the ball) and *process agility* (consisting of software, firmware, and hardware). Market agility is the ability of the *business* to adapt to change in the market and is a function of product genesis. Process agility is the ability of the *organization*, including software, firmware, and hardware, to adapt accordingly through hybrid agility.

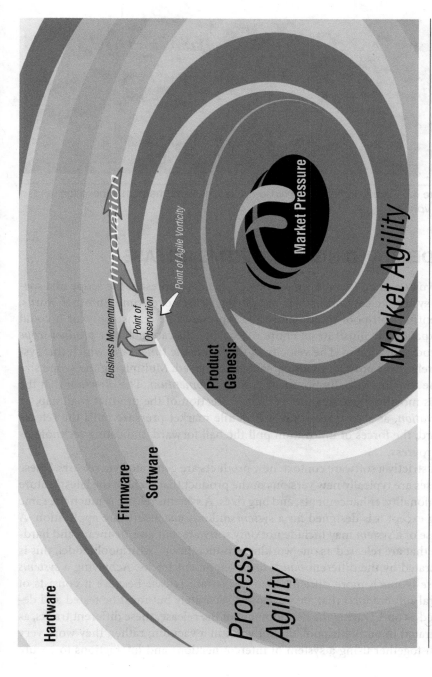

Figure 4.4 *The agile-business vortex*: the ultimate goal of agile orchestration is the management of process and market agility to achieve agile vorticity

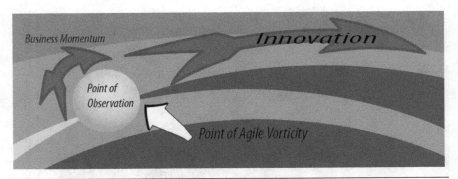

Figure 4.5 *Agile orchestration close-up*: business momentum, innovation, and agile vorticity

UNDERSTANDING THE SYSTEMS RELEASE

The vortex could include a mass or size that can represent the scope of a specific system release or a series of system releases over time. In other words, the entire whirlpool could be used to represent one release only, or it could be expanded to illustrate an entire roadmap. This can include a *product scope* or product roadmap. The velocity of the ball is the *timeline* at which this system release or product roadmap is to be achieved. Multiplying the scope size by the timeline velocity produces *business momentum*. The *direction* that the ball is moving illustrates the technical direction of the product roadmap, or *innovation*, as shown in Figure 4.5. While market pressure pulls the release inward, the forces of innovation pull the ball forward, indicating technological progress.

In strictly a software context, new products are generated via *releases*. These releases are typically new versions of the product that include the latest feature functionality, enhancements, and bug fixes. A systems release is much the same thing except it is designed for a *system* and not just a software application. A release of a *system* may include not only software, but also firmware and hardware that are released as one working product. In our whirlpool model, this is illustrated by the different *bands* or development tracks. Achieving a *systems release* is much more difficult than a software release because it consists of several *sub-products* that are developed separately but must be tested and delivered as one. During the development of the release, these different tracks, as illustrated in our whirlpool, do not work in a vacuum; rather, they work very much together using a system of interconnections and interactions to ensure that the products are compatible and that they meet quality and customer expectations and the goals of the business. This interplay between the different product management, development, and testing teams to come together in creating one cohesive product is difficult to pull off even with a waterfall style process. Accomplishing this in an agile way adds an even greater level of difficulty. Developing the capabilities to generate a systems release in this way is a key component of Metagility. In the following chapters, we will discuss these capabilities and how to develop them.

THE CREATION OF BUSINESS MOMENTUM

In this example, the equation of *momentum* from classical mechanics is translated to a business context. For example, the momentum of a speeding train would be calculated as its mass multiplied by its velocity. It takes large and/or sustained force to get the train moving, and once it does, it will take yet another large and/or sustained force to slow it down. In an agile vortex, the forces of market agility gradually pull the systems release and process agility along with it. As it does, the systems release gains momentum. Development organizations in this situation often see their cycle times decrease. As momentum grows, cycle times become shorter and shorter and accomplishing this tends to become easier. This is what is so interesting about business momentum. The higher your business momentum is, the shorter your cycle times will be and it will take less effort than before to achieve a systems release of the same or smaller size. In fact, it is not uncommon for highly functioning organizations to increase the mass of their systems releases at this point, challenging process agility even more by *managing to the bottleneck*.

$$\text{momentum} = \text{mass} \times \text{velocity}$$

$$\text{business momentum} = \text{scope} \times \text{timeline}$$

AGILE VORTICITY: THE KEY CONNECTION POINT

Finally, the circulation of the water at the point where the ball is located is called its *vorticity*. This is the point at which everything converges. *Market* agility is the ability of the business to reach the vorticity point with its product roadmap under the influence of market pressure via product genesis. *Process* agility is the ability of the organization through hybrid agility to reach the same point of vorticity. A good way to understand process agility in this illustration is an outstretched arm attempting to reach across the organizational rings to reach the ball as market agility slowly sucks it further away. It should be noted that time in this metaphor is ever-present as it would be in actuality. Vorticity is relative to the point of view of an observer at the same point of observation, moving along with the fluid.

Agile orchestration is the creation, nurturing, and closing of an agile business vortex in which market and process agility intertwine to produce a new software release. This was found to be the central problem that all aspects of the organization were trying to solve. These agile business vortices that are created as a result of high market pressure in conjunction with high technological innovation are the central theory of this study. The aforementioned model depicts bringing multiple forces together that create a need to be agile. Each concentric ring influences the point of vorticity where the firm needs to be to successfully produce a systems release.

The systems release is produced by a delivery system, which has been illustrated by the model. In essence, it represents the entire organization. The delivery system can only move as fast as its slowest part. If the different development tracks get too far ahead of each other, this can result in wasted resources and quality issues. Typically, most organizations want their delivery system to reach the point of agile vorticity—the *sweet spot* described by our model that illustrates the point at which a company has achieved maximum agility in a particular product line or market. In most circumstances, the delivery system is lagging behind product genesis and the market agility it creates. In order to catch up, the delivery system needs to manage itself to its limitations, thereby exposing any bottlenecks that may be holding it back. In order to make the delivery system go faster, we must make it go faster at these bottlenecks. In some organizations, managers sometimes choose to slow the system down, not allowing it to go any faster than its slowest member. In other situations, managers try to resolve bottlenecks by throwing people and resources at the problem, basically taking developers and testers from one job and putting them to work resolving the bottleneck. These approaches are commonly used but are marginally effective. Slowing teams down to allow others to catch up simply slows down the production of the systems as a whole. While it may reduce stress among some stakeholders, it reduces overall agility of the system and puts you in danger of losing ground to competition. Throwing people at the problem is also marginally effective because developers and other experts in those situations often must get up to speed on what the *stuck* team is doing, and it often takes an inordinate number of people to pull the bottleneck out of the rut. It is also very inefficient because what happens is that managers will bring in several people from other projects to help out in a confused and uncoordinated, hectic fashion. The problem will get resolved, but many of the resources will have contributed little to fixing the problem while their other work doesn't get done. Additionally, as we can see in our model, the different development tracks of hardware, firmware, and software do not have interchangeable resources. In Metagility, the best way of resolving bottlenecks to achieve the point of agile vorticity is to *push the bottleneck* by removing any unnecessary work from the teams encountering it. Accomplishing this can take many forms. It could mean automating testing, moving lower priority work out of the release, or negotiating with the customer to reprioritize feature functionality to be delivered. In subsequent chapters, we will deconstruct the components of the agile vorticity model to illustrate how this can be done.

THE VALUE OF AGILE VORTEX THEORY TO COMPLEX CONTEXTS

The theory of agile vorticity shows us that there is a point of convergence at which a company or organization has achieved maximum agility in their market and context. This also shows us that it *can* be achieved and that our progress toward it can be measured. High vorticity at the point of observation that we have established (meaning the point where the systems release is developed) means that market agility, or in essence the market itself, is outpacing process agility, or the current run rate of the organization. The goal is for process agility to catch up so that at the point of the systems release, the vorticity measure is zero, thereby meaning that all bands are running at the same speed, and that the organization is keeping up with the market and innovation with the release that it is creating. Thus, it is important to recognize that high vorticity in this context is not good, and the goal should be zero or no vorticity at all.

> *What is the agile vorticity for your company? Would you say that it is high, low, or even zero?*

Agile vortex theory, or the theory of agile vorticity, establishes a measurement by which we can determine how agile our company is within its market. If we find that agile vorticity is high, the company's market and process agility can be tweaked to bring it back down to zero. Highly functioning organizations do just that. This is especially valuable to complex development environments, products, and markets because these make managing agility even more challenging.

As a result, we've used the most complicated case studies possible to illustrate this theory and how it can be applied. Agile vorticity boils the complexity of managing agility down to one central key performance indicator that can be applied to virtually any kind of technology development. In the next chapters, we will illustrate how agile vorticity can be measured, and how your development teams and product organizations can be tweaked to achieve zero vorticity.

5

MANAGING MARKET PRESSURE

MARKET AGILITY

In the last chapter we discussed agile vorticity and how process and market agility work together to reach the point of vorticity. In the next two chapters we will discuss the components of market agility, beginning with market pressure, followed by product genesis. Market agility can be defined as the ability to adapt to market pressures via product genesis. In essence, the business responds to market pressures with a product roadmap based on its understanding of customer needs and the internal capacity to meet those needs. The resulting product scope, or roadmap, creates *business momentum*, which *process agility* attempts to match with the *systems release*. We begin this chapter by discussing the elements of market agility starting with its key driver, which is market pressure. This is followed by a description of product genesis in Chapter 6, which is the company's market agility response to such pressure.

Market pressure in our case studies was found to be composed of six elements. These included four *pressure drivers*: market share, customer base, government regulation, and competition, which were followed by two limiting factors or *governor elements* that served to keep the pressure in check. While most of these elements within market pressure are outside the control of the organization, there are some aspects that it can influence. These elements are outlined in Table 5.1, followed by descriptions of each respectively.

Table 5.1   Elements of market pressure

Elements of Market Pressure	
1. Market Pressure	1.1 Market share
	1.2 Customer base
	1.3 Government regulation
	1.4 Competition
	Governing market pressures
	1.5 Strategic direction
	1.6 Customer appetite

ESTABLISHING AN AGILE MARKET SHARE

Although gaining *market share* is important to any business, findings in our case studies brought forth characteristics that made this context particularly challenging. The embedded devices in one case study consist of new smart grid metering technology. These devices have a long lifespan and are often sold in large numbers. Customer contracts tend to be long term, often spanning decades. Installation of the devices takes place over a period of several months, and once they are installed customers expect maintenance over the life of the product. The customers in question are power utilities, which are often the only service providers in their respective areas. As a result, there is a limited amount of *territory* to be had, and once that territory is sold, it is out of the market for a very long time. These factors have created what one respondent termed a *land grab* situation. Vendors are under exceptional pressure to grab up as much market share as possible before it is all gone. Those who do not are not expected to survive in the business for long or will at least face long-term marginalization in the market. This phenomenon is analogous to the *gold rush* situation noted by Vidgen, which can create very high market turbulence (Vidgen, 2009).

With respect to highly innovative products, such as the Internet of Things (IoT) or related systems, the following characteristics must be considered when building an agile market share:

1. Product service life
2. Length of customer contracts
3. Size and scope of customer deployment
4. Market territory: size and exclusivity
5. Customer acquisition cost

With respect to product service life, it must be understood how long the device will survive before it is completely obsolete. Software can be updated continually, and providers have the option of charging for these upgrades or providing them for free on their own timeline. However, with embedded devices, upgrades can be performed for a period of time, but at some point, the device will have to be completely replaced. Some of this is due to technological obsolescence, but wear and tear and related maintenance agreements must also be considered. Acquisition cost is certainly a factor as the more expensive the product is the longer it may be expected to last. Embedded devices, such as IoT products and cell phones, are expected to last for years. Devices that are integral to smart cities or smart grids, such as streetlights or smart meters, may be expected to last decades. The longer the product service life is, the more limited the market share will be over time as competitors become entrenched. Initiates could possibly end up waiting years for a change to make significant inroads to such markets.

Customer contracts for your product may not be as long as twenty or more years—as with smart grid or smart cities related devices—however, many customers do end up signing long-term contracts for security systems, cell phone service, or smart devices in the home. As with product service life, these contracts can be a limiting factor for new entries into a market where existing players already have significant feet on the ground. Customers may be reluctant to cancel their contracts without incentives.

Deployment of smart devices throughout a smart grid or smart city can be an expensive and long-term endeavor, taking months or perhaps years to complete. However, much may be the same within a single customer's home. A user could spend months installing smart cameras, motion sensors, glass break sensors, and smart appliances. Not everything may be purchased at once, but for most, each item bought and installed is part of a long-term strategy. Interoperable technologies and seamless integration are of key importance here. What needs to be understood is that the size and scope of a customer deployment impacts their decision to keep these devices over time and their expectations of maintenance. Whether your user is a single household or municipality, the number of devices deployed and the complexity of that deployment will affect the ability of new entrants into the market. Customers may be less likely to rip out their devices just to support a new system or technology, and newly acquired devices will be evaluated largely on their ability to integrate with existing infrastructure.

Finally, if the size and exclusivity of the market are such that selling to one customer or a select group of customers means that you have locked down a specific territory, this means that your market share could become limited very quickly. These situations are key contributors to the kind of high market turbulence we are seeing today.

Other considerations when thinking about a new market:

1. Is your business territorial? If so, what does the landscape look like?
2. Are you in a business-to-business (B2B) or business-to-customer (B2C) market?
3. What are the limitations or boundaries of the market you are looking to enter? What are the *barriers to entry*?

Here are some key takeaways for establishing an agile market share:

1. *Time is of the essence*: Market shares in new, innovative markets can be quickly snatched up.
2. *New, innovative markets have a high degree of uncertainty*: Companies should work toward defining a unique strategic position as soon as possible. Those that do will have the best chance for long-term success.
3. *Get testimonials*: In the beginning, focus on a small number of clients who are willing to work with you in getting innovation to market. These can serve as early referrals, which in many industries can be critical in obtaining enough business to become a player to be reckoned with.
4. *Focus on the most willing and innovative customers.*
5. *Leverage agility to assimilate innovation.*

HOW DOES YOUR CUSTOMER BASE IMPACT BUSINESS AGILITY?

Our case studies also noted the relatively small, intertwined *customer base* as being a factor. Although power utility companies are often large government regulated entities, there are relatively few of them. Utilities are part of a small, tight-knit community that readily exchanges information about their vendor experiences. Recommendations from utility customers cannot only help sales, they can make or break a vendor in the business. This gives customers a great deal of leverage when it comes to getting what they want out of the product. We see this issue with a wide spectrum of customers—both big and small—in a variety of industries. Even individual users are often part of online communities that exchange ideas and opinions regarding new products and technologies. Having a positive impact with a few early customers can provide a big boost to new providers. Similarly, one customer's bad experience can have the potential to *go viral* and seriously impact a business to a degree not previously possible.

Customer base can impact agility in the following ways:

1. *Tightness* of the customer community
2. Relative size of each customer

How closely are your customers intertwined? Do they regularly discuss products and services between each other that are common to their business or personal interests? Are your customers part of a loose community of users who are interested in certain IoT devices, or are they large companies that exchange ideas in large trade forums or closed-door meetings? To be agile, you need to understand and connect with your customer base and their community. The tighter the community is and the larger each customer is, the greater impact your agile changes will have on your customer base, for better or for worse. It has been said that bad news makes it around the world before good news has time to get its pants on in the morning. Your connectedness to the customer community will not only be important to spreading the word about positive change, but also to quickly dowse fires before they spread.

Here are some lessons for connecting with your customer base:

1. *Have a social media strategy*: There are many social media tools out there; focus on the ones your customers use. Post content regularly and often and make sure that it is value-added content, not just blatant advertising.

2. *Get involved in trade shows*: In innovative markets, trade shows are more than just entertainment, they are a forum for the exchange of ideas, a chance to compare yourself against potential competitors, and an opportunity to gain intelligence, whether it be about customers or competitors. Don't just focus on having the best presentation or gizmos. Making the most of trade shows, especially in new markets, is a social exercise in information exchange, intelligence gathering, and the building of relationships.

3. *Encourage positive reviews by word of mouth or testimonials*: Try to determine how intertwined your customer base is. The more closely knit they are, the more important word of mouth or testimonials will be. This also influences what kind of testimonials will be important. For example, in a B2C world, there are always people who will say good and bad things about a product, and those customers typically don't know each other. Despite this, they do communicate in specialty forums where they may complain or praise a certain product. In such situations, your product perception will be based largely on the volume of reviews, combined with the forums from which they originate. In B2B markets, you may only need one or two recommendations from key industry players. In these situations, the quality of the review or recommendation, not the volume, is the key determinant on how you or your product(s) are perceived in the market.

4. *Learn the idiosyncrasies of your industry*: Every industry is unique—not just in the products and services it entails but also the culture, people, and expectations that surround it. If you are a new entrant, making the wrong step without doing some research on your new industry could cost you business, hurt your reputation, or worse.

COMPETITION

In addition to this limited customer base, strong *competition* between vendors was also felt by many of our case studies. Other vendors were believed to be more agile and nimble in some cases because they did not have the baggage that is often created by numerous mergers and acquisitions over the years. Competitors were believed to have the ability to respond to the market just as quickly with equivalent feature sets and embedded device support. The respondents felt that this resulted in a constant battle of who could provide the richest feature sets in the least amount of time. As one hardware project manager explained:

> "They [our competition] go to the customer and say, 'Hey, these guys don't have this latest and greatest [feature but] we have it,' so agility is certainly important. Since everybody is responding to the market, if you're the one who is doing it quicker, it helps your business."

New, innovative markets tend to be highly competitive. Chances are, you aren't going to be the only provider in such situations. One key factor is a provider's ability to not only get quality features but also those features that are most desired by the customer base to market faster. Just as you drive your competitors, your competitors in many ways will drive you. This is an integral component of market pressure.

One firmware product manager illustrated this point as follows:

> "I think at least some of our competition are probably using agile methodology and able to cut releases quickly."

In this context, it was noted from the respondent's perspective that the competition was also agile, and able to move new releases to product quickly as a result. In markets with embedded systems, this was true not only with software but hardware as well.

> "I have a feeling our competition does it that way, where they can release hardware in its own project."

What the respondent means by the previous comment is that with embedded systems, where there are multiple development tracks of sub-products, hardware products are often dependent on the software releases that utilize them. In many cases, hardware cannot be released as a stand-alone product without a software or firmware product to support it and be released in tandem with it. He believed in this case that some competitors had managed to rise above this limitation and that being able to do so was an important competitive advantage.

Further, as the comments indicate, they were not the only provider utilizing agile practices, but they believed they were doing it better than anyone else:

> *"(We have) really been successful with that, that we can beat our competitors to the market with products. So I think it's been very successful here."*

So, we see how competition drives us, but what we may not see is the customer's perspective. Agility means providing what the customer needs at the right time. It does not always mean that you provide everything possible that the customer may desire. Just as competition drives you, it also drives the perceptions of your customers. One operations manager put it succinctly and rather candidly when asked how they managed to make the customer happy under very demanding and seemingly impossible circumstances:

> *". . . I don't really know how we pull that rabbit out of the hat, honestly. Unless—I think, in general, in our industry, as bad as things can be here, I think in other places its worse. Somebody at a customer site once said that we're the prettiest girl in an ugly girl dance, basically. So, we're a better dance partner than our competitors and it still doesn't mean we don't step on our dance partner's toes. If that makes any sense."*

To become number one in your market, you don't have to be perfect, you just have to be better than everyone else. A big part of accomplishing this is the manner in which customer collaboration is leveraged and utilized. We will discuss that to some extent at the end of this chapter regarding customer appetite, and then again in Chapter 6 in relation to negotiating with customers.

DEALING WITH GOVERNMENT REGULATION

Governments were also found to be a market driver. Being an international company, this organization was subject to, and worked with, a number of different governments all over the world and even domestically; it was often faced with issues within different states, counties, and municipalities. Although government funding often helped drive the adoption rate of the smart grid technology that the company sold, sudden changes in regulations could have a significant impact on required feature sets and quality standards. As one software project manager said:

> *"In a regulated environment, we find that we are reacting to the whims of government change and having to adopt changes to the products to head off being excluded from bidding on future projects."*

The utility industry is highly regulated. Mistakes in billing and meter reading have garnered a great deal of media attention, and hence, governments have passed strict regulations on billing requirements and feature sets to ensure accuracy. With the proliferation of embedded systems-based products, such government regulation is not limited to products that affect large enterprises such as smart cities or smart grids. As we discussed in an earlier chapter, embedded systems typically have more extensive requirements around quality and reliability, which often have some kind of government oversight. Government incentives are also a factor and not just for large enterprises. We saw a rise in electric vehicle purchases when governments offered incentives to buy them, and once these incentives passed, new purchases took a bit of a dip. To deal effectively with government regulation, one must ensure that they are not excluded from a market based on a new rule or requirement. The following factors should be considered in order to be dealt with effectively:

1. What kind of government regulation, either present or upcoming, may impact your *ability to play* in a market?
2. What government incentives are present or upcoming that could generate a spike in sales and increase the chance of grabbing that critical early market share?
3. What is the process for acceptance or barrier to entry (if any) in a particular area that requires approval from a government? For example, will your company executives have to go before a public service commission or other entity?
4. Are there any negative perceptions or fears regarding your product or service type that could influence future legislation? For example, with smart utility grids, there are still suspicions around the accuracy of the metering and safety of the devices, despite research that has proven there are no issues.
5. What is the public perception of your industry, customers, or products? Remember, governments are subject to voters!

GOVERNING MARKET PRESSURES BY ESTABLISHING A STRATEGIC DIRECTION

Despite the pressures of gaining market share in a turbulent environment, inter-twined customer base, government regulations, and stiff competition, partici-pants agreed that market pressure did not go on unchecked. The organization was adept at employing methods of maintaining a good mix of responsiveness and control. One of these methods was the establishment of a *strategic direction*. In order to get products to market as fast as possible, close customer collabora-tion was often required. The company made strategic decisions to concentrate on those customers who were willing to support this high level of collabora-tion by acting as testers for new technology in exchange for being the first in the industry to obtain the latest feature sets. Such collaboration allowed par-ticipating customers to influence the technical direction of new features. This approach, in turn, allowed the organization to get products to market faster along with the added benefit of conserving resources by using the customer as an extended quality assurance team. Although such customers had to deal with extensive defect rates, they were compensated by receiving higher levels of service. In contrast, customers who demanded proven products straight out of the gate were often ignored. In essence, the company made strategic decisions to adjust customer focus to those who were willing to collaborate heavily in order to maintain its competitive edge. One software project manager summarized this concept as follows:

> *"Some customers are just simply adamant that they get a proven product; they don't want to deal with our problems and, you know, 'It had better come to them tested or, you know, there will be repercussions.' Those are customers that we tend, frankly, not to focus on. If they are going to take that approach that's unrealistic, then they'll get older product and they'll get less attention, because, again, that land grab is the strategic priority."*

When working in innovative markets, it is imperative to concentrate on cus-tomers that are agile enough to accept as much change as your organization can provide. With such products, there are features and functionality that need to be proven out, improved, or ditched altogether in order to perfect the product, thereby facilitating sales to other customers or markets that are not so forgiving. Customers who will accept a high level of collaboration are critical to making this happen. They benefit by becoming an early adopter—reaping the financial and business pluses that go along with that. In our case studies, even though many less collaborative or friendly clients were sold, they never received the level of customer service, attention, or financial incentives won by the earliest collaborators. It is important to note that entire books have been written on strategic planning, and it is not our purpose to cover that topic here in its entirety. However, from an agile point of view, especially when considering customer collaboration, it's important to think in terms of strategic direction within a larger strategic plan. Organizations often overcomplicate strategic planning with SWOT (strengths, weaknesses, opportunities, and threats) analysis, customer/competitor analysis, financial modeling, and so on. There is nothing inherently wrong with these kinds of studies; however, since agile has simplified development, it can also simplify your strategic direction. An agile approach to establishing a strategic direction can be built by following these steps:

1.   Understand the broader aspirations of the company and measure progress toward them. What is the company's current strategic position? What is the desired position and the plan to get there?
2.   What customers will the company choose to play with and which ones will it not? Which customers will best help achieve the strategic goals of the company?
3.   What capabilities will enable wins against competitors? These are the critical capabilities.
4.   What agile mix of processes are necessary to achieve these capabilities?

Put simply, an agile strategic plan can be summarized as one that:

. . . focuses on one or a small set of highly collaborative customers who are willing to help prove out critical capabilities that will enable more wins across the market.

It is important to call out a distinction between strategy and operational effectiveness. Operational effectiveness can be described as leveraging best practices so that you can beat your competitors in the same race. Strategic positioning is the act of creating a unique yet sustainable competitive position—or in short, deciding to run a different race than the competition (Porter, 2008). A good strategy should have a unique value proposition, clear trade-offs, activities that complement each other, and continuous improvement toward the strategic end (Porter, 2008). Concepts such as flexibility, innovation, or even agility alone are not considered strategies. Rather, they are enablers of strategic positioning. In our case studies, agile concepts of customer collaboration and iterative development were exercised to define and refine the unique value proposition, while making clear trade-offs with the customer.

CUSTOMER APPETITE: MAXIMIZING COLLABORATION

Another control on market pressure is customer appetite. Although customers who are willing to collaborate are going to get the latest features and the most attention, there's only so much innovation that they can handle at a given time. The customer must qualify each release before they can accept it, and the continuous release nature of agile development methods can create more work for them. As one firmware product manager put it:

> *"Customers don't have an appetite for numerous system releases because of the complexity of the system release and the level of integration effort and expense on their side to qualify."*

This threshold of customer appetite is one reason why hybrid agility works so well. By combining the gated approach of waterfall with iterative development, it limits the releases to specific timeperiods or gates as opposed to releasing new software all the time; something customers don't want.

So, we've established that customers have a certain appetite for more product, but that there is a point at which they will say, "No more, I'm full!" The point here is that to maximize agility, you need to maximize customer collaboration, and that means pushing your customer to the limits of what they can stand. Obviously, you don't want to overstep that boundary, but you need to reach it. If your customer is still saying *give me more*, then cycle times and iterations need to be revved up. Some of the techniques for saturating customer appetite include:

1. Socialize roadmaps with your customers that enumerate a number of expected releases in a year. These will consist of a certain number of large releases per year, but also smaller releases for feature refinements and defect resolution.
2. Set expectations on the level of testing that each release will require.
3. Be sure that customer involvement in testing is part of your collaboration strategy. This does not have to be relegated to customer acceptance testing but can include an iterative review of features as they are created. Product owners and product managers can provide guidance here, but the more the customer can be included the better.

In summary, the findings show that market pressure is the key driver of market agility. This pressure is created by the drive to achieve market share, the size of the customer base, competition, and in the case of the example used in this chapter, government regulation. At the same time, this pressure is governed by customer appetite and the company's own strategic direction. These elements—outlined in Table 5.1—illustrate how this response to and control of market pressure creates an interesting balance that allows the business to respond to customer needs and *stay just ahead* of the competition without exceeding its capabilities. This paves the way for the company to reach its point of agile vorticity.

6

PRODUCT GENESIS: DETERMINING WHAT TO BUILD

The organization responds to market pressures through the creation and evolution of its product line, or *product genesis*. Product genesis is essentially the organization's market agility response to market pressure. At a high level, it consists of the prioritization and comprehension of requirements, followed by scope negotiation and development of the product roadmap. Table 6.1 illustrates the elements that comprise it.

Table 6.1 Elements of product genesis

Elements of Product Genesis	
2. Product Genesis	2.1 Establishment of market timing
	2.2 Dynamic priorities
	2.3 Requirements comprehension
	2.4 Decomposition
	2.5 Dropping requirements
	2.6 Scope negotiation
3. Business Momentum	

MARKET TIMING: HOW TO KNOW IF THIS IS THE RIGHT TIME FOR YOUR PRODUCT

The process of product genesis begins with the introduction of new requirements. Product managers noted that they serve as the first entry point for these new requirements and are the primary interface to the customer. They play a large part in managing the components of market agility by gathering the initial requirements, establishing priorities, contributing to requirements comprehension, and negotiating scope with both the customers and internal stakeholders. Their first step, according to the respondents, is to create business cases from the initial requirements gathering, and work to determine where in the product roadmap it should fit. This is referred to as establishing the *market timing*. Market timing, in an agile product development context, ensures that the product roadmap is in alignment with current market pressures, as well as internal needs. Respondents stated that the establishment of such timing was subject to a number of internal as well as external factors, which included dependencies on other development efforts, organizational priorities, resource availability, and budget.

> *"So, my role in agility would essentially be a key role as far as getting market timing established, keeping costs down. So, primarily, time, cost, and product requirements."*
>
> —Firmware Product Manager

Primarily established by product managers but also augmented by the development organization, establishment of market timing goes through the following steps:

1. *Criticality of time to market*: This is best understood with a business case. You have customer demand to satisfy a certain problem. It is critical, either for your business or for your customers, to get this product to market at a certain point in time. Doing so gives either your business, your customers, or both a competitive advantage. The potential impact of this advantage and the long-term ramifications of it are key determinants.

2. *Priority and dependencies on other development efforts*: Does this new requirement fit in well with the established portfolio? Can this work be easily added to existing efforts with little to no disruption? If the answers to those two questions are yes, then the timing can be set more quickly.

3. *Resource availability*: When developing embedded systems products with so many interdependencies, resource availability is not a trivial issue. Care must be taken to ensure that a resource is available to work on a new product requirement without compromising another.

4. *Budget*

It is important to note that much of the agile market timing is directly customer driven, as opposed to being based on some analysis of what the market is doing at a given time. One of the first rules for any start-up is to begin with a customer. If you have a customer, you have a business. All too often, new companies make the mistake of developing products based on their own perceptions or beliefs without conducting enough testing or customer validation. A minimum viable product should be created, and this product should be modified and *pivoted* as it is validated with customers. Ideally, a product may be created based on a customer request. Similarly, in a larger organization with established customers and ongoing development, new products or requirements are largely driven by customer demand as one operations manager said:

> *"Growth over the next decade is huge in the Japanese market versus North America. There's still going to be some growth here, but it's more at a plateau. A lot of the big pieces of the grid have already been taken up. I don't think we will be growing as huge in North America."*

In the aforementioned quote, the operations manager is noting that for our case study, the North American market for their products was approaching saturation, but the company was able to find new markets in Asia and South America. Markets can vary widely by geography, demographics, and other factors, and different markets require different timing.

> *"Well, I think it saves us time by not working on something that isn't necessarily going to be the most immediate market need, so that saves time to market."*
>
> —Software Architect

Finally, economy plays a role in market timing. As the aforementioned quote illustrates, resources needed to be focused on the most immediate market needs; not only to get those items out as fast as possible, but also so that resources are not spent on something that will not be used until much further down the road, if at all.

DYNAMIC PRIORITIES: MANAGING EVER-CHANGING PRIORITIES

Once market timing is established for a requirement or feature set, it is then *prioritized*. This prioritization changes *dynamically* as requirements and their impacts become better understood. This understanding is an iterative process of requirements comprehension and decomposition with the input of both product management and engineering. Requirements are decomposed into components that are typically translated into user stories. As these stories are discussed, reviewed, and estimated, the understanding or comprehension of these requirements changes. The priority of the requirements can therefore change as a result of this iterative analysis. This phenomenon was referred to by respondents as *bubbling up* the requirements. As this dynamic priority becomes better established, requirements are then accepted, dropped, or postponed, and the scope for the systems release (and therefore the overall product roadmap) becomes more solidified. The scope of the latest systems release in essence *bubbles up* to the top of the product roadmap. Such prioritization is dynamic throughout product genesis as one software architect said:

> *"Rapid shifts in priorities for what we were supposed to work on and rapid introduction of new features into the system . . . come in, new priorities come into engineering, and we have to shift and say, 'Okay, what do you want to move out to move that in?' . . . And that's what agile actually is pretty good at."*

The previous quote describes—at a very high level—how dynamic priorities impact work from a developer's point of view. In the following section, we review some organizational enablers that research has shown are necessary in order to effectively react to rapidly changing needs. Enablers for dynamic priorities include:

1. *Requirements comprehension*: It is important to be able to quickly document and remember new requirements as they come in and to understand their priority so that when it comes time to plan systems release, the requirements will make the cut.

2. *Use of right-sized sprints*: Sprints can vary by organization, but with embedded systems development we found that two-week-long sprints were ideal. It is imperative to get this right because if the sprints are not sized correctly, requirements cannot be moved in or out as easily.

3. *Always compare new incoming requirements with the existing backlog*: You must ask yourself, "Does it trump the priority of what is already in the queue?"

4. *Plug in sizing*: Once a requirement is deemed high enough in priority to insert into the current release or sprint, search for a requirement that can be removed or pushed out that is the same size of work. This

will make transitioning easier and ensure that the new requirement is developed on time. The trumped requirement can be put into another sprint, release, etc.

5. *Extend dates if necessary*: As we have discussed, hybrid agile development does not always produce iterative releases to the customer. These have to be managed as part of a systems release. However, unlike traditional waterfall, which tends to be more rigid, dates need to be extended if necessary to accommodate new requirements. The key is to obtain requirements comprehension and decomposition as soon as possible so that any date extensions for the final systems release can be made accordingly. Often, by using this technique, date extensions are invisible to the customer because the determination was made earlier in the process before commitments were made.

6. *Understanding business value*: When stakeholders prioritize requirements, the business value of each must be clearly understood—especially new requirements—compared to what is already on the plate.

7. *It's not just about sprints*: Dynamic priorities mean that product portfolios and roadmaps have to change as well.

8. *Focus*: Once you have requirements prioritized and set up for sprints, focus on the work at hand and get it done. Focus on delivered work. Don't worry so much about *what may come down the pike* or *what changes are on the way* or whether your work will be shelved in favor of something else. That's the nature of the beast. Develop the capability to react effectively, instead of constantly peeking around the corner to see what's gaining on you. If you have the right capabilities in form, it won't matter what is thrown at you or your team—you will be able to get it done.

9. *Dynamic teams*: If you were changing one feature for another feature, the team that was working on that previous feature should be able to adjust and start working on the next one. When such exchanges are made, it should be done so with feature sets that require similar skill sets to build so that the teams can quickly adapt and pick up the new item.

Common Challenges with Dynamic Priorities

Even with a very effective organization and detailed requirements comprehension, dealing with dynamic priorities can still be a significant challenge if the requirements are very large in scope, or if the requirement is something totally unforeseen.

Large Requirements

The best way to react to large requirement changes is to build a rapid response team. System architecture teams, who are often separate groups from the developers working within a sprint, can help with breaking down requirements and defining architectural approaches so that larger, more complex changes can be plugged in more easily. The following quote from a software development manager describes how this problem was solved.

> "When we did cellular projects, we were about halfway through a release on Sprint 5 and by Sprint 6, we had teams fully tasked, doing something that wasn't needed in the release at all in Sprint 4. So during Sprint 5, we did a bunch of prep, we had some high-level meetings that had engineers working together to do some design work, make some decisions on approach, and by the next sprint we had switched 25 people into the new requirement. It was a pretty big switch."

Handling the Unexpected

It's one thing if a known priority suddenly becomes more important, and quite another thing when a completely new requirement comes out of the blue. One software architect described this problem:

> "Well, I think we were readily able to address new market demands but, our releases are six months long and we have many competing priorities, so if it's a market demand that we saw coming, well then we can potentially stop for it or change priorities. If it's something that just popped up out of the blue, then it just depends on what kind of impact we take, whether it's upsetting the customer or if it's spending a lot of money to try to bring someone up to speed."

It's important to read between the lines here with what the architect is trying to say. Requirements should be customer driven. But in the instance of significant changes that are a complete surprise, we need to understand if this is critical to the customer's business or just something they think they want due to their own lack of understanding. The new requirement would need to be assessed in terms of budget and timing impact, and then presented to the customer for negotiation. Agile does not necessarily mean the customer gets everything they want all the time. Also, the technology developer is often considered the expert. With technology, the customer is not always right, and it is important to include this technical guidance along with any bargaining that will be needed to determine if the new requirement will move forward.

REQUIREMENTS COMPREHENSION: UNDERSTANDING WHAT THE MARKET NEEDS

So how exactly does prioritization occur? Respondents stated that prioritization is a constant *push-and-tug* process between the business and engineering, or as in the context of Metagility, between market and process agility. It is both dynamic and iterative and becomes better defined as *requirements comprehension* and decomposition progress. Respondents stated that product managers compete with each other as well as engineering stakeholders to bring visibility to their priorities. The dynamism of these priorities is somewhat dependent on their foreseeability and perceived impact. In summary, prioritization is a process of assessment and reassessment of features against company strategic direction, the value of deals coming in, and internal competition between product managers. This process evolves as requirements and their impacts become better understood.

A common pitfall with regard to requirements comprehension is performing it in a waterfall, rather than an agile fashion. This can sometimes occur even in an agile context. For example, in a waterfall process, business analysts will attempt to define requirements by brainstorming or making suggestions as to what they think the customer will need based on their own knowledge, personal affectations, and perhaps an interview of a few stakeholders. The stakeholder interviews are not always comprehensive and analysts are often tempted to make suggestions for features that are not necessarily needed. Product managers and any stakeholders involved will usually not protest because more is always better, right? Not in an agile context. Such situations not only result in unused feature functionality, but also *over-packing the release* by spending precious development points that could be better utilized elsewhere. In even more disastrous circumstances, this has resulted in over-estimating and subsequent loss of business when responding to proposals from customers. When an organization undergoes agile transformation, business analysts are often translated into a product owner role, but they sometimes do not change how they comprehend and break down requirements. They should use their knowledge and analytic skills to collaborate with architects and experts to technically decompose the requirements based on what has been derived from the customer or customer representative. Making endless suggestions for new features should be curtailed.

DECOMPOSITION: HOW TO BREAK DOWN REQUIREMENTS INTO CONSUMABLE CHUNKS

If requirements comprehension is key to the evolution of priorities, then how does it occur? Respondents stated that requirements become better understood as they are broken down through *decomposition*. In order to deliver incrementally using iterations, as agile demands, functional requirements must be broken down into smaller chunks that are digestible by teams. This process focuses requirements on business value. Decomposition was defined by respondents as the process of increasing understanding by reducing complexity. Complexity is reduced by breaking requirements down into manageable chunks so that the technical, financial, and product implications are clear to the stakeholders. The output of this process is typically a series of user stories that can be fed into development sprints once they have been reviewed and accepted for a system release. Once a requirement is decomposed, additional dependencies, requirements, resource, or budget needs often become more apparent. This information is then fed back into the prioritization. Ultimately, the business seeks to understand how much capacity a specific requirement will need, its technical impact, and value add to the company's product roadmap and customer base. This process is a vital input to product genesis because it dictates what features may or may not make it into a specific system release. It is the way in which product genesis *right-sizes* itself as requirements and business needs become better understood and agreement with the customer (or market) is negotiated. The diagram in Figure 6.1 illustrates this cyclical process.

It's important to understand that requirements comprehension and decomposition are critical to the Metagility process. It is also not entirely linear. When requirements are first presented, they are provided high-level estimates or *t-shirt sizes*. As the higher priority items become *penciled in* for a release, they are presented for decomposition. In an embedded systems organization, requirements decomposition is typically conducted by a systems architecture and/or product owner group. This group of professionals consists of systems analysts, business analysts, and system architects with a broad spectrum of knowledge around the company's products and services. They take individual requirements provided by sales and product management and create user stories. User stories are marketable feature components that can be delivered in one sprint or iteration. Such user stories may consist of use cases, wireframes, screenshots, or other artifacts that help the team understand what needs to be delivered. The first user stories created from feature requirements provided by the customer or product management are typically high level. These high-level user stories are referred

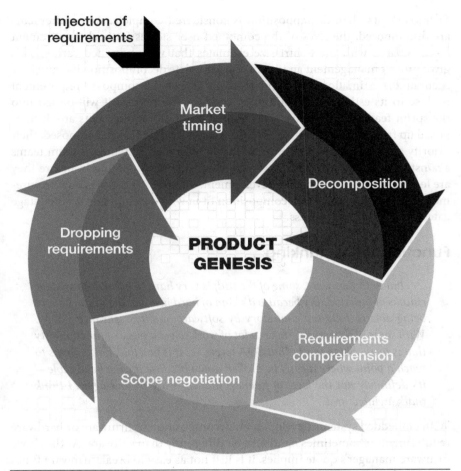

Figure 6.1 The evolutionary cycle of product genesis

to as *epics*. Epics are large groups of feature functionality that accomplish a goal established by the business. Such epics should be traceable to the competitive strategy of the enterprise. In short, epics are large features that should be deliverable within a series of iterations or several months. These parent or *epic* user stories are then broken down into smaller stories, which in turn, can be decomposed into tasks. Although product owners may conduct the decomposition, the sprint teams that are likely to do the work will provide estimates on getting them done. Once the user stories for a requirement are small enough in size to fit into sprints, then decomposition is considered complete. As requirements are decomposed, the sizes of the combined user stories for each requirement are compared with the t-shirt size estimates that were provided earlier. This gives project management an idea of how complete decomposition is—and how accurate the estimations are. If the resulting size of a decomposed requirement is close to its estimate, and still prioritized for the release, it will be fed into the sprint teams. It is important to note that not all requirements are decomposed up front. It is an iterative process. As requirements are decomposed, their priority and business value are re-evaluated by the project and program teams against existing requirements and new feature requests coming in before they are fed into the sprint teams for development. Figure 6.2 illustrates how requirements comprehension and decomposition fit in with development sprints, stage gates, and the Scrum process.

Functionality Chunking

". . . but with firmware, some of the stuff is very hard to break into smaller chunks of functionality because it's kind of hard just looking at stories and being able to fully test that story by software quality assurance (SQA). With some of that stuff, it takes a lot of work to get a piece of functionality that is available to test at that SQA level . . . . It is possible, but it seems to reach a point where it can't be broken down because it can't be testable— it's definitely not the level of fineness that software is, and again I think that's architectural."

With embedded systems development, decomposition of firmware or hardware requirements is sometimes handled a bit differently than software. As the above firmware manager's quote implies, it is just not as easy to break firmware functionality down into very small manageable pieces. The main reason for this is the testing methodology. Firmware and hardware are tested together and must undergo a series of tests for robustness, standards compliance, reliability, and safety, in addition to feature functionality. As a result, work that is fed into the sprints of firmware is often chunked according to functionality. Whereas a software requirement may be broken up into tasks in terms of database changes, application code changes, UI (user interface) changes, etc., which may roll up to a functional requirement that could be released in an iteration, a firmware requirement will be broken down into larger chunks of functionality. For example, a smart thermostat must be able to have a set point created remotely, or a series of daily readings must be obtained from a smart meter. These are *chunks*

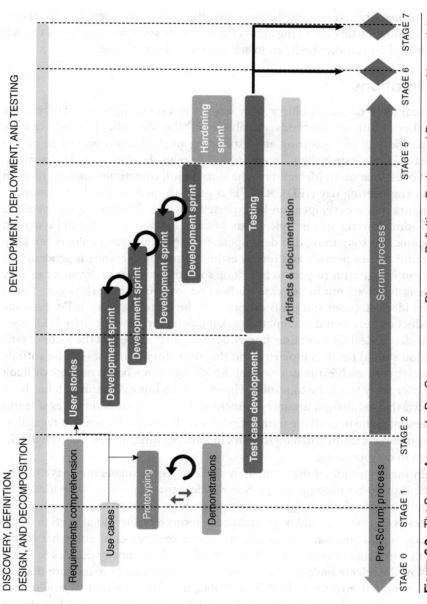

Figure 6.2   The Scrum Approach. Pre-Scrum process: Discover, Definition, Design, and Decomposition and the Scrum process: Development, Deployment, and Testing

of functionality that are vetted along with other testing requirements. The practice of functionality chunking allows the firmware and hardware teams to keep up with their software brethren to achieve the systems release.

Estimations

Typical agile dogma is blurry with respect to estimating work. There are a number of different methods available. With the Metagility process, we have a specific way of measuring and estimating work that has proven to be the most effective, especially with embedded systems development. The defining unit of estimation in Metagility is the story point, sometimes referred to as an ideal engineering day (IED). An IED is generally accepted to be the number of hours that a developer can be expected to code. Accounting for meetings and administrivia, this is typically six hours. This does not have to be written in stone. It is something that developers, managers, and stakeholders can keep in mind as they provide and review estimates so that everyone is generally on the same page with respect to how long something will take. Sprints can vary in length as well, but in our case studies one- or two-week sprints were found to be ideal. If a user story was estimated to be more than five IEDs, then the product owners would attempt to break it down more. Two or three IEDs were considered ideal for most user stories. Many agilists argue that the focus of estimation should be on complexity, and that user story points should be entirely abstract with each estimator or team assigning points based on how difficult the user story would be to resolve. However, with our case studies, it has been shown that estimation accuracy is increased across large enterprises if teams have some kind of unifying frame of reference. It has also shown that regardless of complexity, teams still tend to think in terms of time, or how long it will take them to do something.

In the beginning of the estimation process, requirements may have undergone little to no decomposition. Stakeholders may have very little idea as to what it would take to build out a requirement or series of requirements. Estimates as this stage should be thought of in terms of value. What portion of the release would you want to allocate to certain requirements, and what return on that investment is expected? For example, if the company decides to invest 40% of the release budget, at a cost of $1.5M, but wants to make sure that the return on that investment is at least double, then the requirement would need to be continuously re-evaluated to determine if the return on that investment will meet expectations, in this case, $3M. This return on investment would need to be evaluated against other requirements in the pipeline along with the percentage of the release that each would be expected to consume. This level of estimation is typically performed by senior management.

The next phase of estimation is performed as the teams attempt to determine feasibility. At this point, teams have started thinking about the high-level user stories or epics and probably have, at least at a high level, an architectural approach in mind. Estimates at this level should be abstract, but at the same time, stakeholders should have some range of IEDs in mind. The best way to approach this is through t-shirt sizing, which in turn, can be tied to a range. This approach provides the abstraction needed when performing these high-level estimates, while at the same time providing a framework that stakeholders can go by so that estimations are not wildly different between requirements. This activity is usually performed by director-level and first-level management. Planning poker or a Monte Carlo simulation is a popular method used by teams to provide these estimates. Using this technique helps to eliminate expert or managerial bias and helps remove the ownership and ostensibly the *blame* and *shame* with getting an estimate wrong.

When providing *t-shirt* sizes or high-level estimates, IEDs were also kept in mind. Each t-shirt size was defined as a range of IEDs, as illustrated in Table 6.2. Of course, the larger the t-shirt size, the more time the stakeholder teams would spend reflecting on its value and the team's ability to deliver. As decomposed values of each requirement are compared with their respective t-shirt sizes, the resulting *surprise* may result in re-evaluation of the requirement or dropping it altogether.

Final estimates are generally a two-phase process. As user story decomposition begins, architects, business analysts, first-level managers, and other

Table 6.2 T-shirt estimates: relationships between high-level t-shirt estimates and story points

Size		Range from	Range To
Extra Small	XS	1	5
Small	S	6	20
Medium	M	21	50
Large	L	51	100
Extra Large	XL	101	150
XX Large	XXL	151	250
XXX Large	XXXL	251	500

Numbers represent story points or *Ideal Engineering Days*

stakeholders will review each user story at the time of creation and put a preliminary estimate on it. The goal is to take the prior high-level estimates down to a lower level of granularity.

Another pass is performed once decomposition is complete for all features and epics. The proposed scope for the release is compared with available team capacity. A prioritized product backlog is brought to a release planning meeting where all of the decomposed stories and estimates are reviewed against established vision and risks in the context of the big picture. Participants typically include the entire release team and estimates for every user story are obtained to pass the second stage gate. Again, a planning poker or other Monte Carlo simulation can be used at this stage as well. Such simulations improve over time as the backlog matures, and teams typically like comparing the outcome to what they thought the estimate would be in their heads. Over time, this improves the team's overall estimation accuracy. Although estimates for each individual user story do not have to be spot on with actual results, the number of user stories coming out of decomposition should be very close to ensure overall accuracy of the release estimation.

The key to delivering the kind of product value expected by the business without reducing scope is to focus regularly on the smallest subset of requirements or user stories that the team(s) can deliver, while still realizing the overall product or goals for the release. Many high-level product requirements or features consist of a great deal of ambiguity and the process of decomposition, continuous estimation, and right-sizing assists stakeholders in making the right kinds of trade-offs to maximize value and minimize cost.

DETERMINING WHICH REQUIREMENTS TO KEEP AND WHICH ONES TO DROP

Deciding which requirements to drop for a systems release is a balance between customer needs, capacity, and contractual requirements—with contractual requirements taking priority.

> *"But again, we'll drop the requirements and sometimes whole requirements will move to a future release, or partial requirements will be dropped in conjunction with the market needs."*
> —Software Development Manager

Such decisions are made by the business with an emphasis on continuity. When requirements are removed or dropped, they are done so in a surgical fashion so as not to disrupt ongoing work. A team working on a dropped requirement will tie up the work nicely and put it on ice for the next release and move other requirements into their next sprint. In an embedded systems organization, hardware constraints can complicate this move. One software development manager explains this dynamic:

> *"Once in a while, the business wants to do something that's big, but the hardware is coming from another country and it won't be available until about the same time we want to release the software to the customer, so we have to do that coordination and it's going to cross into the next release. So we'll do as much work as we can in this release, but until we get that hardware we can't verify that it's good in the next release, and again, those releases are gated because customers don't want software every week."*

In this section, we will discuss the four key drivers used when determining which requirements to drop: customer needs, customer-driven priorities, quality, and over-commitment.

Customer Needs

Customer needs can be defined as those features requested by a customer for a specific release. These may or may not be contractually committed requirements. Respondents often stated that customer needs were sold first and then they determined how those needs could be accommodated in a release later. In many cases, such needs may be placed into a release in hopes of satisfying a prospective customer. Dropping such requirements is a strategic decision among the leadership. As one product manager stated:

> *"One is part of the senior leadership decision-making process about which risks to take with input from the product management, VP, the CTO for R&D, and the general group of executives who have all the skin in the game to get that contract delivered."*

Dropping a requirement is a risk-taking exercise where the potential value add is balanced with the cost of trying to keep it in. Our case studies regularly pushed their capacity to the limits and beyond, adding additional resources when necessary, as the following quote from a software project manager illustrates.

> *"Yeah, and in the past, we've been well over capacity and we've contracted with third-party organizations to help us do the development. We've hired*

more people. Those customer needs definitely impact how much work we do here and how much we decide to take on. We've been managing a consulting company for the past few years and we just don't have enough internally to complete the work, so we have to hire outside to get it done."

Customer-Driven Priorities

Beyond customer needs, there are customer-driven priorities that are absolute *must haves*. These could be bug fixes of high severity, or features or fixes that directly impact a customer's revenue. In these situations, our case studies admitted that the loudest source of a requirement got the highest priority, or in essence, the *squeaky wheel* was the one that got the grease.

Commitment to Quality (CTQ)

Most embedded systems development efforts will require some level of quality commitments. These are important measurements or benchmarks related to performance or data quality that are contractually committed. In many cases, such commitments may be derived from government regulation and are therefore non-negotiable items. These commitments are typically determined early in conjunction with the customer.

> *"Customer input and collaboration are key. So, early on, when we are selling something, the customer determines what they want as benchmarks or the type of measurements that they need out of the system and its at that point where we start to determine what the CTQs are and if they are even achievable."*
>
> —Software Project Manager

When CTQs are determined early on, the development organization works backward from the proposed delivery date to determine how much quality can be committed to within a certain period of time. Customer committed CTQs must be met, although there may be internal CTQs set within the teams to help sell other products or customers. One software project manager illustrates these two points:

> *"There's a number of CTQs that we determine that we're going to implement. Usually we determine when the release is going to go out the door and then from there we back into how much development can we squeeze in and how much quality are we willing to accept within this period, and if it works out then that period stays."*

"Well, we have contractual agreements with customers. Some of those CTQs have to be met and if we need development efforts to help meet that, then we have to put that as scope. We determine if there is some internal CTQs that we want to manage to improve our product and help us sell something else."

Over-Commitment

As alluded to earlier, the organization stretches itself to the very limits of its capacity and beyond when it comes to packing the systems release with features and fixes. Many architects and managers felt that this was an example of extreme over-commitment. Such managers felt as if each release was over-subscribed, that contracts were too aggressive for the capabilities of the organization, and that they were always playing a game of *catch up* with contractually obligated work. Despite all of these misgivings, the organization always managed to *pull the rabbit out of the hat* so to speak and satisfy its customers with the results of the systems release. Only by pushing themselves to the limits were they able to reach the point of agile vorticity. Customer negotiation techniques, as we will discuss in the next section, allowed the organization to *make its customer* happy with what eventually ended up in the systems release.

Table 6.3 contains a decision matrix for dropping requirements.

Table 6.3 Dropping requirements decision matrix

Query Point	Yes?	No?
Decision makers should bear in mind the established priority for the requirement made during release planning when satisfying the following queries.		
Is the feature contractually committed or a need?	Retain the requirement	Ensure that the priority of the requirement in the backlog is set accordingly.
Does the feature or fix impact company or customer revenue?	Retain the requirement	Ensure that the priority of the requirement in the backlog is set accordingly.
Does the requirement impact a quality commitment?	Retain the requirement	Ensure that the priority of the requirement in the backlog is set accordingly.
What is the level of urgency with the customer?	If the level of urgency for the customer is extremely high, determine the impact on the customer's business and base retention on whether they are impacted from a revenue or regulatory standpoint.	If only moderately urgent, perhaps this item could be negotiated for the next release.

How far have we over-committed? Can additional resourcing deliver?	If the requirement can be delivered with modest additional resourcing, and particularly if it impacts the aforementioned items 1–4, then it should be retained.	If over-committed with no additional resourcing, negotiate with customer to push back to the next release, perhaps a maintenance release.
What is the risk of dropping? Can this be added to the next release?	Risk commonly takes the form of possibly losing business. If this probability is high, retain.	Low risk and can be added to the next release, do so.
Are there any dependencies hampering delivery that cannot be mitigated for this release (hardware availability, technology availability, vendor products)?	Determine what these dependencies are and a potential mitigation strategy for each. Prioritize based on the viability or non-existence of a mitigation strategy.	Drop the requirement only if there are no other options.
Has decomposition proven the requirement to be much larger than expected?	The business value of the requirement should be re-evaluated against constraints.	If decomposed estimates fit well within the t-shirt size established, congratulations!
Has requirements comprehension revealed critical gaps in knowledge or resource availability?	The business value of the requirement should be re-evaluated against constraints. Try to determine what was missing during earlier planning.	Retain the requirement unless it is edged out by others.
Has the priority of the requirement changed from a customer or product management perspective since it was originally set?	The requirement should be re-prioritized against the other requirements before being fed back into the product genesis cycle.	Drop if it is edged out by other requirements.

HOW TO NEGOTIATE SCOPE WITH YOUR CUSTOMERS

An agile organization typically has a prioritized list of scope for a particular release that can change rapidly day by day. In our case studies with hybrid agile organizations, they attempt to pare this scope down as closely as possible by the second stage gate. This practice of early pare down helps the teams get to work early at focusing on the highest priority items, as illustrated by one manager's comments:

"So, agility here saves us time because for a release we will have basically 100 features that are being desired. Well those 100 features were pared down from 200 items . . . "

"I think reaching a scope decision early on is probably one area where we struggle, and probably one of the biggest wins we can have because if we reach our scope early enough, and focus on decomposition, then the teams work on the right things, right out of the gate."

That does not mean that scope cannot change after the second stage gate. The organization works to pare it down as closely as possible, but it can still flex in an agile way. If a feature becomes less important for scope, and work has been done on it, it is tied off and completed so that the team can move on to something else. This reduces jeopardizing the integrity of the release because they were able to implement at least a simple or partial component of a complex feature. If additional scope is added pushing the release to its limits, more capacity may be moved from quality testing to development.

So, we can see how the hybrid agile organization handles scope changes, but how are these negotiated with the customer? Field trials, workshops, and pilot projects are tools or negotiation points that allow the company to better understand customer needs and requirements, get early feedback on work that has been completed, and move products into production faster by allowing the customer to perform much of the testing. The next sections will describe in detail how these methods work.

Field Trials

Field trials are particularly useful with embedded systems products because the process allows for early testing of hardware, firmware, and software together within the customer's actual environment. The field or beta test must be conducted with customers before the product is released to the larger market. Such testing is commonly conducted with existing customers who already have some experience with an earlier release of the product and are in the process of evaluating new hardware functionality. The practice of field trials allows the development organization to not only leverage the customer's resources in order to conduct testing, but also to get feedback on improving their own testing techniques. As one product manager illustrates:

"We essentially had very big installations for a few customers in Texas, and I feel the customer played a key role in improving our quality with

their feedback . . . and that's the first chance for us to get some feedback on our quality. Our customers in Canada, they do a really, really thorough testing of our products. I would say sometimes even more detailed testing than us, so we take that feedback and it helps us to improve our quality of tests—that's certainly a good thing."

Since embedded systems products are relatively complex with higher standards for quality and safety, the customer is typically more than willing to participate in field trials; in fact, these may be a customer requirement.

Workshops

At times, a customer may ask for something quite complex or may have trouble expressing his or her own needs. In these situations, a vendor may hold workshops with the customer. This usually includes product managers, product owners, and systems engineers sitting down with customer stakeholders to gain an understanding of their issues and determining what solutions will best suit them. Often, what a customer thinks they want is different from what they really need. These workshops improve customer service and satisfaction because it makes them feel as though their needs are being heard. At the same time, product managers and engineers can propose solutions that satisfy the customer requirements, but also are not as complex or costly as what the customer may initially have proposed. It is a good idea to hold these workshops periodically even as requirements and release work are being performed. The earlier feedback can be received, the easier it is to make changes.

Pilot Projects

Similar to a field trial, a pilot project is where a small number of devices or products are tested in a controlled environment at a customer site. Pilot projects are usually conducted earlier than field trials. With field trials, the purpose is to leverage the customer to help with the testing so that development can refine and perfect the release. The pilot project is conducted earlier and is more of a fact-finding mission to determine what the customer wants and to verify the viability of a particular device or concept.

"We work with the customer to set expectations that we are going to pilot things with them instead of giving them a proven, field-ready, tried-and-true product, and the customers, to their credit, have generally accepted

*some of these decisions and worked with us as long as the expectations
were managed."*

—Software Product Manager

With innovative products and industries, customers are usually interested in
participating in pilot projects. It gives them the opportunity to test out and
potentially implement new technology before their peers do and gives them a
hand in the development of new products and services.

Release Acceptance

At some point, after all field trials, pilot projects, and workshops have been
completed, the final release is provided to the customer. This release must, at
some point, be accepted. This release acceptance provided by the customer may
vary from region to region, but it typically consists of the customer conducting a series of release acceptance tests, and then providing a formal letter of
acceptance. Only then is the project closed out. Much of this may sound more
waterfall oriented, but the release acceptance phase is not as final as it sounds.
Requirements that were moved out of one release will quickly be moved into the
next, and there may be a series of smaller maintenance releases provided to the
customer to correct defects or refine a particular feature. Figure 6.3 provides a
release process overview that maps the release planning to the stage gating and
development phases discussed earlier.

Cultural Differences Affect Negotiation

*"Some of that is cultural, some of that is we're an American company,
we're working on a Japanese product, and there is some inherent distrust
there. I think our North American customers, we tend to work a little bit
better with. Perhaps that's just cultural similarities though at that point."*

—Operations Manager

It is no surprise that cultural differences between countries can affect negotiation practices. Field trials, workshops, and pilot projects are all still viable
options to augment and push forward products in countries all over the world.
However, the more vast the differences are in culture, the more extensive such
testing efforts may become. For example, workshops in Japan may take days or
weeks to conduct with a large variety of stakeholders. Field trials may be more
extensive. Customers from other cultures may be less inclined to take what the
vendor says at face value without significant verification. However, although

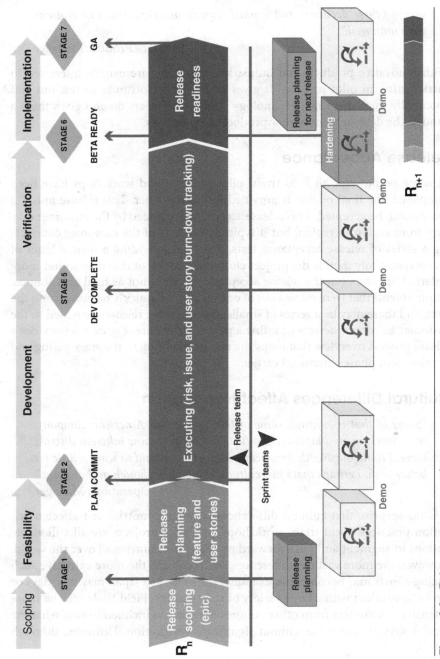

Figure 6.3 Release process overview

they may take longer to conduct, these techniques will still allow for products and services to reach the market much faster than they would with traditional non-agile methods that do not utilize extensive customer collaboration.

CREATION OF THE ROADMAP

Product managers like to build roadmaps. As technology developers, we are attracted to the idea of knowing where we are going, and our customers will want to know what our plans are as well. However, even in a hybrid agile development environment, the roadmap may not always be very clear, especially when looking more than six to twelve months out. The most effective hybrid agile organizations use the following techniques in developing their roadmaps:

1. Detailed roadmaps are developed no more than 18 months out—and even that is a stretch. Although product managers may have a good idea as to what is coming down the pike two or three years down the road, there is too much potential for change to create a detailed roadmap that far out that could be socialized with confidence both internally and externally. If roadmap items that far out are indeed on the table, they are typically left as only footnotes or high-level goals until the time frame gets closer.

2. Roadmaps may focus more on goals than on specific requirements. For example, a company may want to be a key player in the smart cities market and may decide that they will provide networking technology that other vendors can attach devices to and communicate with. The details of this roadmap goal may need to be worked out in conjunction with contractual requirements and work already in the pipeline; however, it may be socialized as part of a larger agile roadmap. Many product managers in an agile environment shy away from creating detailed roadmaps at all for fear that they may change. Goals are one way to alleviate this stress by noting what the organization intends to do without being held accountable for details that cannot be known at an early date and most certainly will change to some degree. The fact that requirements can change over time in an agile environment should not dissuade product managers from creating roadmaps. Just like the products they are creating, the roadmaps should be changeable in an agile way, but it always helps to know where you are going, or at least where you think are headed at a particular time. Inquiring customers will want to know!

3. Roadmaps can be tailored to specific customers. Product management in agile organizations often provide different roadmaps to each customer depending on their needs and interests. With large, complex product lines, customers may not be interested in roadmaps with items that don't pertain to them. Customer-specific roadmaps increase the collaboration aspect of agility, making them more amenable to participation with pilot projects and testing.

INSTILLING A CULTURE OF AGILITY

In the end, company culture plays a large part determining the level of market agility. According to one software product manager:

> *"It is probably a cultural strength, and the reason for our success is that we are used to change and it's not a cliché.*
>
> *Our corporate parent pushes aggressive expansion and fortunately the culture can stand it because it's used to it in the North American business. There are jobs I've been in where the cultures couldn't stand it and that usually ended up with a bunch of people quitting when something moved to a different mode of operation or went from domestic to international business."*

To summarize, we have shown that market pressure is driven higher through the need to gain more market share. Such pressure can also be driven by a small, tightly knit customer base or community that readily exchanges detailed information about the vendors, their offerings, and their customer experiences. Government regulation can drive market pressure in this industry through government mandates to utilities to adopt certain technologies, enforcement of billing standards for embedded device performance, and government financial incentives. These market pressure drivers are tempered by a company's strategic decision making to accept or ignore certain pressures, and the appetite for customers to accept innovation at a given time. Product genesis is the business's *agile response* to this market pressure. It begins with establishing market timing for a set of feature functionality, and dynamically prioritizing these feature sets as they go through a requirements comprehension and decomposition process. As this process arrives to completion, some features are dropped or retained as the final scope is negotiated. What remains is the scope and timeline that the organization strives to *reach*. This scope and timeline creates *business momentum* that the organization often finds itself chasing after. This business momentum influences the roadmap, which is comprised of a series of system releases, each of which have a scope and timeline, as created via product genesis.

A RECAP OF BUSINESS MOMENTUM

As described in Chapter 4, business momentum is the scope of the release or product roadmap (release mass) multiplied by the velocity or timeline in which the organization is attempting to achieve it. The direction in which this flows is in the direction of technological innovation. As market pressures increase, this business momentum can be sensed within the organization and can feel as though it is increasing or building over time. It begins with an aggressive initiative to gain market share, which feeds into the product genesis and results in the size and speed of the system release. Managers noted that as this momentum builds, it creates a ripple effect that can be felt throughout the organization. As it gains speed, managers, developers, and engineers may feel as though they are always *behind the curve*, never having enough time to build in robustness or form long-lasting and architecturally sound solutions. The following comments illustrate this sense of momentum:

> *"It seems to me that we're always behind the curve, and we've just got to get it done, and there's not enough time to do architectural work and make sure it's being done correctly and for long-term extensibility."*
> —Firmware Manager

> *"We don't usually get the time, just don't have the resources, at least not for the last couple of years, to really look ahead and evaluate new technologies. It feels like we're always a little bit behind the curve and reactive."*
> —Hardware Architect

Despite all of this, the development organization attempts to rise to the challenge and match this momentum. As one firmware architect explained:

> *"There will be a call for extra hours, weekends—to try and make it. I wouldn't say we change the deadlines, we just roll over them and we get in the 'as soon as it's done' mode. We try to condense when things change."*

The *condensation* expressed in the previous paragraph is one example of how the organization attempts to match this challenge. Although market agility sets the tone through product genesis and the momentum it creates, the development organization uses its own form of agility—described in the next chapter as *process agility*—not only to match the momentum but to influence it as well.

7

ORGANIZATIONAL (PROCESS) AGILITY: BUILDING THE CAPABILITY

HOW DO HYBRID AGILE IMPLEMENTATIONS WORK? ARE THEY SUCCESSFUL?

In our embedded systems case study, each of the three domains, software, firmware, and hardware are capable of releasing independently and at different speeds. At some point, however, all three domains must work together to create a *system release*. A system release is one where components of all three domains are developed, tested, and released together as one cohesive product. Doing so often stretches the capability of the organization to its limits. It is this crucible where process agility is flexed or adjusted in order to reach the same point of momentum that the business has been leading via market agility. The organization makes this happen via a hybrid agility implementation.

Hybrid agility can be defined as a delicate balance of agile development methods and stage-gate processes. For example, in a hybrid vehicle, electric power is utilized as much as possible to maintain economy, but it is augmented by gas motorization when extra power is needed. Hybrid agility makes use of its stage-gate and agile Scrum components in much the same way. Agile Scrum methods were employed across domains to allow the development organization to *rev high* when needed, while at the same time, stage-gate components served as a sort of *throttle* for this capability. Table 7.1 outlines the elements that were used to create this balance. It illustrates how agile development methods allow the organization to *stretch* or *reach* when it needs to, while the stage-gate aspects keep the entire process in check. Doing so allows all three domains to work together at an optimum level to achieve system release.

Table 7.1 Elements of hybrid agility

4. Hybrid agility	4A. Software	4A.1 Employs mostly agile/Scrum methods
		4A.2 Serve as the early responders
	4B. Firmware	4B.1 Employs some agile methodologies
		4B.2 A shared resource: the middle domain
	4C. Hardware	4C.1 Employs waterfall process
		4C.2 Prototyping
		4C.3 *C-Level* projects
	4D. Customer management	4D.1 Managing expectations
		4D.2 Customer negotiation
5. System release		

It is important to keep in mind that many organizations may have a combination of agile and waterfall processes, but it is getting the right mix of the two that makes the difference between success and failure. All too often, companies retain certain aspects of waterfall for the wrong reasons, or they inhibit the agile component of their strategy by approaching it from a waterfall perspective. A common pitfall is transitioning business analysts into product owners without coaching them on how to do agile decomposition. For example, a business analyst often focuses on expansive creation of features based on his or her own belief system, rather than on customer need. This is a waterfall mindset, the idea that you must plan ahead for every contingency by trying to anticipate every possible thing a customer may want. A highly capable research and development organization with all of the agile processes in place can be brought down to a slow grind if product owners create and decompose requirements in a waterfall fashion, as opposed to an agile fashion.

Metagility focuses on the mix of waterfall and agile that has proven to have the highest success rates, or rather, the case studies that leveraged their hybrid agile strategy to become number one in their market.

The following are some considerations that highly performing organizations have used in order to determine their mix:

1. The mix is driven by the market and business needs, not by internal employee pressures
2. Using Point 1, this means considering the following:
   a. Product type (software, embedded systems, etc.)
   b. Maturity of the market
   c. Maturity of the technology

HOW IS AGILE ADOPTED DIFFERENTLY BETWEEN SOFTWARE, FIRMWARE, AND HARDWARE DEVELOPMENT?

Our case studies indicated that each domain approached agility differently. The claims in Table 7.1 outline these differences from one domain to another. One software project manager attempts to explain why some of these differences exist:

> "The problem we found in agile was morphing and meshing that set of work to the waterfall methodology for hardware development."

Figure 7.1 attempts to illustrate the characteristics of each domain and how they fit together. It is important to note that these *agile characteristics*, which vary from one domain to the other, are largely unique to the embedded systems context. For example, the software domain acts as the *early responders* for high-priority issues when the other domains cannot respond as quickly. Firmware is a shared resource for both software and hardware domains, and hardware will often employ rapid prototyping or will fast track projects to keep up with its nimbler domain cousins. These characteristics enable the three domains to work together as one cohesive unit. Further, all of the agile characteristics within each domain are collectively grounded by the stage-gate components of the process. In addition, customer management activities are typically performed with the input of all three domains acting as one cohesive unit when communicating with the customer.

Although merging agile and Scrum with the stage-gate methodology may have been driven, in part, by the need to incorporate hardware projects more effectively, it also served as a series of *sanity checks* for the organization as a whole. The purpose of this sanity checking is to ensure that the system release matches what the business needs. It is how process agility lines itself up with market agility at a specific point. In short, the stage gate acts as a control or checkpoint on agile methods. One product manager explains these *toll booth* characteristics:

> "[The merging of agile methods] to a gate-driven process is more or less like a toll booth. Before you go on to the next section of road, do you have the right fare to get through? And did you get the right checks of the requirements? Did you get the right financial backing? Did you get the right details in the technical pieces and how you are going to get to the next toll gate? That is our new product introduction gate-driven methodology."

This kind of sanity checking is often necessary in an embedded systems environment due to the complexity of the solutions, interdependencies, and the

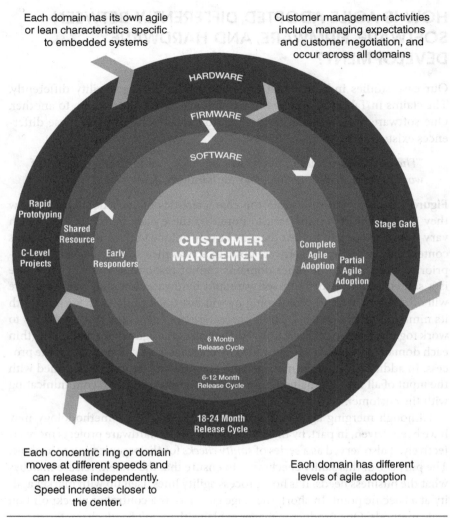

Figure 7.1 *Hybrid agility in embedded systems*: key characteristics

need to eventually roll components up from all three domains (software, firmware, and hardware) into one comprehensive system release. As one firmware manager explained:

> *"That complexity [of] firmware, the head-end, and the hardware in order to release it is what contributes to the waterfall methodology of a system release."*

The next sections describe the domains of software, firmware, and hardware within an embedded systems environment, and their role in hybrid agility. Yet another element of hybrid agility is customer management. Although product management may serve as the primary interface to the customer initially, the engineering organization is not without a voice. Respondents noted that the organization's *voice*, as well as the business side, was a critical component to hybrid agility success.

WHAT IS DIFFERENT ABOUT AGILE IN SOFTWARE DEVELOPMENT AND HOW CAN THIS DIFFERENCE BE LEVERAGED?

As with the other domains of firmware and hardware, software can release independently, but it is also linked to the other domains. Respondents repeatedly noted that the software domain had adopted the most agile development practices. These included regularly scheduled sprints, Scrum meetings, retrospectives, and agile methods for requirements management and estimation. Software development in an embedded systems environment can be just as conducive to iterative agile development as software alone with the exception that it has some constraints or linkages to the other domains from time to time. This is due to the fact that software can be more easily decomposed into testable chunks of code. Because of these factors, the software domain is capable of cutting new releases in an little as six months, compared to hardware, which could be up to 18 months or 2 years.

Respondents also noted that as the most agile domain of the three in the organization, software often serves as the SWAT team or *early responders* for the company. Whenever there is an urgent need, or even if it is not urgent but merely a process of decomposition, the organization strives to achieve *software only solutions* where it can bypass firmware and hardware when possible. This tactic contributes to the process agility of the entire embedded system.

MANAGING SHARED RESOURCES: RESOLVING CONFLICTS AND GETTING THE JOB DONE

Firmware development employs many of the same agile Scrum processes that software development does with a few exceptions. Although firmware teams manage requirements through user stories and have regular Scrum stand-up meetings, the story estimations and sprints tend to be longer and more flexible. This partial adoption of agile is due in part to the fact that firmware development cannot always be broken down into testable, iterative chunks as software can. Respondents stated that the size of the *chunks* impacted team velocity and sprint management, making it much more difficult to monitor and manage firmware development in the same way as software.

From a process perspective, firmware must straddle the organizational divide between the pure agile methodology of software and the waterfall process of hardware development. More important, both software and hardware domains often require support from firmware resources to complete their tasks, which can produce a sort of organizational tension. A hardware architect explains:

> *"Given that firmware is kind of a shared resource across all these different products and they're following a sprint cycle—it creates some tension in terms of [interdependencies]."*

Firmware's ability to *stretch* resources in support of the other domains is critical. In many ways it serves as the *glue* that keeps software and hardware connected.

Case Study Interview: Firmware in Embedded Systems Development

Firmware development holds a unique position in the embedded systems environment. There are typically many interdependencies between firmware and the other two domains of software and hardware, and the firmware often has to act as a go-between. Firmware development is often poorly understood, especially by those who work solely in a software context. There's really no better way to understand this than by talking and listening with the principals themselves. The following interviews were conducted with an architect, an engineering manager, and a product manager in the firmware domain in order to share their unique perspective on how agility works in their environment.

Interview questions focused on the four key tenets of agility, and the respondents' perception of each in the context of their organization and role. As such, the responses are in some cases very candid, and reflect the frustration level that some may be experiencing. In these cases, it is important to note the differences between perception and reality. On the one hand, the situation is probably better than how some of the respondents may perceive it to be. On the other hand, perceptions of stakeholders and experts are important, and they shape the behavior of the teams and organizations as a whole. In this respect, perceptions can indeed influence or become the eventual reality. Thus, these interviews are of great importance—not only because they give us a rare glimpse into the firmware development of embedded systems, but also because they shed some light on the challenges that managers and executives may face in changing perceptions and company culture. If you are in the process of adopting agility in your organization or if you have done so recently, chances are that many in your own company have the same or similar views to those of our respondents. As we progress through the interview, we will interrupt with summaries, clarifications, or notable points. The interview begins with an introduction:

> Interviewer: Alright, thank you very much for volunteering. First question up is, just tell me about your role here, a little bit about what you do here.

> Firmware Architect: I'm a lead firmware developer, and I write code to meet customer requirements and industry standards.

> Interviewer: How would you describe agility in your organization today? Or for example, when I say agility, how we manage change and how we adapt to new customer requirements.

> Firmware Architect: In the embedded firmware department?

> Interviewer: Yes.

> Firmware Architect: I would say we are a bit sluggish with managing changing requirements.

> Interviewer: Okay. What would you say is the process that led up to that? Or the processes around how we do manage it? For instance, when someone comes to you with a requirement, what do they do? Or how do new requirements get fed to you and how are they evaluated and prioritized?

> Firmware Architect: Can we pause this for a second?

> Interviewer: Oh, sure.

[INTERVIEW PAUSE]

In this pause, the respondent is concerned about the confidentiality of the information he is about to give and his anonymity. Once this was assured, he was willing to proceed. It is important to note that organizational processes and the issues that surround them—whether agile, waterfall, or whatever—are often hot-button issues within technical companies. Among the rank and file employee, such processes can appear ineffective and unnecessary. This is why executive engagement is so important; if hybrid agile processes appear to evolve without purpose, apathy and disillusionment can set in. Early executive engagement and communication downline can nip these issues in the bud before they occur. The firmware product manager's response below is a bit more relaxed. The firmware manager's introduction was removed for brevity:

> **Firmware Product Manager:** My position—I am a senior product manager. Specifically, my role is to gather market requirements, create a business case for the market requirements, and ultimately, have those requirements consolidated into a product that we can bring to market. So my role in agility would essentially be a key role as far as getting market timing established and keeping costs down. So, primarily time, cost, and product requirements.

> **Interviewer:** Okay. Would you say you work mostly from a hardware perspective or a firmware perspective—or a combination?

> **Firmware Product Manager:** I would say I, primarily, historically, have worked both hardware and firmware. Often, a firmware release will have to be made off cycle from a hardware product release.

As discussed in the previous chapter, this illustrates that product managers have a key role in product genesis, including establishment of market timing and requirements comprehension. We can also see here the interdependency between firmware and hardware, even at the product level.

Agile Adoption and Assimilation

The questions that follow here center on the current state of agility in the organization and how it evolved:

> **Interviewer:** Okay. How would you describe agility in our organization today?

> **Firmware Product Manager:** I would describe it as using certain pieces of what I understand to be the agile methodology, but I think those pieces are still rolling up into my understanding of waterfall in that everything rolls up, be it a hardware project, an

embedded-code project, a software head-end project all rolling up into what's called a system release—and it puts constraints on the way we do things, and we're not truly agile where you can actually cut a release and release a product at any time.

Interviewer: Okay, so it all kind of rolls up into a system release then.

Firmware Product Manager: Right.

Same question (How would you describe agility in our organization today?) posed to the engineering manager:

Firmware Engineering Manager: I'm not sure we accept change very well. It seems to be that change in customer stuff causes ripples through and between the development, testing, and definition of requirements. It kicks off a whole chain of events that goes on so I think there's always a lot of momentum going with project schedules and stuff. If you have something that changes midstream within a project, then it's very hard for us to change direction there, and it's got to be kind of planned into future releases.

The respondent in this case makes reference to business momentum, a concept introduced previously. A side effect of this momentum is the difficulty it sometimes creates with change management. The current can be so strong that significant change can be difficult to actuate unless it flows with the tide.

The firmware architect chimes in on how his tasks are prioritized:

Firmware Architect: Whoever's highest on the food chain takes priority in the order structure. For example, all the requirements in the project I've been on for the last 6 or 8 months have come from engineering. I had no visibility to any product management requirements generation.

Interviewer: Right. Okay, and I know that—I think maybe at one time that wasn't true. I think at one time, a lot of firmware developers worked directly with product managers, but it seems like that's changed now.

Firmware Architect: It's changed, I think, just because of the pace of the current project. There are very aggressive deadlines.

> Interviewer: Can you describe the events that led up to this current state based on your experience here? How did it evolve? Or has it evolved very much?
>
> Firmware Architect: Well, from my perspective, we still have a process that we intend to follow—we would like to follow. It seems pretty well defined. We end up abbreviating the process due to time constraints, and some of it is where the technical expertise lies. So, I find myself playing multiple roles sometimes: systems engineering and firmware developer.

From the perspective of the firmware architect, he is performing multiple roles, helping to define and decompose requirements and perform design, as well as develop code. In an agile environment, this is typically expected. As part of a Scrum team, the architect should be able to make suggestions with respect to requirements, design, etc. However, from the architect's perspective here, he did not think that was the intention. So, it is important early on to set the expectation of what architects and developers are responsible for in an agile framework, and then empower them to do it.

> Interviewer: What do you think contributed to the development of our agility strategy here in this organization? It certainly sounds like our aggressive timelines have been a contributor of how and what we follow but . . .
>
> Firmware Architect: I think it's been an ongoing theme around here for years to try to increase the quality of our product, and that's what led us to try to put an agile process in place. We have struggled with a true agile process because, in my opinion, the nature of embedded software is not quite a perfect fit for the agile methodology because people aren't interchangeable resources. Each of the developers have a sort of compartmentalized expertise. So, we tend to tailor the process to that a little bit.

The firmware architect makes several interesting points here. He notes that many of his requirements were generated by engineering, or from within, as opposed to product management or the customer. When it comes to firmware and hardware development, this can be quite common due to their interdependency. He then talks about how the agile process is abbreviated at times due to time and resource constraints, and about how he has to *wear different hats* to help compensate. Finally, he mentions what we now know—that pure agile is not necessarily a best fit for embedded systems development and that hybrid approaches are often the result. The firmware engineering manager echoes many of the same sentiments:

> **Firmware Engineering Manager:** I think early on, there were some processes when I came on board that were kind of already in process; then we've had some agile coaches that came in and kind of helped tweak and optimize our processes and specifically trying to make sure you had focused Scrum teams. Firmware engineers are a limited resource where we had to wear many hats, and there were always a lot of distractions that would come in and prevent us from staying focused on the sprints. That goes with the sprints, and I think that is something that we've never really addressed today. Where we are with Scrum, I don't see the agility. I don't see any of that activity. Any of the processes that we had in place have kind of fallen by the wayside, so I don't see a whole lot of agility going on today.

> **Interviewer:** So in the firmware space you were doing Scrums at one time I believe, but you're not doing Scrum meetings anymore necessarily?

> **Firmware Engineering Manager:** No.

> **Interviewer:** And you think that's because it just didn't help with agility or was possibly counterproductive in some way?

> **Firmware Engineering Manager:** It was—a lot of people didn't like—a lot of the engineers didn't like Scrum. The daily stand-up meetings and that kind of stuff, they thought it was overhead that wasn't needed. As you are aware, there was a change that came in, a change in leadership, and that's where a lot of things have kind of, in my mind, changed the behavior of the team.

> **Interviewer:** Right, and so it sounds like part of that is because when it comes to firmware resources, there's a premium on those resources so much so that perhaps even those daily Scrums are just too much of a resource drain.

> **Firmware Engineering Manager:** Yeah.

It should be noted that Scrum meetings phased in and out of this organization but were finally instituted on a permanent, although less frequent, basis. It took time for the firmware engineers to become comfortable with the idea. These developers often worked alone, on siloed projects, and some did not welcome the visibility and exposure that Scrum meetings demanded. If done properly, a Scrum meeting should be very short, and should not be a terribly significant burden on a person's time. More important, Scrum meetings should be sold to teams as a way to make suggestions for improvement, have a voice in what is going on, and bring forward any issues that may be blocking their progress, as opposed to being a way to put a spotlight on what they are doing. The same questions are posed to the product manager:

Interviewer: Can you describe the events that led up to this current state of agility, how it evolved?

Firmware Product Manager: Well, in the years I've been with the company, we definitely started with a true waterfall approach. We had experienced folks come in from different software industries that wanted to bring the agile method and we're to a point where we're using pieces of it, but I can still see us using the historic waterfall method with regards to planning a system release with X-number of requirements and being very systematic in that you can't cut a system release whenever you want.

Interviewer: Right. So, would you say on the software side they've adopted more of the agile processes than perhaps with hardware or firmware?

Firmware Product Manager: Absolutely. Hardware projects are definitely not agile. I would say the firmware to some extent gets wrapped into the agile pieces in that firmware is typically released with the system release. We just have to anticipate and plan and ultimately hope that the hardware projects align with that pseudo-agile system release.

Interviewer: What do you think contributed to the development of agility strategy here? What factors do you think contributed to what components that we do use from agility and what components we don't?

Firmware Product Manager: I think the complexity of our system contributed to, again, I'll use the term pseudo-agile methodology that we use. Our system releases consist of a head-end system, firmware, hardware components, often even different types of firmware running on different radios in our hardware products. So it's quite complicated and the ultimate goal is to test all of those at the same time. A lot of that is due to the complexity of the system, but the drive to test them all at the same time is a product of resource constraints also.

Interviewer: So we've got multiple versions of firmware, probably multiple hardware types, multiple meter types that we're trying to integrate into this one big system release and hopefully get tested all together.

Firmware Product Manager: Right. Now, don't get me wrong. There are certain features within a system release that fall into agile methodology in that it is a feature. It will be implemented and tested such that it should be releasable. However, that is just one piece of it, and like I said, that complexity given that you need the firmware, the head-end [software], and the hardware in order to release it is what contributes to the waterfall methodology of a system release.

What the product manager is describing here is that due to the fact that an embedded systems product is an amalgamation of different smaller products released as one unit or *systems release*, that the *stage-gate* approach of waterfall is utilized to keep all the moving parts in sync. It serves as a control, which benefits the organization but also the customer in terms of not overloading their appetite. Although much of the development is iterative, not all iterations are released to the customer. Rather, they are accumulated into the systems release. The engineering manager describes some of these challenges in detail from a hardware perspective. Hardware development consists of rapid prototyping or experimental development that does not always result in a deliverable product after an iteration, and *board spins* can either slow down or advance beyond software development, which are often linked. Again, it is the stage-gating process from hybrid agility that is necessary to allow these different tracks to maintain synchronicity.

> **Firmware Engineering Manager:** With firmware, we have had system releases that were very driven by the agile process, but then we had hardware projects that were very waterfall-type projects, and that was always a challenge to try to keep both feet in and work with one that was a waterfall kind of mechanism and the other one that used agile methods.

> **Interviewer:** You guys are kind of caught in the middle, basically.

> **Firmware Engineering Manager:** Right, yeah.

> **Interviewer:** And you have to sort of almost adapt to both sides of the house. You've got to adapt to hardware's waterfall schedule and then the system release's agile schedule in many ways.

> **Firmware Engineering Manager:** With some of the tools that were required for use with hardware development and factory development, they had a lot of difficulty trying to get those tools integrated into the hardware project process, and sometimes it was part of the challenge of managing resources. They would tend to allocate resources and try to incorporate functionality needed for hardware projects into the scope of a system release project. For example, tool development was part of the software release scope, but then as that hardware project kind of slowed down or sped up or that kind of stuff—particularly they will slow down because of some board spin or a hardware issue comes up or some other external dependencies, how do we then keep in sync with this waterfall project that's going on where you've got an agile thing that seems to have its own timeline?

> **Interviewer:** Right. So leaning in on that a little bit, describing the process that you use in managing agility—what processes are involved

to keep that all together, making sense of it and managing it when you've got your hardware, your firmware, and your software moving at different speeds?

Firmware Engineering Manager: The biggest thing is just prioritizing and planning the order of your stories that you're going to execute. One thing we've at one point tried to get is hardware requirements pushed into the agile system and generating user stories to work hardware issues. With the New Product Introduction process, you tend to get some activities that are kind of—I don't want to say open ended, but experimental kinds of things. It's kind of hard to capture some of that stuff and user stories or requirements that are going to produce a deliverable kind of code. We developed user stories for most of the work at least to identify activities of the work, and we try to prioritize that against the software. To me, it's all release planning and trying to meet everybody's objectives and your external dependencies.

Individuals and Interactions

In the next portion of the interview, we focus on individuals and interactions involved in managing agility. Interactions over processes and tools is a key tenet of the *Agile Manifesto*, but exactly what those interactions are supposed to be is not really called out in traditional agile documentation or textbooks. In Metagility, although there are certain informal interactions, there are a series of interactions that are specifically planned. Chapter Eight will discuss in detail the kinds of interactions that are needed, and the following interview illustrates some of these:

Interviewer: Describe the individuals and interactions involved in managing this process. What individuals do you interact with in terms of the roles, and then what do those interactions consist of? For instance, what meetings do you go to and who attends those meetings?

Firmware Product Manager: I'll start from a hardware project. A hardware project will have its project steering meeting, which is primarily the meeting where you're going to be talking about the hardware and firmware development specific to that piece of hardware. For that piece of hardware to be implemented at a system level, you also need to participate in the steering meetings for the system release which that hardware is anticipated to be aligned with. So, within that meeting, that's where they talk about the software implementation and possibly the firmware implementation and testing that needs to be done. So, those are just the meetings associated with each individual project. There's also meetings on issues that come in that need to be either determined to be a requirement, which would funnel it back through an agile process, or a defect, and a defect would be managed in real time through a triage-type setup. There are additional meetings called the project operations review, or the POR, which is a summary for executives and project and product managers on all the active projects in an organization and their status: green, yellow, or red. Any issues essentially bubble up in that meeting. There are release architecture meetings, which also discuss the issues pertaining to a complete system release. Essentially, lots of meetings on the software side that are all attempting to be in alignment with the hardware project meetings.

Interviewer: So, it sounds like the software side is sort of driving it, driving the whole process. Is that a fair statement? Or is that an overstatement to say that?

Firmware Product Manager: Yes, that's a fair statement. The software somewhat incorrectly gets associated with being the system release, but often you'll find a system release meeting will be focused solely on the software, whereas it needs to take into consideration the firmware and the hardware and the project efforts around them.

Interviewer: Why is that do you think?

Firmware Product Manager: I think a lot of people's experience with productization has to do with software, and I think agile is primarily for software, so it's a level of comfort. I think that's again what led to that pseudo implementation of agile where it's mainly waterfall, and the reason we got to stay waterfall is because that's how the hardware projects work. But we want to stay agile or claim we're agile with the software that's associated with it.

As discussed previously in Chapter 4, the software development track is the most agile in embedded systems and considered to be the *first responders*. The firmware engineering manager and architect in the following interviews describe the interactions they are involved in, primarily with respect to incoming work or requirements. Unlike at the product management level, formal interactions are few for the rank and file firmware developers.

Firmware Engineering Manager: Requirements come from the product management team, as well as trying to figure out: is hardware defining requirements potentially from a factory perspective? There should be requirements coming in from them. Some of that stuff is funneled through product management. I'm not sure if it makes sense that all of them should be. Systems engineering is responsible for the decomposition of the requirements and the user stories, and they could, in theory, in my mind, produce requirements as well from a system perspective. Other folks involved are project management for managing the projects and overseeing the execution of a project that ties into what ultimately is defined as the scope of user stories that go into a project. Then there's release architecture meetings that includes architects and subject matter experts—just to review user stories, provide estimates, and flush out the details.

Interviewer: How would you say that progress is monitored? Are project managers just pulling statistics from a central repository for firmware work or is it just like pinging people and saying, hey, where are you on this or . . .

Firmware Engineering Manager: They were pulling from version control looking at percent completes, or completion of user stories being completed. I don't know if they were looking at hours. I don't think that they were always looking at hours and that level of detail; it's more of either stories complete or not complete.

Interviewer: And did it seem like with firmware stories that perhaps there was usually a larger epic story or a master story and then there were typically a lot of tasks that the developer might break the requirement down into?

Firmware Engineering Manager: Yeah, so there are parent stories, and then they are decomposed into smaller stories which are then decomposed into tasks or stories.

Interviewer: And do you have to participate in change meetings, change control meetings, or anything like that?

Firmware Architect: I do as needed. Typically, management will do that. I will interact with systems engineering and systems might go to the change meetings. Systems would also act as the go-between between product management and firmware.

Tools

Tools were found to be important to communication and requirements management. Respondents noted that getting rid of *disparate* tooling and focusing on one application that could do everything was of the highest importance. Simplified tooling makes everything else easier. In the clip below, the interview references prior tools that were deprecated and phased out. The conversation focuses on a requirements management application primarily used by product management. That group was initially reluctant to give up this tool, but eventually did so after recognizing the inefficiencies and overhead that it placed on the organization and the fact that much of its feature functionality was not being used.

Firmware Product Manager: My contribution; I use Microsoft Team Foundation Server (TFS) and that's essentially it. Other tools for requirements management, such as Accept, have gone away.

Interviewer: There were some strong proponents of it, then we moved all the way to TFS. Do you think it's really just all about having everything in one tool or was there more to it than that?

Firmware Product Manager: I think it's about eliminating the complexity of having to move requirements over into TFS so that they can be decomposed by systems engineering. Additionally, I think product management as a whole agreed that it was unnecessary, it was over-complicated. I would say probably 80 to 90% of the features of that tool weren't even being used.

The firmware architect chimes in with the fact that he uses the same tool, but also briefly describes the requirements management process it facilitates:

Firmware Architect: We use TFS for user stories and defects. And so in a typical situation, systems would create a user story, possibly ask me for some guidelines on estimating a certain user story or whichever developer is likely to execute a story, and then I'll give them that feedback. Product management and my team management would then prioritize those and then it would eventually filter down to me. It's a similar process with defects, only those are managed in a weekly change control board meeting and they're triaged and assigned to developers.

Responding to Change

In this portion of the interview, the respondents discuss how the organization typically handles changing priorities, and the part that agility plays or could play in this situation:

Firmware Product Manager: Product management receives new requirements and changes to requirements very often. Our response to that is often an understanding that we're really not going to be able to address those in a real-time fashion given that we have one or two system releases a year. So, it becomes a game of quickly documenting, making sure we remember these things, and making sure we understand the priority of them so that when it does come time to plan a system release that they make the cut.

Interviewer: Okay, and I guess there's a prioritization effort as well, right? To determine what that priority is with the customer.

Firmware Product Manager: Right, and often it happens right when we're doing our gates for the system release. Prior to Stage 2, there's an objective to get everything that's been gathered since the last system release or even fallout or defects from before the last system release and have those in a prioritized fashion. Accounting for revenue, customer urgency, and other factors ultimately determine whether or not the feature makes the cut for the system release.

Interviewer: Okay. So we talked about revenue and urgency, obviously, as factors for prioritization. Can you think of any other factors that might cause something to bubble up to the top in terms of priority?

Firmware Product Manager: Urgency is broad in that it could be we're causing a customer to not be able to realize the full benefit of their system because of the way we implemented something; it urgently needs to be resolved in the next system release. Or it could be a defect that is also partly an enhancement, which we would need to work for a particular customer. Sometimes, we just need to put things in system releases in order to do something like a proof of concept in order to gain more business. Many times, proof of concepts for bids have tight deadlines around them, which could drive their urgency.

Firmware Engineering Manager: The whole organization has to respond to a change in requirements, and it's got to start at the requirements level and make sure that we have a clear understanding of what the new requirements or modified requirements are going to be, and then developing user stories to execute that requirement and implement it. Whether we scrap existing user stories and write new ones or modify existing ones, clearly where it happens in the life cycle of the project also drives the impact of testing, and if it happens early in the project then you can accommodate some changes earlier on.

So, it is important to take a moment to note the key factors in managing change in environments like this one:

1. Is revenue affected (either customer revenue or vendor revenue)?
2. Is the customer not realizing the full benefits or functionality of the system due to a defect or misunderstanding in requirements?
3. Is there a need to add a feature that would be critical to winning new business?
4. Risk: the later changes are added and the larger they become, the greater the risk.

In an embedded systems development organization, changes don't always come from the customer, and are often generated by the other domains. Integration is a big issue with embedded systems or other kinds of multi-track development. More often than not, internal changes are the result of integration problems, either with other internally developed products, or supporting products provided by outside vendors. Integration should always be near the top of the agenda for every interconnection or interaction in a hybrid agile environment.

Interviewer: Where do such changes generally come from? For instance, on the software side, obviously many of them come from customer requests, but it seems like on the firmware side you might have changes coming from many different directions, maybe from hardware, maybe from software, and maybe—

Firmware Engineering Manager: Yeah, I would say a lot of times integration. I can remember where we've taken and tried to do some of that work ahead of software, and then when you come to integrate the software, it doesn't work. That's one source of changes. The other would be hardware; for example, if we have some optimizations or getting battery endpoints with battery life. Hardware testing doesn't happen until later on in the project. They had an issue where we had to remove a battery. We had two batteries on the commercial gas, had to remove one battery, and that means that battery life is more critical since we just had one battery. We had to go and optimize some of our processing to accommodate changes in battery requirements. Some of that stuff you don't know until the end and it becomes a little bit more difficult. There might be a few customer things that come in with field issues and that stuff too, but I don't think that's a lot that we see changing throughout a project.

How Does Agility Contribute to Economy?

The concept of *nimbleness* and the difficulty in achieving it with embedded systems is very real. Pushing innovative technologies out the door can be a difficult proposition. How much should you test? Can you really test enough? Technology in these situations limits the validity of testing environments and test cases. In these situations, finding a large number of bugs as soon as the product hits production is not unusual. The question is—how do you manage that? The organization compensates through a process called *hardening*, which is an extensive system-level test that allows the entire solution to *sit* for a period of time while it is being tested in the hopes that any bugs that were previously unforeseen will rise to the surface. However, as the product manager laments in the following interview, this can have an impact:

Firmware Product Manager: I can't say that it's saving us time and money now. I would say it could if we were more nimble in our development and test methodology—then we could get more releases out, more revenue-generating features out in ideally a shorter period of time rather than waiting for an entire backlog to fill up and then pile them into either one or two slots per year. We could greatly improve time to market and it could also give us the opportunity to get revenue features out sooner than a scheduled system release.

Interviewer: So, it sounds like when you say *more nimble in test and development methodology*, you're talking about breaking out of this system release.

Firmware Product Manager: System hardening for 30 to 45 days and that type of concept where we have tests that go on a meter farm before a system release; and all that's even after, like I mentioned earlier, each individual feature has been tested. Now it's all consolidated and tested again as a system; and if you find an issue when you're doing this now mega-consolidated test, then it really breaks the process.

Interviewer: Right.

Firmware Product Manager: Where do you go back? Do you go back all the way to the individual feature and test that and skip redoing the consolidated system test? Or do you do it all over again if an issue is found? So it brings up some questions. There's lack of clarity. It's not very nimble.

Interviewer: What do you think is driving that? For example, that 30 days of hardening?

Firmware Product Manager: I think we have a significant defect backlog and with each system release, more often than not, we find critical issues sooner than later. In the mode that we're in, we find critical issues in live deployments nearly immediately with each system release, so I think it's used as a comfort to say, 'well, we're going to look at this for 30 or 45 days and that'll be the equivalent of a system release in a real production environment'—but it's not.

How Is Quality Perceived Within the Organization?

The *agile triangle* emphasizes quality in addition to value and constraints. However, what is quality? Quality can be both intrinsic, as well as extrinsic, meaning that it may be perceived differently by internal stakeholders and external customers. Respondents discuss these perceptions and the need for cost of quality analysis:

Firmware Product Manager: I think quality is perceived often in a negative connotation, in that a lot of times issues are found with each system release nearly immediately when they're brought into production. However, quality is seen as a necessity. It is, unfortunately, I don't think given enough attention. I think there's some powerful things that could come out of quality—like cost of quality analysis that really drives some change because it shows, 'hey, this issue, this coding defect, or this oversight in software quality assurance, for instance, costs the company this much money'—and I think a lot of that, more often than not, is buried, and I think if cost of quality was brought forward on a lot of defects, it would be eye opening and would bring about some positive change.

Interviewer: There's often two types of quality: there's extrinsic quality where we or the customer define quality based on what we think a quality product is; and then there's intrinsic quality that we build into the product from an engineering perspective. Do you think that we look at both ends of the spectrum in terms of quality or are we more concerned about what the customer thinks? Or are we more concerned about building quality in based on what we think is a quality? Or a combination?

Firmware Product Manager: I think it's a combination. I think often you'll find roles like product management step in. I'll give an example. It may not be a big deal to an SQA tester or an engineer that there's misspellings or columns don't align or something like that in a graphical user interface. However, if a customer sees that, it makes it look like a very poor quality software product, even though it's extremely minor in the grand scheme of things as far as what the system's doing for you but, again, I think product management often steps in that role and says, 'no, that's customer perception. You need to take care of customer quality.' I've definitely seen an improvement on putting yourself into the shoes of a user or a customer and considering what is quality to them. So, it's improving. I see it from both sides.

Interviewer: So it sounds like you work pretty closely, collaborate pretty closely with our customers to help to find that quality and build a quality product.

Firmware Product Manager: Yeah. Our customers are our best testers.

Whereas the product manager may have a good perception of both intrinsic and extrinsic quality, engineering managers are typically focused more intrinsically on *bugs* or defects as a quality measure:

> **Firmware Engineering Manager:** One metric that we measure is the number of bugs that come up in the field that are reported by the customers. That's the main thing. The number of bugs that came out during hardening was another metric we used to monitor.

> **Interviewer:** And what do those metrics look like? How many bugs do I have to have before I realize that this is not so good? What do the thresholds look like?

> **Firmware Engineering Manager:** The severity of the bugs is the main issue. It can also depend on the customer, too.

It was interesting that while the manager was focused on bugs or defects, his architects emphasized *robustness* as a quality measure:

> **Firmware Architect:** I would say what suffers in this situation where we press to meet a deadline or we're past the deadline, is robustness. We might do very well developing and testing the successful path, but corner cases and unsuccessful paths would suffer. [Such as] fault handling . . . things like that. I am not aware of any metrics like that. What determines a quality product all comes down to the highest level of success delivering the data that we've committed to deliver to the customer.

> **Interviewer:** Right, and that's usually based on the customer's testing they do once they get the product.

> **Firmware Architect:** Yeah.

How Customer Needs Are Balanced with Release Commitments

The previous discussion on quality shows the differences between intrinsic and extrinsic perception. While internal stakeholders may be focused on defects or *robust* code, all are aware that the ultimate test is customer satisfaction. Such defects or lack of robustness often takes a back seat to any customer concerns in a hybrid agile environment.

Firmware Product Manager: Customer needs are balanced with release commitments. Again, it's often a very brutal process that we go through right before a stage-gate review to determine which customer we are going to disappoint and which one we're going to make happy; and often it's taking emotion out of it. Decisions need to be based on revenue opportunity, but the reality is that there is some of that urgency that plays into it as far as relationships down the road and reference accounts and whatnot that play into selecting what customers need compared to what actually makes the system release.

Firmware Engineering Manager: Ultimately, customer requests should come in through the product management perspective and be planned into a release, and that's their responsibility to manage stuff, but as far as addressing questions from a field or issues in a field, for firmware that's always a challenge. We don't have the luxury of a separate development team and a separate sustaining team, so you've got folks wearing multiple hats; so if you've got a lot of field issues and investigations going on, then that tends to take away from the current release that we're developing and working.

Firmware Architect: Well, our release commitments, I guess in theory, do come from our customers or from our customers' interactions with product management. Again, I feel like we as a company tend to over-commit a little bit. While we might meet a deadline, the quality might not be as high as it should be. My personal philosophy is to roll back on the commitments a little bit and deliver a quality product which would be better than under-delivering on everything. That's how I estimate things as an engineer.

Managing Documentation

Documentation is a huge issue when discussing agile versus waterfall style development. Hybrid agility makes use of documentation, but it is not emphasized, and artifacts are typically created on an as-needed basis. The upcoming portion of the interview describes what kinds of documentation are typically created and expected in a hybrid agile environment:

Firmware Product Manager: Product management is essentially responsible for the content of all customer-facing documents and, more often than not, it's the product manager that goes in and writes a draft or is editor-in-chief of a draft that technical documentation has already produced. It goes through review cycles, sign offs, and technical documentation primarily controls the publishing and formatting aspect of it. The content product management is responsible.

Firmware Engineering Manager: We don't have a whole lot of processes around design documentation. We have some design documentation that's maintained, but it's just very simple maintenance. As you change the code, then you try to keep us up-to-date, but there's nothing that identifies documentation to get updated.

Interviewer: So you're not really writing something like a design document like you would in traditional waterfall where you would be writing a complete design document for everything.

Firmware Engineering Manager: No.

Interviewer: And is it fair to say that most of the documentation is probably in the code itself?

Firmware Engineering Manager: Yeah.

Interviewer: And as far as customer-facing documentation, that's probably just mostly in the form of release notes and things like that?

Firmware Engineering Manager: Yeah, we maintain engineering change notes, detailed changed notes, and then on a release, we will sit with the product management and they will develop the customer-facing release notes. We will kind of help them out with explaining to them the details so that they can bubble it up to a customer-facing level.

Interviewer: Do you have to provide any design documentation directly to the software or hardware teams for them to do their work or is part of that information exchanged? Do you consume any documentation from them?

Firmware Engineering Manager: I know with the gas stuff we provide some documentation, as far as defined configuration tables and interface documentation for the gas products. I think some of the stuff for end points and stuff is maintained by systems, you know the protocol definition document, but we provide input into those documents for systems.

Interviewer: And how would you describe the PDU document, what its purpose is, and its content?

Firmware Engineering Manager: The purpose is to just define the messages exchanging—the messages that are shared between the end points and Command Center. It defines just the message headers, the fields associated with each message ID, just parameters.

Interviewer: So, when you develop something, you're not having to write any documentation on it at all, pretty much?

Firmware Architect: Pretty much.

Interviewer: Is that a fair statement?

Firmware Architect: That's fair.

Interviewer: Do you think—is anyone else involved in writing documentation for it? Like, do they have a meeting with you and say, 'hey, I'm writing a document, can I get this from you?'

Firmware Architect: There's some customer-facing user documentation that gets developed in that way, but as far as design documents and things like that, no. We do, I should say, the hardware team, does a fair amount of documentation; but on the firmware team, we don't do a whole lot. We add comment(s) [to our] code.

With respect to firmware, product management produces customer-facing documentation, while technical documentation exchanged between teams is mostly limited to code comments. Very little design documentation exists, and there is no specific process around the documents that do get created. In a later chapter we will discuss the concept of tribal knowledge, how it is disseminated, and how this method is how knowledge is transferred in a meta-agile environment.

Organizational Readiness to Respond to New Market Demands

Firmware Product Manager: I would say that we have an understanding of market demands. I would say, again, as far as that nimbleness of being able to respond, we're not nimble. We're not able to respond in a timely manner or probably in a manner comparable to our competition. We're pretty slow.

Interviewer: So, you think the competition is responding maybe a little quicker? What are they doing differently?

Firmware Product Manager: I think at least some of our competition are probably using agile methodology and are able to cut releases quickly and get products out the door in time periods not necessarily aligned with system releases where you have got a piece of hardware or you're either waiting for a system release or you've passed it and then you need to wait another half year to get it in a system. I think there's smarter ways to do that. I have a feeling our competition does it that way, where they can release hardware in its own project and not be dependent on another project altogether to get it out the door.

Interviewer: Don't they have some of the same complexities that you do or are they somehow simpler?

Firmware Product Manager: They do, but some you could argue are simpler in that they're not the conglomeration of companies that are now the company we work for. So I think a lot of our complexity also is probably driven by, again, we are an amalgamation of various communication technologies be it PLC (power line carrier), RF (radio frequency), or cellular communication technologies and several different variants of RF communication technology as far as firmware goes. There are several different head-end systems. That mix creates a complexity which some of these smaller start-up-esque-type companies don't have; they're starting fresh. They don't have that noise of all these other technologies to deal with.

Firmware Architect: I would say we are ready to respond to new demands. We have a pretty capable team of people participating in standards, bodies for the next wave of new technology in this industry. They've got their ear to the ground, so to speak.

Interviewer: So, it sounds like that readiness is based on highly capable, highly trained staff—staff that have a strong high level of expertise in specific areas, as opposed to having just lots of people.

Firmware Architect: Yeah.

Although there was a perception that the organization in this case lacked some *nimbleness*, this was largely due to the integration of various solutions available as a result of several corporate acquisitions. Complexity versus simplicity is another important issue in evaluating agility. Agile is supposed to help in reducing complexity, and the frameworks supporting it should be simple. However, this can prove to be a daunting task indeed if the organization in question is complex by design because of corporate amalgamation.

The preceding interview provided insight into one of the most challenging contexts for agility—firmware within embedded systems development. The following sections provide an analysis of how the hardware domain adapts to agility and how customer collaboration can be maximized in these situations to achieve agile vorticity.

IS WATERFALL BEST IN CERTAIN SITUATIONS?

Out of all the domains, hardware moves the slowest with release cycles of up to two to three years in length. Like the other domains, it can release independently, but it is constrained to a certain extent by linkages to the others, particularly when a systems release is needed. Hardware's linkage to manufacturing, longer product life, and the associated costs of *spinning boards* makes it difficult to manage requirements in the same way software and even firmware can. As a result, it operates largely within a waterfall context. One of the main reasons cited for this is hardware's inability to drop features as development and manufacturing progress, as cited by a project manager:

> "With software, you can be agile as you go along and you can drop certain features as needed. With hardware, the reason it hasn't been adopted is you can't really do that."

In addition, the product lifespan of the hardware warrants more extensive quality assurance requirements than the other domains. As a hardware manager explained, this means it cannot flex or compromise in these areas as firmware and software often do:

> "On the hardware side, we commit 15 or up to 20 years of product life, so since our products are installed, they are exposed to the elements and [must withstand] severe or extreme weather conditions and humidity conditions, so we have to maintain our quality and put a lot of effort in testing and validating."

Another reason for waterfall methodology is the cost of spinning boards. If new hardware needs to be created due to changing requirements, that can be expensive. This characteristic does not lend itself well to *continuous iterative* development. Additionally, customer appetite is a limiting factor here as well. Hardware development, especially in an embedded systems context, typically requires extensive customer validation and financial investment. Whereas upgrades in software or firmware may require a swift download and testing validation before disseminating to production, replacing hardware requires shipping costs, truck rolls, and hands-on installation. The customer is burdened with customer service, logistics, and validation issues that are associated with new hardware installs, which can be significant. In short, once hardware is purchased and installed, it is expected to last for a significant amount of time before it is obsolete due to the investment it warrants. In these kinds of situations where iterative development is not as feasible or economical, a waterfall approach may prove to be the best option.

The waterfall process used by hardware serves as the foundation for the gating process employed by Metagility and the hybrid agile implementation. This provides concurrent engineering and quality checkpoints throughout the development phase, which as we discussed in earlier chapters, is so much more critical with embedded systems development. There are seven gates overall in the process, which are summarized in Table 7.2 (refer back to Figure 3.3 for a visual).

Table 7.2 Phases and stage gates: including gating requirements from a hardware domain perspective

Phase	Stage Gate	Gating Requirements
Discovery	0	1. Basic architectural foundation 2. Constraints established
Scoping	1	1. Release vision
Feasibility	2	1. Feasibility assessment including high-level estimates
Development	3	1. Technical specifications and product requirements 2. Supply chain analysis performed
	4	1. Rapid prototyping is conducted until a satisfactory design is obtained 2. Product delivered to software and firmware tracks to support their work
	5	1. Product is considered feature complete
Verification	6	1. Testing is conducted
Implementation	7	1. Engineering support and documentation provided

Prior to the instantiation of a release, or at Stage 0, a product roadmap should be available and work performed to identify high-level features for future releases. At Stage 0, a basic architectural foundation should be in place and constraints of time and budget should be established. Prior to Stage 1, a release vision and a list of *must-have* features should be established:

- *Pre-engineering Stage 1*: Ensure that estimates of feature functionality are in line with business constraints. Ensure that the anticipated return on investment can be delivered based on the identified scope.
- *Development Stages 2–3*: Design
  - Inputs include technical specifications, project plan, and/or a product requirements document. In these stages, the product architecture is determined, along with detailed specifications and schematics. A supply chain analysis is performed to ensure availability of components. Design reviews are conducted with cross-functional teams that include systems, firmware, and circuit designs.
- *Development Stages 3–4*: Prototyping
  - Inputs at this stage include schematics and circuit designs. Prototypes are built and tested until a satisfactory design is obtained. A test specification is typically written for use in manufacturing. Design specifications are updated as needed.
- *Development Stages 4–5*: Development verification
  - Using the updated schematics and specifications from the previous stage, alpha units are manufactured, and development verification testing is conducted. Final test plans and documentation are completed. At this point, the product is delivered to firmware and software development for use in their work.
- *Verification Stages 5–6*:
  - All quality testing is conducted during this phase with documentation being updated accordingly. Regulation compliance tests and the requisite submissions are also typically performed.
- *Implementation Stages 6–7*:
  - Engineering support is put into place, along with the necessary production-level documentation.

PROTOTYPING TO ACCELERATE PRODUCT DEVELOPMENT

Although the hardware domain does not use agile methodologies as the other two domains do, comments from respondents showed that it does contribute to process agility using agile or lean techniques. These include rapid prototyping and bypassing the stage-gate methodology when necessary.

Rapid prototyping is one way in which the hardware domain attempts to *keep up* with the agility of the other domains without outright adoption of agile methodologies or Scrum. In essence, it is exercising an agile capability in contribution to the organization's hybrid approach. Using this method, the hardware team begins with a working prototype, and then rapidly and iteratively develops subsequent prototypes as requirements change. This is often performed in tandem with firmware development. Firmware requirements are often tied to software and, thus, change more frequently. As a result, rapid prototyping as firmware and hardware requirements change before a systems release provides for higher levels of innovation than what a typical waterfall approach would allow.

MAKING USE OF *FAST TRACKING*

The hardware domain has the ability to bypass the stage-gate process under certain circumstances. These situations were referred to in our case studies as *C-Level* projects. These were projects given special priority due to their visibility and relatively low cost. It is one way in which the hardware domain can suddenly become more agile on demand, as the following comment explains:

> *"There are smaller hardware projects that can be more agile where it's just having to change out one part on a board that's already designed and verify it's good, and those . . . don't need as strict following of the NPI process [waterfall]. We call them C-Level projects and they're managed real loosely. They only have to basically go through two gates—a planning gate and a project closure gate—and then the team is allowed to be free in between. We do have many of those type projects and I think they work well if the team plans it well from the beginning. So those are where we're able to take the more agile approach on the hardware side."*
> —Hardware Project Manager

These projects are typically low-budget efforts. In a sense, they work like a stand-alone development iteration that can be initiated on demand. Unlike the firmware and software domains, the hardware domain is managed without the use of sprints, Scrum, or other commonly accepted agile methods. Through prototyping and *C-Level* projects, however, the hardware domain still has an agile or *lean* contribution. This demonstrates that forcing agile approaches and processes onto every domain might not be a good idea. In the case of embedded systems development, a mixed approach for hardware domains works best.

MANAGING CUSTOMER EXPECTATIONS FOR AGILE VORTICITY

Although the business side serves as the primary communication interface to the customer and the market at large, the engineering organization is not without a voice. Like market agility, process agility not only attempts to reach the momentum set by the business, but influences it as well. This is done through managing customer expectations and negotiating from a technical perspective when necessary. Such communication is performed by all three domains within embedded systems. As one operations manager explained:

> "It can also slow the project down if the customer isn't managed in a way that lets them know 'we're demoing something you asked us to do and here's the result and the limitations.'"

Even though agility demands extensive customer collaboration and adaptation, these must be tempered and controlled for the good of the business. The company cannot respond to any and all demands every time. Through managing expectations, the business *grounds* what may often be lofty or unrealistic expectations by the customer with respect to quality and feature functionality.

CUSTOMER NEGOTIATION TECHNIQUES FOR MAINTAINING BUSINESS MOMENTUM

Not only must expectations be managed with respect to technology and capability, but the deliverable must also be negotiated with the customer. This illustrates that not only does the business have a voice with the customer when it comes to deciding the scope of the systems release, but the development organization does as well. Although the business leads, while the organization largely *reaches*, there is a symbiotic interaction here where the organization may offer more technical input to the roadmap than the business was, or is not capable of, seeing. As a result, the organization and business, or the process and market agility respond, respectively, to influence and adapt to customer demands. The following comment illustrates this:

"If certain issues are not fixed or if you realize that you won't be able to fix it in time, then they work with the customer to get some kind of a resolution on when that commitment could be satisfied; so in an ideal world, you provide everything to the customer, but in reality sometimes you have to go and tell them, 'hey, yes, this is our commitment, but right now it's not working.' With my experience, the customers understand that as long as there is a reasonable time frame to fix or close that gap, I think they always work with us."

—Hardware Product Manager

In this way, business momentum is maintained. The organization *keeps its eye on the strategic ball* always, never losing site of the customer, but leveraging and supporting them to the extent that it satisfies their own strategic vision. Many companies lose site of this, responding blindly to whatever the customer wants, whenever they think they need it, in crisis situations. Knee-jerk reactions must be curtailed to reach agile vorticity and maintain momentum.

As explained previously, the process agility response of the organization is the hybrid agile implementation. The product of this implementation is the *system release*. System releases are complicated embedded systems developed in a hybrid agile environment. The environment in this study has organically adopted the optimum mix of agile and waterfall processes to make the system release happen.

System releases are strategic as well as practical. Feature functionality that makes the system release can be driven by the desire to gain new business in a specific area, as well as satisfying existing customers. In this way the company can increase business momentum with each release in the direction of innovation. As one firmware product manager explained:

"Sometimes, we just need to put things in system releases in order to do something like a proof of concept to gain more business. A lot of times, proof of concepts for bids have tight deadlines around them which could drive their urgency for requirements."

The system release seeks to match the business momentum that the business side has established. However, it is important to keep in mind that both influence each other. Since all three domains within embedded systems can release independently, business momentum can affect each in different ways. For example, hardware may experience a stronger momentum than software due to the fact that it has a more difficult time adjusting to dramatic change and the *larger mass* of their releases. This, in turn, may impact the scope of such releases. The customer management category within hybrid agility is utilized by the embedded systems development organization to negotiate scope modifications when these situations occur. In this way all three domains are kept to some level of synchronicity within the embedded systems context through utilization of its hybrid agile implementation.

WHAT SITUATIONS BENEFIT MOST FROM A HYBRID AGILE MIX?

In this chapter and others, the benefits of a hybrid agile approach have been discussed, including a method for determining if such an approach is right for a particular organization or company. As has been shown, a hybrid agile mix can be of particular benefit to organizations which meet the following criteria:

1. Hardware development and/or embedded systems development
2. Multi-track development
3. Significant interplay between different domains
4. A high level of interdependency between product lines and/or development tracks

What is not considered good criteria:

1. *Company culture*: It is never good to combine agile and waterfall practices based on internal political pressures or the special needs of a few, yet often vocal, individuals who are resistant to change. This would constitute a failure to do what's good for the business before other considerations.

Some organizations stick to a hybrid approach to agile not because of product or technology constraints or the needs established by research, but because of cultural ones. A hybrid agile implementation should be utilized for the good for the business and what makes sense from a development perspective, not necessarily what is popular or comfortable. Removing components of agility because certain employees feel like it's too difficult is not good enough. Catering to these kinds of demands will result in an ill developed implementation that will be agile in name only, providing lackluster results and only marginal improvements. Ultimately, it will result in the company experiencing high agile vorticity, low business momentum, and being left behind in the market. In order to meet market demands, organizations and the people that compose them have to adapt to keep up. How can such a company assimilate innovation and match market pressures if its people cannot? In the end, it's all market-driven, right down to the individual contributor. Market pressure drives the whole process, even to the mix of agile and waterfall processes itself.

Part 3

Practical Issues and Applications

8

THE ART OF METAGILITY: BRINGING IT ALL TOGETHER

METAGILITY IN COMPLEX ENVIRONMENTS

As has been established, agile is a challenge to implement and manage in complex development environments. One of the most complex is an embedded system where software, hardware, and firmware are developed on different tracks at different speeds but must be tested and delivered as one cohesive product. The act of integrating these different development tracks together takes the agile concept of individuals and interactions over processes and tools to an entirely different level. We should be reminded that although agile emphasizes the former over the latter, this is not to imply that processes or tools should be entirely negated. Indeed, our most successful case studies used a skillful combination of both. With reference to interactions, there are a variety of formal and informal communications that are required to manage multiple development tracks. At the same time, certain metrics have proved useful—at both the project management and executive levels—in not only monitoring and measuring progress, but facilitating communication and understanding. The following sections detail formal and informal interactions, the metrics, and the fine-tuning techniques that allow for complex hybrid agile implementations to be managed for maximum efficiency.

Embedded Systems: A Case Study in Agile Orchestration

Agile orchestration can be defined as the activities required to make agility happen within an organization. One of the key purposes of Metagility is to break down these activities into well-defined components so that they can be replicated and implemented in other organizations and contexts. Although the *Agile Manifesto* recognizes the importance of interactions, it does not specify any details around them. Analysis of the data in our case studies revealed that the activities of orchestrating agility fall into two main categories: interconnections/interactions and making adjustments. Table 8.1 outlines these categories and their elements. Interconnections consist of people interactions and technical connections that communicate, monitor, and synchronize with each other. The enterprise uses these interconnections to make adjustments, thereby bringing market and process agility closer together.

Table 8.1   Elements of Agile Orchestration

6. Agile Orchestration	6.1 Interconnections and interactions	6.1.1 Dependencies
		6.1.2 Interdependencies
		6.1.3 Linkages
		6.1.4 Status points
		6.1.5 Decision points
		6.1.6 Touchpoints
	6.2 Making adjustments	6.2.1 Customer acceptance
		6.2.2 Scope adjustment
		6.2.3 Resource adjustment
		6.2.4 Constant re-assessment

INTERCONNECTIONS AND INTERACTIONS

One of the key tenets of the *Agile Manifesto* is the emphasis of individuals and interactions over processes and tools. However, the details regarding what this entails are rarely discussed. During our research study, we worked to put some definition around what kinds of interactions were conducted regularly within a successful agile implementation. More important, we worked to determine how these interactions differ in complex situations, such as embedded systems development. Interconnections are intersection points between different domains within the embedded systems environment. These interconnections can be interactions between people or dependencies based on technology or resources. The major categories that arose from the data included dependencies, interdependencies, linkages, decision points, status points, and touchpoints. Dependencies and interdependencies are involuntary connections that are forced due to the nature of the technology and the product(s) being developed. The remaining connection types are voluntarily initiated connections created by the organization in order to manage the first two. Table 8.2 provides

Table 8.2   Understanding interconnections and interactions in hybrid agility

Connection or interaction type	Formal or informal	Definition
Dependencies	Informal	One domain has a technical or resource dependency on another
Interdependencies	Informal	Two or more domains have technical or resource dependencies on each other
Linkages	Formal	Scheduled meetings between *domains* for collaboration and coordination
Status points	Formal	Monitoring points and metrics
Decision points	Formal	Formal meetings or process points between *stakeholders* for making decisions; these could be agile in nature, such as a demonstration for user acceptance, or more waterfall based, such as decision gates in the stage-gate process
Touchpoints	Informal	Informal interactions that occur to resolve potential problems or follow up on progress; largely intuitive in nature

a summary explaining the connections or interactions. The following sections describe these different categories and their relationships to each other.

Managing One-Way Dependencies

Dependencies are just that; they are situations where one domain has a dependency on another to complete a task. As is often the case in embedded systems, one piece of the solution, such as firmware, may have to be completed to a specific level before hardware can complete their work, or vice versa. This is a technical dependency. In addition, respondents in our study noted the presence of resource dependencies. Often, one domain may require expertise or consultation with another domain before it can move on. This may require a resource or subject matter expert from one domain to stop what they are working on to help out with another.

Often, the result of these dependencies is that one domain must put its work into a *sleep state* until the other domain is ready. As one hardware architect explained:

> *"If firmware resources are diverted, then the project basically is just in a sleep state until it gets resurrected."*

This presents some practical problems in that once resurrection occurs, resources must be re-engaged. This may become difficult if the original participants are not available, and new resources must be brought up to speed. Domains attempt to mitigate these dependencies and the *sleep state* situations through proactive communication and coordination. Each domain communicates to others what changes they are making that could impact them. For example, if hardware is changing the way a circuit operates and firmware needs to know about it, they will communicate that to them. If hardware needs additional test modes, they will communicate those changes as well. Although this communication or *agile interaction* is often informal, the results must be coordinated for the domains to keep in sync. This synchronization can put limitations on iterative development. The following excerpt illustrates that although firmware utilizes development sprints, they cannot keep *developing until they are done*, as is usually the case with an agile Scrum methodology:

> *"And so, a lot of times we have to coordinate, so the firmware team can't just say, 'well, we're just going to deliver features until we run out of time.' We have to build those three features about a month before software needs them, so software can do their work."*
> —Software Development Manager

In summary, dependencies are managed through a series of informal agile interactions, as opposed to a formal process. Synchronicity between the domains is maintained by either proactively planning so that one domain does not have to wait on another, or by putting a project into a sleep state until the dependency is resolved.

Intertwined Solutions: Managing Interdependencies

Dependencies in embedded systems can be particularly complex in that there may be multiple interdependencies intertwined between multiple domains. While dependencies can be described as *one-way* situations in which one domain is reliant on another, interdependencies consist of *two-way* dependencies between two or more domains. For example, one or more domains may be waiting on another domain, while at the same time that domain will need feedback from yet another before work can proceed. As one hardware architect noted:

> *"Hardware quality doesn't want to finish its final product testing until they have a final version of firmware. That may be dependent on the [software] release."*

The organization mitigates these issues by using iterative development to provide enough material for dependent domains to proceed. As one software development manager explained:

> *"So, they generally have major milestones or target dates for deliverables of features and they'll deliver us a [device] that has 30% of the features set*

on it. We'll take that, we'll implement that 30%, test it, and then by the time we've done that, they've delivered the next 30% of the feature set and we'll work with them."

Interdependencies in embedded systems are essentially a complex web of intertwined dependencies that must be carefully monitored and managed to ensure that projects keep moving. To summarize, they are a form of interconnection in which two or more domains are symbiotically interdependent on each other. Such interdependencies can come in the form of shared testing and development needs, and they are often managed by one or more domains, providing iterative functionality that allows the other domain(s) to proceed. This is one way in which process agility is managed.

Defining Formal Linkages: Developing Productive and Impactful Meetings

Different from dependencies or interdependencies, linkages are *scheduled* interactions between stakeholders for the purpose of sharing information, coordination, collaboration, and decision making. These consist largely of a series of formally organized meetings attended by progressively smaller, yet more executive-level, teams as issues and the status move from the ground up to C-Level. Such meetings include release architecture meetings, Scrum stand-up meetings (including a larger Scrum of Scrums meeting), project operations review (POR), and change control board (CCB) meetings.

At the lowest (or development team) level resides the daily Scrum stand-up meetings. Scrum is a commonly accepted lightweight process to manage iterative and incremental product development. It consists of small teams of generally less than ten people, using tightly time-boxed iterations or sprints, which typically last two to four weeks at a time. As the development organization is divided into Scrum teams, each has its own *stand-up* within the software and firmware domains:

> *"There are daily stand-ups by sprint teams. Those are attended by the Scrum Master and/or the key people on the team. They discuss what they're working on, how they're progressing, and issues they're encountering."*
> —Software Project Manager

As the development organization employs two-week sprints, sprint team meetings are held bi-weekly. These meetings are where requirements or user stories are reviewed with the engineers and product management to resolve issues and negotiate what the final outcome may be for a set of user stories within a sprint. Each team focuses on producing a usable increment of work with each increment building on a prior one. There should be clearly defined deliverables and responsibilities for team members, and there should not be any changes to these during the time-boxed sprints. Figure 8.1 illustrates the sprint framework and the interactions that compose it. Sprints begin at Stage Gate 2 of the hybrid agile process and end at Stage Gate 5.

Due to the size of the organization, large distributed teams report in to small Scrum of Scrums meetings, which roll into an even larger one. This is one way in which an embedded systems organization allows the various distributed teams to *roll up together* into one Scrum. As one software project manager explained:

> *"We have a Scrum of Scrums, which is where we meet with all the software managers, firmware managers, and the leads, and we discuss how the sprint teams are performing and any issues that they're encountering."*

Depending on the needs of the release or the project, there may be multiple *Scrum of Scrum* meetings broken up by function as a software project manager explained:

> *"There's even a smaller Scrum of Scrums that meets a couple times a week and that is a little bit higher level than the stand-ups and a little bit lower level than the project Scrum of Scrums, and those have been broken up by major functional areas."*

At the next level (release management level) are the release architecture meetings. As a software project manager explained, these meetings are attended by most first-level managers, product managers, project managers, systems engineering, and other stakeholders who may have issues on the agenda for discussion:

> *"And so, we have release architecture meetings multiple times a week, which is where we review what's going on in the release. That's attended by software managers, firmware managers, systems engineers, architects, and some key experts as needed, and in there we review what's targeted for the scope and get things slated up for sprint work."*

Release architecture and Scrum meetings typically only involve software and firmware domains. Hardware is brought in at the POR meeting, which consists primarily of first- and second-level managers in conjunction with the executive team:

> *"We have a project operations review every week, which is where we bubble up everything out of the project systems meeting and present that to basically everyone else in the company, the executive review board, the VPs. We give them insight into the project. We give them the opportunity to weigh in or help us with an issue or address any questions they have."*

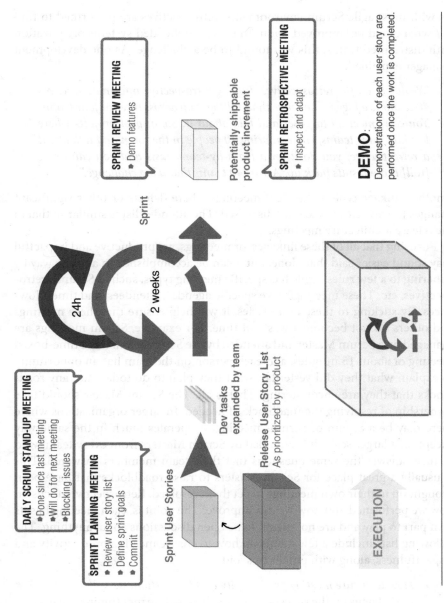

Figure 8.1 *The sprint framework*: illustration of the sprint framework and the interactions that make it happen

As with most agile Scrum environments, retrospectives are performed to find out what could be improved upon. In a large embedded systems organization with distributed teams, this was found to be a challenge. As one development manager explained:

> *"Yeah, we do the retrospectives. Rolling retrospective information across 40 teams is a bigger challenge than rolling it up across three or four teams. You can't meet all together and talk about it. So, in past projects where I've had three teams, you can bring 20 people in the room and talk about a retrospective, you do it on a team-by-team basis and you can bring [roll] those results back up. Across 40 teams that a big challenge."*

Another linkage type is the CCB meetings where defects or other significant changes to *released* software are discussed. The attendee list is similar to that of the release architecture meetings.

Ensuring that all of these linkages, or meetings, are productive and impactful may sound easier said than done, but it can be accomplished in an agile way by adhering to a few rules. Agile has specific meeting types, such as Scrums, retrospectives, etc. These meetings have specific agendas, attendees, and time allowances. By sticking to these boundaries, it will help ensure that these meetings and others do not become a waste of time. For example, Scrum meetings are managed by a Scrum Master and attended by the Scrum team. It is a time-boxed meeting of about 15 minutes, and each person on the team has an opportunity to explain what they did yesterday, what they plan to do today, and any roadblocks that they are encountering. That is all. The Scrum Master should take ownership of resolving the roadblocks if needed. In larger organizations where there may be a Scrum of Scrums meeting, it operates much in the same way except on a larger scale. It is attended by Scrum Masters from every team, who in turn, answer the same questions that their team members answered. This is usually a great place for Scrum Masters to raise roadblocks that have been brought up in their own meetings to get them resolved. Retrospectives focus on how we performed and how we can improve. The point is, each meeting has its own part to play and are not meant to be open discussions about anything. The following lists include a few points on how to ensure meeting productivity and impactfulness, along with pitfalls to avoid:

- *How to ensure meeting productivity and impactfulness*:
    1. Focus on the successes, or positives, before mentioning the negatives or failures. People tend to be much more accepting of criticism when they know that their positive contributions have been recognized.

2. Have a clear agenda, and make sure it matches up with the type of meeting being held. Make sure that attendees are aware of the agenda and that they have time to review and prepare for it.

3. Time box the meeting as well as responses from each person in the meeting as necessary. Offer to take deeper discussions offline as needed.

4. Document the meeting with minutes or a tool that makes it easier. Be sure to document any decisions that were made in the meeting and send those out after the meeting has closed.

5. During the meeting, if discussions become haphazard, a good technique is to start writing people's comments on a whiteboard. Direct everyone's attention to what is being written. This helps everyone focus on what's being discussed, and you will find that they will do a better job of editing themselves and making sure their comments are relevant and not wildly off base.

- *Pitfalls to avoid: the reasons most meetings fail*:
  1. **Lack of clear agenda**: The lack of a clear agenda or failure to socialize that agenda ahead of time is a recipe for failure.
  2. **The right people are not invited**: This is a very common problem in technology development. For some reason, principals will not invite certain people in hopes of obtaining a decision unfavorable to those who are absent. If you need an expert, go out and find one. Having a meeting without the necessary expertise will result in needless churn and bad decisions. You might end up paying for it later.
  3. **Attempting to solve a managerial problem with a technical solution**: This is also a very common problem in technology development. Ron Heifitz, author of *Leadership without Easy Answers* and a Harvard researcher, discusses this phenomenon in his talks about adaptive leadership. In an effort to avoid the *real* problem, project leaders will sometimes have meeting after meeting to find a technical solution in order to avoid raising it with upper management. The root cause of any problem needs to be brought forward, and if it is a technical problem that can be resolved, so be it, but if it is the result of a bad managerial decision, then it needs to be escalated to a principal who can resolve it. Having endless meetings that burn the time of your developers and testers in hopes that some kind of technical workaround can be found can result in huge losses of time and resources. Unless executive management has specifically requested it, do not search for technical solutions for management problems.

4. **Failure to referee or manage the agenda and time-boxed responses**: There is always a person in every meeting who likes to hear him or herself talk. These people typically don't pay attention well. Everything comes out of their mouth, and very little goes in their ears. It is important that a meeting leader time box the responses of each person in the room so that everyone who needs to speak, can. It is also important to move on from one agenda item to the next so that the entire agenda can be covered. If something needs more discussion, create another meeting for that item with the needed attendees.

5. **Managing by consensus**: This is a technique often used in change management meetings. Discussion of changes and the decisions made to make or break them are often relegated to these meetings, which may have a certain set of attendees. Each attendee is given a chance to object to a change and, if needed, discussions may ensue. This works fine if agendas are published ahead of time so that attendees can decide if they need to be there, and if any decisions that are made are published and subject to review after the fact. Managing by consensus can become a problem when a leader who is responsible for making a certain decision decides to move it down the line, or when a project manager or leader is attempting to have developers and testers make a decision about a certain technology problem without the proper expertise present. It is important to know who the experts and leaders are and who is responsible—then make them so. Consensus management should only be used when the situation warrants it.

6. **Failure to escalate**: This can be related to *managing by consensus*, when a meeting organizer for one reason or another is assigned a problem to resolve that clearly needs escalation. Trying to obtain a decision from others to avoid escalating to management can lead to wasted resources and bad decisions. Use the experts to gather the appropriate information and develop a set of options with pros and cons, and perhaps even recommendations, then escalate this issue to management for a final decision.

In summary, linkages are a form of formal interconnection (or interaction) that usually consist of a set meeting or meetings that serve as formal contact points between domains. They are part of how agile processes are orchestrated across the enterprise. Table 8.3 summarizes the meetings that are utilized in a Metagility or hybrid agile environment.

Table 8.3 Summary of formal or planned meetings in a hybrid agile implementation

Interconnection Description	When?	Who?	What?
POR	Weekly	Executive team	Review of portfolio and project status
Delivery management	Weekly	Engineering and product management directors	Scope adjustment; cross organizational escalation point Resource adjustments
Project status meetings	Weekly	Project team	Discussion of project status
Release architecture	Weekly	Project stakeholders including analysts, product managers, project managers, development managers, and delivery leads	Determine business priorities on which requirements should be prioritized for decomposition and estimation (preparation is key to success in this meeting); stakeholders should be prepared to discuss their requirements and priorities
Sprint planning	Once per sprint	Sprint team members	User stories are pulled from the back-log, broken down into tasks, work hours are estimated for each, and a commitment is received to delivering a certain number of user stories
Sprint demos and reviews	Iteratively during the spring	Sprint teams and product managers	Review the output of the sprint and gain acceptance of user stories
Scrum of Scrums	Bi-weekly	Project and development managers, and Scrum Masters	Discuss sprint progress and areas of overlap and integration between teams; raise awareness of potential impacts and resolve inter-team roadblocks
Daily stand-ups (team Scrums)	Daily	Scrum team members	Each member discusses what they did yesterday, what they plan to do today, and any roadblocks they are hitting up against
Retrospectives	After a release	Sprint teams, managers, and product stakeholders	Discuss what we set out to do, how we actually did, and what we could do differently to improve
CCB	Bi-weekly	Project stake-holders including analysts, product managers, project managers, devel-opment managers, and delivery leads	Reviews changes that are being considered for development and release; defects are commonly reviewed here

Metagility Metrics: Predictive Analytics Dashboards for Executives (Status Points)

In this study, we've coined the term *status point* to indicate a form of agile interaction or connection that is used to provide a status, or measurement, of some value relating to program, project, or portfolio management. This section begins with a review of the current research on metrics and measurements in an agile context, thereby revealing that agile vorticity and business momentum fill existing gaps in the ability to measure agility itself. This is followed by a description of common, usable status points from Metagility, and how these can be leveraged to function, along with gauges and dials to achieve zero vorticity for your organization.

General Principles of Metrics Development

Measures Begin Within the Context

One may expect to find in the literature a seminal work on general principles of metrics development that could be applied to any context. After conducting such a review, however, it was found that metrics are developed almost exclusively within the context of what is being measured. Skaistis (2008) establishes that measures should focus on indicators that need to be improved and such indicators should be established at a *high or macro level*. For concepts that are weakly defined, such as agility, Giachetti et al. (2003) state that building the determinants should begin with an audit of factors that correlate with the measure. Other examples follow a similar vein. In developing an assessment tool for lean services, Malmbrandt and Åhlström (2013) begin with a literature review specifically on assessing lean adoption, out of which they develop a set of characteristics for a measurement instrument, which they, in turn, compare against existing lean service measurement tools. Van Horenbeek and Pintelon (2014) follow similarly by beginning their measurement development with a review of maintenance performance measures and maintenance performance indicators in the literature. In developing a metric for evaluating the understandability of state machines, Bae et al. (2013) begin with defining what is to be measured (understandability) and discuss basic structural metrics that have been proposed for state machines.

Measurement Focus: Output, Outcomes, and Structural Properties

Most measurement systems focus on operational measures that adhere to a decision theoretical framework, such as financials. Such frameworks identify key factors, obtain quantification from management, and aggregate the factors into a score (Giachetti et al., 2003). A good example of such a measure is a *balanced scorecard*. Giachetti holds that decision theoretical approaches such as these cannot measure fluid concepts such as flexibility or agility because they measure only past *outcomes*; they cannot say to what degree a system possesses a structural property. Yauch (2011) disagrees, stating that such properties can impact agility, but do not represent such concepts in and of themselves. She states that a measure should be based on results instead of characteristics. I would argue that *structural properties can and do have an impact* on the outcome and, therefore, both should be carefully considered. It is important to know not just what the performance outcome is, but what structural properties give us that performance.

Example: Flexibility

The relational measurement theory that Giachetti proposes is one framework that can be used to build a formal foundation for agility measures as they have been used with similar concepts such as flexibility (Giachetti et al., 2003). Flexibility has been defined as the ability of a system to adapt to external changes while maintaining satisfactory system performance (Morlok and Chang, 2004). In the literature, flexibility has been related to strategy, organizational structures, uncertainty, environmental, and technological factors. Although Morlock and Chang's study concentrated on maintaining performance at a satisfactory level, other measures could have been pursued such as rate of return, profitability, and system cost. Such flexibility measures have been built with an absolute scale as opposed to ordinal (as with agility). However, this is largely due to the fact that flexibility has been studied much longer than agility measures (Dove, 1994; Goranson, 2000).

Measuring Agility

Agility Measures in the Literature

Agility metrics have been considered difficult to define largely because of the multi-dimensionality and vagueness of agile itself (Yauch, 2011). Despite this, there is a significant body of research on measuring agility that focuses mostly on *external measures*. These measures in the literature usually focus on one of two areas, external company performance in relation to its business environment, or performance of specific projects in relation to cost, time, and commitments. Examples include:

- A quantitative agility metric is developed that *provides the desired time-based performance rating which reflects the agility of a manufacturer during product development* (Sieger, Badiru, and Milatovic, 2000).
- Another approach is to define a key agility index, which is a *ratio of time taken to complete change-related tasks and the time taken to complete the whole project* (Lomas et al., 2006).

- J. Highsmith (2010) defines the iron triangle as *value, quality, and constraints* as opposed to the traditional *scope, cost, schedule.*
- Skaistis (2008) states that agility should be measured as the time it takes to respond to a new requirement. Agility factors should be established based on elapsed time, cost, and quality.

Since most agile research and implementations have been concentrated at the team or project level, established measures have largely focused on operational measures as well (Giachetti et al., 2003). However, agile is more than a method, it is a strategy and business philosophy. Such strategies are based on structural properties of the organization such as system architecture, technology resources, system controls, and policies (Giachetti et al., 2003).

Some measures do attempt to look beyond tasks or projects with a more business-level view of agility. *Business agility requires both intrinsically agile IT systems support and a low impedance path from the specification of business change to a specification of IT change* (Caswell and Nigam, 2005). In this example a model is presented based on business artifacts to evaluate the extent of the gap between the business system and the IT system. However, this method examines only one dimension of agility as it relates to IT infrastructure and applications, not product development. Another approach related to software development utilizes fuzzy logic to assess project velocity as the indicator of agility, taking into consideration a number of variables such as technical complexity, programmer capability, and software-testing requirements (Kurian, 2006). Again, this type of measurement looks only at specific projects, and not organizational agility.

Measuring Organizational Agility
Is organizational agility measured based on the organization's structural properties, or its outward performance? Agile companies have been described as those responding successfully based on cost, time, robustness, and scope (Yauch, 2011). This response has been, in some cases, measured against environmental turbulence. This turbulence has been assessed in four categories (Sharifi and Zhang, 1999, 2001; Zhang and Sharifi, 2000; Christian et al., 2001; Ismail and Sharifi, 2006; Toward et al., 2003):

1. Intensity of competition;
2. Dynamic customer requirements;
3. Supply chain turbulence; and
4. Other changes related to the social, technological, environmental, economic, and political business environment.

However, this method measures only the outcome. Measurement frameworks based on the measure of structural properties in an enterprise system could be very useful in the evaluation of new measures for agility as well (Giachetti et al., 2003). True agility could consist of a combination of both, or perhaps other factors, such as complexity.

Complexity as a Measure of Agility

The primary dimension of the agility of a system is its ability to respond to change. Whereas traditional software projects are commonly assessed using the iron triangle, agile development must be measured on responsiveness as well (Ramesh, Mohan, and Cao, 2012). Dove holds that complexity hinders agility because it inhibits this response (Giachetti et al., 2003). Conversely, Dove argues that a measure of complexity would, in turn, measure agility. Giachetti takes this to another level by stating that complexity can be intrinsic or structural. To adapt to change, agility must be a structural property of the system (Giachetti et al., 2003). Goranson argues that when actors and their relationships increase so does complexity (Giachetti et al., 2003). In one study, the time to effect change was measured in both a complex and non-complex business process. The low complexity process took less time and was therefore considered to have greater agility. The problem with measuring agility based on complexity is that it fails to identify potential changes that the system must respond to. It is not proactive. Additionally, measurement of ease of change can be variable and subjective, and as a result, more work is needed to explore the link between complexity and agility (Giachetti et al., 2003). Further work is also suggested to establish a link between ambidexterity in an agile context and performance (Ramesh, Mohan, and Cao, 2012).

Agility and Measurement Indexes: Capability Maturity Models (CMM)

Studies examining both agility and CMM have found them to be quite compatible with little to no impact on each other (Fitzgerald, Hartnett, and Conboy, 2006; Dybå and Dingsøyr, 2008). It has been suggested, however, that although they do not appear to conflict, there needs to be more explicit support for agility in CMM (Boehm, 2002). Indeed, CMM should integrate measures for agility, such as agile vorticity, to determine an organization's *agile maturity* even in hybrid implementations.

Other Agility Indexes

Dove developed a five-level maturity model to determine the agility of a company, but the measurements were determined solely based on the opinions of senior managers (Giachetti et al., 2003). The literature shows that such opinions can be flawed. One study indicated that people with more agile experience had a more favorable perception of it. Those with at least three or more years of experience in traditional methods had less favorable views (Laanti, Salo, and Abrahamsson, 2011). Crucially, a person's background was found to influence their perception of agility and, as a result, measures based on such perceptions could be influenced (Laanti, Salo, and Abrahamsson, 2011).

Metes, Gundry, and Bradish (1998) extended the work by Dove with a scorecard that maps standard agility domains against agile networking capability. Kumar and Motwani (1995) developed an agility index based on the enterprise ability to accelerate activities on the critical path and to compete on time. In this time-based index, firms assessed themselves on agility determinants such as technology, human resources, information flow, and time on critical path for product design and prototyping (Giachetti et al., 2003).

Change as an Agile Measure
Agile adoption is being driven by a number of factors:

- Availability of technology
- Accelerated pace of technical development
- Rapid expansion of access to technology
- Globalization
- Environmental responsibility
- Resource limitations
- Increasing customer expectations

Enterprise agility should be measured in the context of one of these changes (Arteta and Giachetti, 2004).

Measuring Information Systems Development (ISD) Agility
One study on agility found four implications for software management:

1. Cost and quality do not drive agile; speed is paramount
2. Project management is considerably different between agile and traditional methods; projects do not end, they tend to be ongoing
3. Maintenance is merged into ongoing development
4. Human resources management can be more challenging; obtaining highly functioning developers with more creativity and courage would be required as resources become less interchangeable

Conceptual studies are required to develop much-needed instruments to assess the agility of ISD processes and teams (Baskerville, Pries-Heje, and Madsen, 2011).

Compliance as an Agile Measure
The lack of a conceptual foundation regarding agility in ISD does actually present significant problems for practice. Such an absence means assessing agility may be attempted by measuring compliance to commercial agile methods such

as XP and Scrum. There are a number of limitations with this measurement (Conboy, 2009):

1. *Compliance-based assessment of agility* places adherence to a method over the result and may discourage improvement. There is no consolidated body of knowledge of agile solutions to suggest how they may be improved upon.
2. The literature has shown that the vast majority of agile adopters use a hybrid approach. Strict adherence to agile methodology in its purest form is as low as 5%. This makes assessment that is based on compliance difficult.
3. Hybrid methods that are adopted are largely dependent on the context.
4. Dependence on the environment may be unsuitable for agile. The nature of an environment can influence performance. The literature has shown that agile methods may not be the best approach in certain environments (Ramesh, Mohan, and Cao, 2012):
   a. Large teams
   b. Distributed teams
   c. Greenfield sites
   d. Educational environments
   e. Open source development
   f. Outsourcing situations
   g. Systems maintenance
5. Assessment that is based on the adherence to overall values and goals of agility is one way of looking at compliance. However, the literature has shown that these are poorly defined (Conboy, 2009).

Agile and the Iron Triangle

Highsmith states that agile is a business philosophy, not just a development method, and that if agile adopters do not change from the traditional iron triangle of measurement, agile will be relegated to just another technical approach. He contends that adopters must move from measuring projects by scope, cost, and schedule, to value, quality, and constraints (Highsmith, 2010):

- *Value*: to build a releasable product
- *Quality*: to build a reliable product within acceptable constraints

When management is measuring against one set of parameters while projects are measured against another, there will be a core problem with agile adoption. It creates a situation where agile teams are striving against one set of goals while executives are measuring against another. As a result, there are many successful agile projects, but few successful agile organizations. True agile transformation requires changes in organization, process, performance measurement, alignment of business and technology, governance, and culture (Highsmith, 2010). Performance measurement is the most important according to Highsmith because it is the feedback loop for the others.

Technical Debt as an Agile Measure

According to Bavani (2012), an acid test for agility is frequent delivery of business value at least every one to four weeks depending on customer preference. Although this measure is obviously directed at the agile team instead of the organization, adapting to the changing needs of the business at a sustainable pace is an agile characteristic. This pace cannot be maintained in the face of technical debt (Bavani, 2012).

Technical debt consists of repairs, architectural improvements, or much needed changes that are delayed or placed into a development backlog due to time and resource constraints. Technical debt can ruin predictability, which in turn, impacts market capitalization. The results are unrealized roadmaps and an inability to respond to customer issues in a timely manner (Bavani, 2012). Bavani states that there should be continuous integration tools to measure technical debt. Measuring technical debt, as an indicator or at least an impact to agility, could be a key component to any agility measure.

Quality as an Agile Measure

Highsmith (2010) holds that there are two types of quality:

- *Extrinsic*: customer perspective—perceived quality from the customer's point of view
- *Intrinsic*: engineering perspective—quality built into the product internally from the engineer's perspective

Although the customer may be satisfied in the short term by sacrificing quality, technical debt will eventually catch up. It tends to increase as customer satisfaction decreases. The ability to deliver value over time is linked to this intrinsic quality (Highsmith, 2010).

Value as an Agile Measure

Highsmith (2010) suggests that value is a defining characteristic of an agile organization. He defines this as the ability to *deliver a continuous stream of value to the customer with high quality and within scope, cost, and schedule constraints*. He further suggests that a value measurement should include low cost, increased revenue, and improved service well into the future.

Shortening the Tail

According to Highsmith (2010), shortening the tail is a powerful metric for measuring progress toward agility. This measurement consists of the time period from code slush (or freeze) to release. Highsmith attempts to put a number on ISD agility by stating it in terms of software releases. He speaks of *shortening the tail* (or the feedback loop) with customers and management to less than six months, or else such a team could not be considered agile. Indeed, this shortening of the tail is critical, although not the only factor in achieving agile vorticity.

Shortcomings of Current Agility Measures

Much of the current research on agile measurements falls short in the following ways (Yauch, 2011):

1. Some are too narrow or too broad in scope to apply to a single enterprise (e.g., software development, product development, or supply chain agility).
2. Many do not result in a single, quantitative index of agility. A single number allows researchers to use agility as the dependent variable in statistical analyses.
3. Often, they do not enable comparisons to be made between companies in different industries.
4. Most do not explicitly incorporate a broad assessment of the dynamic business environment, which captures the myriad sources of turbulence and triggers for change faced by an organization.
5. Some are singular in dimension, for example, measuring only responsiveness or the number of releases in a given year.
6. Some studies have developed *key agility indexes* using the ratio of time taken to completed change-related tasks and time to complete the whole project. However, these types of indexes are relevant only to new product development and do not gauge organizational performance.
7. Measures based on perceptions can be easily influenced.
8. Compliance-based measures are too dependent on the context, environment, and tailored adoption, and do not account for performance.

Status Points: Agile Interactions and Connections in the Form of Metrics

Status points are monitoring points and metrics that managers use to observe progress and alert the proper authorities of potential problems. This activity is not limited to development but starts early, even as new requirements are decomposed and understood. In addition to the usual burn down charts, managers employ a customized dashboard that monitors progress based on requirements activity. The first of these metrics is the *decomposition rate*.

As mentioned earlier, decomposition of requirements is key to understanding them. This activity takes time, and it is important that it is monitored. The following excerpts explain how the decomposition rate is created and monitored:

"So [for] a feature that hasn't been broken down or well understood, it [dashboard] shows an estimated value of that, and we compare that to the total decomposed value and also the percent complete based on each."
—Software Project Manager

"So [in] that decomposition process we have a percentage. I'm simplifying the math, but if we start with 10 requirements and they have between five and 20 stories each, on day one, the decomposition percentage would be zero and then as the business analysts and the product owners work and start generating stories, we'll start checking off stories that have reached a gating point."
—Software Development Manager

In addition to the decomposition rate, the progress of user story development and the tasks they consist of is monitored via the dashboard and a burn down chart. These burn down charts are broken down to the team level and to the individual level. These statistics can also be rolled back up to project level, which shows how many *ideal engineering days* (IEDs) (based on approximately 6.5 work hours per day) are in each sprint and the entire release. System releases typically consist of 10 such sprints.

Another important metric is velocity, which is based on how many IEDs a team has completed in each sprint. Velocity performance is compared to previous releases in order to gain an understanding of how teams perform over time. It also serves as a benchmark for capacity and as a predictor for scoping the next release.

Of course, no executive dashboard would be complete without financials and general project performance data. Budgets are tracked to the actuals of the company's financial spend. Project dependencies are monitored as well as past release metrics. Measurements of how long it took previous system releases to go from one stage gate to another and their respective financials are actively compared to current efforts.

Yet another important status point is defect metrics. The incoming arrival and closure rates for defects are monitored, as well as their customer impacts. All this metric data is maintained internally in a central repository accessible by the project team.

In summary, status points are a form of interconnection that consists of monitoring points that the organization uses to keep track of what is going on with feature decomposition, development, and testing. They serve as inputs to decision making and agility management. The Web Added Value (WAV™)

materials provided with this book (located at www.jrosspub.com/wav) include a metrics guide with numerous measurements and aligns these metrics with the agile triangle so that you can develop your own *gauges and dials* that you deem necessary in order to reach agile vorticity!

Decision Points: The What, When, and Where of Metagility Decision Making

Another type of interconnection is the decision point. These don't always occur in a meeting or specific venue and can happen throughout scoping and development. As requirements understanding is taking place, decisions are made collaboratively by the executives from engineering (process agility) and the business (market agility). These include decisions regarding what kind of work and how much can be taken on for the next systems release as one software product manager described:

"Before we sign up for it, they're evaluating at different levels whether we're ready to take on the next big one, and that would be when they look at their revenue plans and they see the top-line utilization of the R&D assets."

While software and firmware tend to be more agile in the way they approach decisions, hardware is much more rigid and waterfall based, requiring a feasibility study in the beginning to help decide whether, when, and how the work could be taken on. During the progression of the systems release, stage gates are integrated into the agile process as *check points* on the progress and reliability of the release. These check points allow all three domains to maintain synchronicity. If the project has met its gating requirements, it will be allowed to proceed to the next gate.

Not all decision points are grounded in the stage-gate process. Important decision points are made at the user story and requirement levels as well. The final decision point for any requirement is the demonstration. Stakeholders, typically the product manager, will observe and sign off on the demo if it meets expectations. Respondents felt as though the size and complexity of the organization contributed to a more formal demonstration process. As one manager noted:

"Our demo is more formal, much more formal than it has been in other companies, and I think the reason for the formality is because we have a lot of product managers, a lot of different people, and a lot of developers in place."

Such complexity contributes to limitations elsewhere, such as change management. Even in a hybrid agile environment, change becomes more rigid beyond a certain point. Although the ability to change is an important component of market agility, it does not mean that it is constant throughout the development process. As the system release progresses, it becomes less impervious to change. With embedded systems organizations in particular, the release tends to be more rigid where hardware and multiple domains are affected. The following excerpt from a software project manager illustrates how change is managed after the systems release has passed its stage gates:

> "After that, change still happens but it's a process. It has to go through change control, it has to be well documented and with that, the team agrees that, 'hey, this is the change we need to make, it has all the right buy-in and has the right business specifications, so let's make it.'"

A hardware engineering manager explained how such changes tend to be much more rigid in his domain:

> "Before that can happen, an engineering change order has to be written that explains what's being changed, what it effects, and why it's being changed, and then this error correction coding is routed through the various functional groups: electrical, mechanical, firmware, supply chain, manufacturing, hardware quality assurance, and systems quality assurance. It communicates the change and all these functional groups have to approve that change, and it also notifies them of what's changing and what the impact is on that functional group."

To summarize, decision points are a form of interconnection where the stage-gate process and agile methodology synchronize and sanity check each other. In other words, it is where the agile and waterfall sides of the organization come together, hence the management of hybrid agility.

Informal Interactions for Maximum Agility: Eliminating *Forgetfulness*

Less formal interconnections are *touchpoints*. Touchpoints are informal interactions that are performed by managers and other stakeholders in order to *check on* what may be going on in another domain or team. It is a form of tacit communication that is ongoing, yet it is not formally required or stated. The initiating of such communication is largely intuitive but has proven effective in making sure tasks are being performed, roadblocks are removed, and that processes are being orchestrated as expected. These touchpoints can be one-off communications for follow-up or ad hoc meetings to resolve issues or to continue requirements decomposition. One manager described this as:

> *"Helping [to] ensure that the teams are completing what they need to complete, when they need to complete it."*

Systems engineering plays a significant role in managing these interactions, along with project management. They ensure that business requirements are properly broken down into technical requirements for each domain, and serve as the primary communication conduit from the engineering organization up to the business:

> *"I will interact with systems engineering and systems might go to the change meetings. Systems would also act as the go-between for product management and firmware."*
>
> —Firmware Architect

These communications occur at all levels of management as one software project manager explained:

> *"I work with product managers on a regular basis, as well as the directors and the VPs to assess the project, determine where we are, and how we need to proceed. They let me know if there are issues with scope or some new customer commitment. I meet with them, kind of on a regular, not a scheduled basis, but a regular basis."*

One hardware architect stated that documentation can sometimes take the place of interpersonal interaction as a touchpoint:

> *"So usually the way that those touchpoints happen would be us developing a technical specification."*

Touchpoints are a form of interconnection that consists of ad hoc meetings, documentation, and personal follow-up. It is a largely intuitive part of the process because it may be initiated by the project manager or other stakeholder based on feel, discomfort, or output from a monitoring tool that lets them know they need to initiate a meeting or contact a stakeholder for status. The concept of touchpoints maximizes interactions for increased agility and eliminates *forgetfulness*. It is a form of *always-on* communication that should be encouraged.

FINE TUNING: HOW TO OPTIMIZE

As the information inputs from the various interconnections and interactions are realized, the company makes adjustments. Promises are made intuitively and quickly with little information and are actively balanced with contractual workload. Adjustments to scope, resources, and customer acceptance in particular are an important component of agility management. These adjustments are updated via a process of constant reassessment.

Customer Acceptance

Customer collaboration is a key tenet of the *Agile Manifesto*. Respondents indicated that much of their work involved influencing customer acceptance of the product. By working with the customer to develop different modes of acceptance, products could be brought to market quicker. As mentioned in a previous chapter, these modes most often consisted of field trials and pilot projects. Field trials are where the customer receives an early version of the product and is allowed to test it and provide feedback. With this technique, the customer benefits by getting a new product quicker and having the chance to influence product direction, while the vendor company saves resource costs by essentially outsourcing its testing to the customer as a hardware product manager explained:

> *"And that's the first chance for us to get some feedback on our quality. Our customers in Canada, they do really, really thorough testing of our products. I would say sometimes even more detailed testing than us, so we take that feedback, and it helps us to improve our quality of tests—that's certainly a good thing."*

Pilot projects are another method of agile customer collaboration. Using this method, the customer's expectations on quality are lowered in exchange for the opportunity to *be first*. This allows the vendor company to bridge customer needs with organizational capabilities as a software product manager explained:

> *"We work with that customer to set expectations that we are going to pilot things with them instead of giving them a proven, field-ready, tried-and-true product, and the customers, to their credit, have generally accepted some of these decisions and worked with us as long as the expectations were managed."*

Manipulating customer acceptance is one way in which the organization makes adjustments to manage agility. Through the use of field trials, pilot projects, and other modes of acceptance, the organization influences as well as adapts to the business momentum generated by market pressures.

Scope Adjustment

As with managing customer acceptance, adjusting scope is one of the necessary evils of managing agility. Due to the high unknowns of new technology and changing customer needs, capacity is pushed to its limits and is often overestimated, then it is gradually adjusted as the requirements and business needs become more apparent. This refinement occurs gradually as requirements are better understood. Often, this may continue after decomposition and well into development.

One operations manager noted how they over-estimate capacity or *pack the release* with the expectation that items will be pulled later:

> *"I get a lot more of, 'well, I want you to prioritize three times the capacity of the project because I really don't know which bits and pieces I'm going to pull to be able to fill up the actual capacity.'"*

Another respondent recounted how requirements are selected for the release as they bubble up to the top:

> *"We pick the highest priority items off of the top of the pile and slate those to a release, haggling over what's really a priority and so forth [until it] is finally settled."*
>
> —Software Product Manager

These scope adjustments are often strategic. They may be based on obtaining business from a specific customer or sector or be due to the lack of profit in a specific product line. Respondents noted that revenue generation tended to be a key component of the company's strategic direction. For rapid scope adjustment to work, the organization must be flexible in its ability to abort gracefully on requirements, features, and/or products. One software manager described how this ability is one of the most important pluses of utilizing agile:

> *"What I see the agile process does is allows you to abort gracefully and much sooner. In an agile [environment] when it's going south, you can often make that decision at the 30% mark to say this isn't working and drop it. . . . [With] agile a lot of times it becomes obvious sooner that you're not going to succeed in the marketplace and you don't invest that money for whatever reasons."*

These requirements may be postponed or dropped altogether. Resources can then move quickly from one aborted task to a more important priority. Although such decisions are ultimately made at the executive level, the business or product side works in tandem with the engineering or organizational side to make the best recommendation.

Resource Adjustment

Resources must be adjusted, as well as scope. Analysis revealed that the organization cultivated an ability to flex resources in a variety of ways. These consisted of maintaining team flexibility, outsourcing when needed, and most important, relying on a core group of engineers with high expertise. Such flexibility is much higher within the software domain than the firmware or hardware domains, but it still exists. The reason for this difference was cited by many respondents as being due to the lack of interchangeability of resources. Such interchangeability is less prevalent in the firmware and hardware domains due to the specialized level of expertise required.

Teams have the ability to optimize the use of this high expertise when necessary. The agile concept of self-organizing teams and pair programming allows them to organize the required expertise according to the current scope. Although expertise may be high and specialized, respondents noted that the teams are smart enough to organize the *right mix* of people. Having these self-organizing agile teams was found to be critical in maintaining capacity as one software project manager explained:

> *"If we don't have agile teams, if we are constantly swapping in new features, if Team A only works with one type of code or one type of functionality and that feature is now pulled from the release, well now that team goes unused and they have to scramble to do something else or we're going to lose capacity."*

Embedded systems development brings with it its own set of challenges with regard to high expertise and self-organizing teams. As mentioned previously, firmware sits in the middle of the technological solution between software and hardware. Resources from firmware are often strained because the other domains require their support. Managing this *resource rotation* is a continual challenge. These resources tend to be even more specialized and less interchangeable than other domains as a hardware engineering manager explained:

> *"We have firmware guys that are rotating in and out, say for instance, 80% of the time they're supporting the software group and 20% of the time they're supporting hardware. If I've got a firmware guy that's supporting hardware efforts and he gets moved over halfway through the life of development to support software, and we bring somebody else in that knows nothing about this hardware development, it's a challenge for him to get up to speed."*

The most severe example of this flexibility is referred to as the *hero model*. Often as a last resort, the organization will draft one (or more) highly capable expert to solve a problem or meet the goals of a release entirely outside of the agile processes as a lead architect explained:

> *"The hero model, which we know doesn't really last forever, it's not a good thing to build a company on, but sometimes when you've got to get something done really quickly and you don't have time to track story points and break it down, you can just give it to a group of very capable people and say, here, you just need to get this done as quick as possible."*

Kaizen Culture: The Importance of Constant Reassessment

Kaizen culture is one of constant improvement or reassessment. It is a two-part philosophy. On the one hand, the organization needs to create events where improvement can be assessed, reassessed, and discussed. Retrospectives play a large part in this process. More important though, there should be a culture of reassessment where each stakeholder works to find ways to improve their job or the technology they help develop. The process of Metagility supports this idea of constant reassessment both ways—by process through hybrid agile development and by culture through the way adjustments are made based on discoveries from interconnections.

The organization must continually adjust the correct resource mix across the range of domains and projects. This adjusting is facilitated by a constant process of reassessment of the business's current position against its strategic direction. In this way, the business reassesses all of its adjustments.

Respondents noted that much of this reassessment activity arose from the hybrid agile implementation. The stage-gate method forces re-evaluation at each gate that many felt makes the organization more agile, despite its waterfall nature, as a software project manager explained:

> *"Because it's within that waterfall process, it probably makes us more agile because we have to constantly reassess and re-evaluate where we are and what we need to complete versus just finishing what we finish."*

Metagility is the group of activities used to orchestrate and manage agility across the enterprise. It is how process and market agility are managed to achieve a common goal. There are two major categories of agile orchestration, which are interconnections/interactions and making adjustments. Interconnections consist of dependencies of one domain on another, interdependencies between two or more domains, formal linkages or key meeting points between domains, status points for monitoring and maintaining status, decision points for executive decision making, and informal touchpoints that stakeholders establish intuitively to keep the process moving. Decision points and linkages also serve as the connecting points between the agile method process and the waterfall process, and they therefore assist in managing the hybrid agility implementation that the organization has employed. It is important to note that the kinds of interconnections and interactions developed within this study are largely influenced by the embedded systems context. The *agile characteristics* outlined in Figure 7.1 enable all the domains to work together as one cohesive unit and agile orchestration ensures that this cohesion occurs. The interactions and interconnections are designed to bring all domains within embedded systems together both informally and formally when necessary to ensure the production of the systems release. The necessity of this cohesion and the agile characteristics and orchestration it demands are specific to embedded systems.

The business then uses the outputs and inputs from these interconnections to adjust customer acceptance modes, scope, and resources to manage the agility of the organization. The process of making these adjustments is one of continual reassessment. Inculcating this *kaizen* culture of constant reassessment is critical to the success of Metagility.

9

SOFT SKILLS FOR MANAGING AGILITY

"...and there were always a lot of distractions that came with the sprints that would prevent us from staying focused on them, and I think that is something that we've never really addressed."

—Firmware Manager

ADDRESSING COMMON PROJECT MANAGEMENT CONCERNS

One of the most worrisome fears that project managers have is the invisible drain that distractions have on their precious resources. Fighting fires, side projects, meetings, and spending time supporting colleagues and customers can dramatically reduce time spent by resources on a project or user story.

This is compounded by the fact that in challenging contexts, such as embedded systems, resources are not always interchangeable.

"We have struggled with a true agile process because, in my opinion, the nature of embedded software is not quite a perfect fit for the agile methodology because people aren't interchangeable resources. Each of the developers has a sort of compartmentalized expertise."

—Firmware Architect

This compartmentalized expertise and the resulting lack of interchangeability means that time must be carefully managed, much more so than usual. As a result, a squeeze is put on any task that does not directly impact development; documentation being chief of these tasks. Most developers will say that the need to create documentation is where their greatest amount of time is spent, other than development itself. Therefore, a key component of minimizing distractions and managing non-interchangeable resources is managing documentation effectively.

Documentation

A key tenet of the *Agile Manifesto* de-emphasizes documentation. However, this is not meant to imply that documentation is not important—only that working software is more so. Studies show that documentation is still very important to the success of any technology development effort. It is needed by customers to understand and support the product, and it is needed internally to transfer information between teams, development tracks, and releases to ensure integration integrity and viability of solutions. The question is, who does the documentation—and when? Developers and engineers have the knowledge to write the documents, but do not always have the time or inclination to do so. Technical writers do not always have the necessary expertise to create the kind of documentation the organization needs. During our study, we found that the most effective organizations managed documentation in four ways:

1. Use of technical publications teams
2. Bottom-up documentation
3. Using user story repositories to gather information
4. Iterative reviews

Use of Technical Publications Teams

Most engineers or developers simply do not have time to write the bulk of the documentation that is needed. If they do, it will take up an inordinate amount of time and detract from development work that they need to perform. As a result, technical publications teams, or tech writers, are a *must have* to alleviate this pressure. The challenge is that these teams are often still reliant on the developers and engineers for the more technical aspects.

Bottom-up documentation is one technique that helps with this conundrum. What this means is that documentation that changes less frequently is done by the engineers, while faster changing tracks rely more heavily on the technical writers.

> *"The hardware team does a fair amount of documentation but on the firmware team, we don't do a whole lot."*
>
> —Firmware Architect

The slower moving (yet still quite agile) hardware track produces much of its own documentation because it is less tolerant of errors and fixes are not as easily implemented. Faster moving tracks, such as firmware or software, still provide input but typically do not take direct ownership of the documents.

For tracks such as firmware and software which have higher rates of change, the documentation is gleaned from user story repositories.

> "So, if it's a documentation for a release, we have our documentation team review what's in the release; they tag user stories that need to be created to track documentation whether its release notes or whether it's a specialized white paper or installation guide or anything like that. So, they track the features of release and they can run queries on what documents need to be created, and then all through the process they are ensuring they receive drafts and have ownership of the right items,"
>
> —Software Project Manager

Information gleaned from these user stories, if done properly, can be collated and wordsmithed to create release notes, software development kits, white papers, and other documentation for both external and internal audiences.

Finally, *and more often than not*, it's the product manager who goes in and writes a draft or is editor-in-chief of a draft that Technical Documentation has already produced. Typically, Technical Documentation controls the publishing and formatting of it.

Product managers and system architects typically serve as *editors* of these documents, which includes coauthoring, review, and final approval.

Iterative reviews between stakeholders ensure that new changes are integrated as new user stories are worked, and that all stakeholders get at least a chance or two to review the document before it goes out—due to their limited availability.

TEAM MANAGEMENT

Two of the most important agile team constructs in large enterprises are the Scrum teams and product owner teams. Scrum teams are generally a cross section of expertise necessary to create the product. Participants in the team include business analysts, developers, testers, systems engineers, and even technical writers. Once formed, Scrum teams should remain together over time to reduce distractions and overhead, but most important, to establish a stable velocity. We will discuss team velocity in a later section, but it is essentially a measure of the rate at which items can be completed. Having a stable velocity across teams helps to ensure that we have a predictable delivery capacity across the enterprise. If teams are constantly changing, the true velocity and capacity of the organization will remain unclear.

In Metagility, product owner teams are a separate group, usually consisting of both business analysts and systems engineers working closely with product managers to translate the needs of the business into user stories that are ready to be consumed by the sprint teams with minimal discovery. In essence, the product owner team enables the Scrum or sprint teams they support by assisting in requirements comprehension and removal of blocking items. Typically, the product owner team is empowered to make decisions that the sprint teams are not. Primary responsibilities include:

1. Requirement decomposition
2. Serving as the representative of the customer or other external stakeholder(s)
3. Creating and prioritizing the product backlog
4. Reviewing and approving the work that has been completed by the sprint teams and providing guidance for correction
5. Serving as communication conduit between sprint teams and the business
6. Initiating and communicating changes in direction if necessary

Another important team in Metagility is the release architecture team. The release architecture team focuses on prioritizing items in the backlog for the upcoming releases. This team is also responsible for determining changes in direction at the release level. Although product owners typically lead these team discussions and implement the resulting outcomes, they consist of a number of additional stakeholders. These include product managers, technical architecture, and first- and second-level management.

Since these are some of the most important teams in a hybrid agile context, what follows here is a short reference on how to understand and build them.

Understanding Tribes and Building Agile Teams

A tribe is a social order consisting of a group of people with common ties such as bloodline or culture. For centuries, tribes were a way for humans to improve their odds for survival. In a workplace context, tribes have become a way of increasing odds for success on the job. Tribes tend to form naturally with leaders that may or may not be influenced by an organizational chart. Tribal influence can dictate whether changes in an organization will work, and whether they will be accepted and supported by the group. Often, the leaders who are listed on an organizational chart may not be the actual functional leaders of the tribe.

To manage tribes, leaders need to first identify these groups. This step is a bit intuitive, but not difficult. Observe which groups of people congregate together and who they talk to. This will give you a good idea of the tribal structure. The next thing is to listen to the group and the language that they use. Successful groups use a common language that everyone in the group understands. If a leader is brought in who does not speak that language, they will have difficulty. Some tribes are lazy and lack productivity, while others can be highly productive. This level of productivity is influenced by the tribal leaders. Strong tribal leaders who focus on improving the standing of the tribe in the organization are often rewarded with great loyalty from its members when successful. A development organization may consist of many tribes with some moving in different directions than others. Some have friction, and some do not, while others may attract high-talented people and others not so much.

Leaders assigned to managing agile teams should embody the following characteristics: trust, humility, and exceptional communication skills. Much of agile is built on what is often termed as a *servant leadership* mindset, the idea of leading by example by taking on a more supportive, nurturing approach to managing teams, but also having an accommodating and flexible attitude to customers and the business by always asking the question "How can we help?" as opposed to the "We cannot do that now" phrase that is often heard in a waterfall environment. Managers and other leaders in these contexts are typically so busy *pushing back* that they develop a reputation with other parts of the business as being *difficult* and too intractable. Although protecting one's team is important, a good agile leader should focus on:

1. Setting the example for the team;
2. Removing barriers or dependencies between teams and team members;
3. Keeping the team focused on the requirements and goals for the project;
4. Ensuring that team members are free of needless meetings or distractions, while at the same time making sure they have the information and updated news necessary to do their jobs; and
5. Ensuring that the methodology is followed.

Successful agile implementations require high-functioning teams. In order to have high-functioning teams, it is important to inculcate a high-functioning tribal culture to encourage the initiative, motivation, and the independent thought that is needed in the kind of developers and testers that make agility successful. If a group has a very bureaucratic, staid culture, and as an agile consultant you come in and tell them that anything is possible, you will not get a very positive response. The way to get past this barrier is to push agile values one at a time. Select a person in the group who seems to desire change and who seems to have some influence with the team. Inform this person that they have the potential to utilize their creativity and initiative to make the product(s) better. This can be referred to as the *I'm Great* concept. You are convincing a person that they have greater potential. Eventually, as one or two people are convinced, they, in turn, will convince others of the same and the tribal culture will change. The next step is to figure out what the individual team members value by asking them a series of questions and then requiring them to work with others to achieve those desires or solve those problems. This could be referred to as the *We're Great* stage, and that's what you want. By organizing Scrum teams and setting up pair programming, you encourage people to work together. The needs of the individuals have been transferred to making the greater team a success.

Sprint team leads are critical in making this kind of success happen by guiding the teams from both a social, agile, and technical perspective. Building the kind of high-functioning teams that the organization needs means that sprint team leads must build up the tribal culture one person at a time. In many development organizations, formal training and documentation are rare or nonexistent. This kind of expertise is transferred informally via what can be termed *tribal knowledge*. This tribal knowledge is passed from one person to the next over a period of time. As a new agile team member moves through the tasks of their first assignments, they gain knowledge here and there from their peers, which grows as they are assigned more complicated tasks over time. As this knowledge grows, team members should be given more opportunity to ask questions of product owners and make suggestions for improvement. High-performing teams need to have very good communication skills, so it is very important that they learn to talk to the business as well as each other, with the ability to switch gears from the typical *developer* language to the *business* language when necessary.

Self-Organizing Teams

The concept of self-organizing teams is an important one in the agile/Scrum lexicon. While in the throes of agile transformation, many managers and individual contributors ask whether this is required or not, and they argue about the benefits or lack thereof. The truth is, you don't have to do self-organizing teams if you don't want to. It is perfectly acceptable to have the manager or other lead create the teams themselves. However, you may find that by denying teams the empowerment to their own team destiny, they may not be as *proactive and high-functioning* as many high-performance agile organizations may require.

Development of self-organizing teams has three phases, and it typically takes an agile coach—someone external to the organization—to bring individual contributors forward into creating their own teams.

The first phase is fearful resistance. You may find that the suggestion of self-organizing teams makes many people express high school-level behavior. They will recount memories of grade school where the slow- or low-performing kids were the last to be selected by their peers and were often sidelined on the bench. There will also be cliquish behavior, where groups of people will tend to stick together with their *friends* without creating balanced teams. When this is challenged, some will weaken and suggest that the manager simply *make the selections themselves* to avoid putting anyone else on the spot.

To move the group past this phase, it is important to emphasize that if the manager is going to make the decision, then they will lose a vital and important chance to change their destiny and experience a higher degree of freedom, empowerment, and creativity in their job than they have ever known. Next, make each person fill out their three most important skills on a sticky note and place it under the name of a team. The number of teams should be decided ahead of time and listed on a whiteboard. Emphasize to the group that each team needs to have roughly equivalent expertise. At this point, the teams will be filled, but probably unbalanced. Take a look at the whiteboard and the skills for each team member. It will most likely be obvious that at least a few people need to be moved around. The key here is to accomplish a breakthrough, where at least one of these people who needs to move comes to this realization themselves and takes the initiative to move their own sticky note out of the *comfort team* and into the team where they know they are needed. Emphasize again that if the team cannot self-organize and the manager has to do it, a big opportunity will be lost. Usually, at least one of these people will get up and take the initiative to move themselves, and when that happens, you have accomplished a breakthrough.

The last phase is realization. Once one person gets up the gumption to make the difficult decision of moving themselves, others will follow suit, and it won't be long before you have a group of well-balanced and self-organized teams. Now that they have the confidence to organize themselves, they will tend to work in a more agile fashion during sprint work, offering up more accurate estimates, better suggestions, and higher velocity overall. You may even find that people will work much better together in general, resulting in fewer managerial issues or drama that can be a drain on everyone's time and energy.

Again, you don't have to have self-organizing teams in hybrid agility, but it is highly recommended.

MANAGING DISTRIBUTED TEAMS

In today's globalized working environment, distributed teams have become ubiquitous and vital components of any development organization. Although such teams could be housed anywhere, even in the same country, typically such teams are the result of offshore outsourcing initiatives, which have become a popular and accepted method for quickly adding additional resources. As we have established in earlier chapters, managing agility with these distributed teams can be quite a challenge. As one product manager explained:

"We have a lot of offshore resources and those teams do not work as well in an autonomous, self-directed mode; they require a more structured deliverable to be given to them to build to a spec or to a highly granular detail level of user story that can then be measured and more repeatedly checked for quality against the original requirements."

It is important to understand the underlying factors as to why this difficulty exists. The reasons are twofold:

1. Lack of communication
2. Inability or unwillingness to build highly capable teams

Many agile organizations will attempt to flex or extend the capabilities of their existing local teams by adding distributed (i.e., offshore) resources. One challenge with these resources is getting them up to speed on the technology. Local developers are often not inclined or incentivized to share knowledge. There is very little cooperation, pair programming, or training going on between the local teams that know the products and services and the offshore or distributed teams that are entirely new. This slows down the effectiveness of the distributed resources.

Additionally, one of the key characteristics of successful agile teams is that they are highly capable and willing to take the initiative. Creativity and autonomy are encouraged. However, distributed resources often feel constrained when attempting to take the same initiative due to the lack of available knowledge and training that the local teams have. Local development organizations are sometimes unable or unwilling to dedicate the time and resources necessary to get the distributed teams up to speed. Consequently, distributed teams typically consisting of offshore contract resources want to make their customers happy and do not want to burden their host with requests. As a result, the work they do, as our product manager's comments suggest, must be closely managed.

Our most successful case studies in Metagility succeeded in solving this problem in a couple of ways. The first was heavy communication. Anytime you are working with remote resources, regardless of their location, lots of daily communication is required. This goes beyond the typical stand-ups or Scrum meetings and into knowledge-sharing sessions, code reviews, architectural design sessions, and other venues that allow for knowledge transfer and better understanding between teams. Local architects and developers must be incentivized with the understanding that conducting such services is what makes the difference between a senior or *lead* developer and one who is not. Lead developers must be imbued with the understanding that leadership of distributed teams as well as local teams is critical to their own personal success and that of the team. The idea of *hogging knowledge* as a guarantee for job security needs to be soundly discouraged. Lead developers need to understand that their expansive knowledge is much more valuable to the company if they share it with others so that the organization draws a greater benefit as opposed to keeping it secret among themselves so that they cannot be replaced. This outdated mindset of controlling knowledge in order to preserve oneself needs to be completely removed if agile teams are to be successful. Such leads need to understand that it is not their specialized knowledge per se, but their initiative, creativity, and ability to motivate and lead others that is the path to self-actualization and success. These concepts should be integrated into the performance review process for all developers and testers on agile teams. Doing so will ensure team growth among all teams—both local and distributed.

Another method that our case studies used to bring distributed teams forward was personnel exchange. Like officer exchange programs in the military, offshore resources were brought onsite to work with local teams, as well as local experts being sent to the offshore locations. This exchange was conducted regularly and proved to be very effective in transferring knowledge, fostering pair programming, and assimilating distributed teams to the agile processes and procedures used by the local groups.

INTERCHANGEABLE TEAMS

Development organizations want interchangeable teams. This does not always mean that expertise is entirely duplicated from one person to another or even one team to another. What it does mean is that if one feature is changed out for another, an agile team should be able to adjust. It allows the organization to have a leaner staff. It doesn't take as many system engineers to write stories. Not as many development teams are required because the ones that exist can focus on many different pieces of functionality and technologies so that development can focus on what's the most important thing to the business at that point in time. The inability of agile teams to adjust can result in significant loss in capacity. As one project manager explained to me, they often had projects where new features were being swapped in for old ones as the needs of the clients became better understood. This was particularly true at the beginning of the project. In order to preserve capacity and maintain momentum, the teams had to be able to wrap up their work on the old feature and start work on the new one as seamlessly as possible. Old features are never thrown away, they are placed into the backlog and often resurrected later.

However, being able to conduct this *feature swapping* in a smooth and agile fashion is easier said than done. One way architects and managers build this interchangeable skill set into their teams is by carefully selecting the kind of work assigned to specific team members. New members are assigned work that builds knowledge of the *core* product, which is then followed by work that builds on this knowledge in a natural way so as to eventually grow expertise around the entire system. As one development manager illustrated:

> *"They're not quite as interchangeable as we'd like, where anybody can work on any story. You can do that, but it's not efficient. So, you want to give people kind of a growth path, so you start with a new requirement of the core product, then move to another requirement that enforces that knowledge, and then move through the system in a logical manner. If it's a contractor, they probably will never get through the whole system. I think employees take a year or two before they feel comfortable talking about most of the system. Being able to get in a conversation where questions could come up about the majority of the system probably takes them a year or two to be comfortable."*

It should be understood that this does take time. Considerable investment among managers, team leads, and architects is also required for this to be a success.

TECHNIQUES FOR BRINGING YOUR TEAM UP TO SPEED

Teams Are Not Equal

Teams are not always equal, nor do they need to be. In our case studies, some teams had higher levels of expertise than others, but were not really specialized. This allowed for a greater level of interchangeability of work. If one team finds out that work they thought would take three sprints ends up taking four, then the work they were going to do in the fourth sprint will need to be moved to another team. This other team may not be the exact equal of the first, but they should have the skills to pick up the work and do the job.

Another type of team difference is, of course, size. In our case studies, sprint teams were initially six people, which was eventually paired down to three in some cases. These smaller teams were able to do work that did not require larger teams. A challenge here was keeping track of pace because the velocity of a six-person team is very different from a three-person team.

Training

Despite the concept of tribes, transference of tribal knowledge, and the influence that sprint team leaders can have over these entities, formal training is still important. This kind of training needs to occur with some level of regularity, at least in the beginning, to reinforce the changes needed. As one project manager explained:

> *"I think constant training is needed because as you grow an organization, you just get used to the fact that you've been agile, and that's the way it's always been, and that's the way it's always going to be—so when new team members come on board, you must train them and have them go through a formal process of why it is we are using agility and how it benefits things and what the process is instead of less informal training. I think that's key because I see issues sometimes when new teams or new people are coming onboard and they're not being held accountable or aren't following the process like they should."*
>
> —Software Project Manager

Pair Programming

Pair programming is the agile practice of pairing developers into teams of two so that they can work together, support each other, and learn. It is one way that helps new team members get up to speed more quickly on a new product or codebase. Pair programming has a number of benefits. Paired developers put *pressure* on each person to do their best. It also results in more accurate estimates as developers get a better sense of what they and their team members are capable of accomplishing in a period of time. Most important, it creates a sense of comradery, which enhances overall team performance. It is important to note that in order for these dynamics to continue, pairs should be broken up and re-paired with other people on regular intervals to prevent complacency.

EXECUTIVE MANAGEMENT: MANAGING YOUR MANAGERS

Managing large, complex environments and the challenges surrounding them is a recurring theme among most of our case studies. In previous chapters, we've discussed how large environments can communicate and maintain synchronicity via a series of well-defined interactions. However, harmonizing research and development between teams is one thing, but ensuring that accurate performance data gets bubbled up to upper-level executives is another one entirely. As mentioned before, a successful agile transformation requires executive support and buy-in. By the same token, executives need access to the right kind of information to enable this support. Executives in our case studies described the following three most significant challenges as it relates to managing agility in their organizations:

1. Real-time strategic alignment
2. Decision making based on the agile triangle
3. Adequate program and portfolio management

Real-Time Strategic Alignment

Gathering performance data across a large number of distributed teams, many of which may be using agile in a slightly different way, was cited as a major challenge. Such data is often managed in spreadsheets and can be a monumental effort to gather. By the time the data is actually compiled and presented, the actual status of many of the teams may have already changed. The goal post moves faster than the organization's ability to compile and report information. This lack of real-time intelligence and the inability to align this intelligence across large organizations was cited by many of the executives in our case studies as a chief frustration. As a result, they were unable to provide transparency to internal business partners and stakeholders on millions of dollars of investment each year, or perhaps more. Evaluations were based on stale data that could not be entirely trusted.

Decision Making Based on the Agile Triangle

As has been discussed previously, the agile triangle demands that decisions for new products and services should be based on their *value*. Executives often mentioned that they lacked the ability to determine the flexibility of resources to make value-based decisions because they had no insight into how engineering was performing on a regular basis. Executives needed a way to assess team performance, skills, and capacity across the entire organization. Leaders attempted to compensate by having more daily and weekly status meetings to provide updates, but this simply created more overhead. A lack of the ability to accurately assess value itself was also mentioned.

Adequate Program and Portfolio Management

Due to points one and two of the most significant challenges mentioned previously, large organizations today require more sophisticated tooling in the form of program and portfolio management applications. Having such tools solves the crucial problem of knowing what is going on across all teams and development tracks. Being able to see where a company stands from a technological, developmental, and financial perspective from top to bottom is important. Such intelligence is critical—managing investment dollars to maximize value delivery, cutting off bad investments, and focusing on products that are working out best for the company. This is a key enabler for achieving agile vorticity.

So, the challenge then becomes: how do we create and manage intelligence that meets these requirements? In Chapter 8 we discussed a series of metrics based on hybrid agile implementations that have been best found to facilitate team and project management. The next challenge is: how do we roll these metrics up into more of a business intelligence (BI) solution for program and portfolio management? Coming up is a set of guidelines for creating, managing, and using such a solution, which is followed by a series of examples. Remember, the ultimate goal (or indicator) is agile vorticity.

Management and Usage
Before building a program or portfolio management solution, one needs to understand how to properly apply it.

1. *Using tools as dials as well as gauges*: Many proponents of agile measures have warned against using them as a lever to drive behavior instead of just feedback. This is based on the idea that if managers start inquiring or criticizing team leaders about the performance of a certain measure or metric, than the leaders will focus too much on satisfying the metric, and will eventually engineer a way to make the numbers look good without solving the underlying issues, or perhaps in doing so, create more problems than they solve in other areas. A good program management solution provides more than a series of metrics; it takes this information and combines it with others to create actionable intelligence. If you take one particularly poorly performing metric and beat your teams up with it, chances are they will figure out a way to game the system. But if your project portfolio management solution is intelligent enough to link performance metrics with resource allocation in a real-time way, it can provide a *dial* that you can turn to change this allocation in order to improve the situation. Not only is this a more elegant solution, it gives the power to the executive or leader in charge to effect change. Executives are going to use data to make decisions, why not give them the tools to execute as well?

2. *Measures should align with the agile triangle*: In the old waterfall context, metrics were largely based on the iron triangle of scope, budget, and timeline. These are all factors in an agile triangle as well with

additional emphasis on quality and value. Concepts such as productivity, responsiveness, predictability, quality, and customer satisfaction are all important when it comes to providing insights into development work and decision making; but in the end, each one can—and should—roll up into the three components of the agile triangle.

3. *Failure to support quantitative measures with qualitative information*: One mistake that many organizations make when managing a program management solution is having policies that automatically trigger certain alarms or processes based on when a specific metric hits a certain threshold. Every metric or measure should be augmented with qualitative information. That is to say, the context of the situation should be understood. If certain measures are too high, there could be extenuating circumstances that the executive needs to be aware of before making a decision. Such decisions should certainly not be automated. A good program management solution makes available qualitative as well as quantitative information to executives so that informed decisions can be made.

4. *Spending as much time creating measures as doing work*: It is important to avoid situations where obtaining the data needed to update the program and portfolio management solution becomes a drain on your teams. Most of the data that is needed should be obtainable from good downline systems that provide detailed CRM, financial, and requirements and version control information with minimal manual input from developers and testers. Be sure that the value of any measure is assessed against the time and resources needed to create it.

5. *Avoid information overload*: Many program and portfolio management solutions have more information or tooling available than what an organization may need. A search for *executive dashboards* on any search engine will undoubtedly lead to a smorgasbord of dizzying screens, reminiscent of a dashboard from a jet aircraft. Understanding what all of these metrics mean and how to use them can be complicated and difficult to learn. Focus on selecting measures and indicators that are fully relevant to your business and that your leaders understand. A good project portfolio management solution should provide a simplified, elegant, top-level view that can then be broken down into detailed components. Attempting to flash all of this detail up front on the initial screen is confusing and overwhelming to most users.

6. *As a communication facilitator*: Few things communicate better than numbers. Regardless of culture, country, or language, everyone throughout the world understands statistics and corresponding qualitative intelligence when collated and presented in a cogent way. A program and

portfolio management solution should serve as one way to communicate status, trends, and analysis between distributed executives, leaders, and teams all over the world. For a global company—as many are today—this approach is a requirement for doing business.

Creating Solutions

A modern program and portfolio management solution includes both business analytics and BI. In some disciplines, business analytics is the process of providing predictors for change, innovation, market differentiation, and process changes. Similarly, BI has typically been a gathering of current and past performance data that can track change and processes over time. The building blocks of any BI or analytics solution are key performance indicators (KPIs).

KPIs for your business are just that. They are indicators driven by your *business* that leaders use to inform their decisions. Such indicators are typically part of an executive dashboard or portfolio management solution.

It is important to note that as we drill down *lower* in the organization to the team or project manager level, the KPIs tend to be less complex and transformative in nature, and nothing more than basic metrics. For more information, refer to "Key Performance Indicators: Ideation to Creation" in the March 2018 edition of *Engineering Management Review* (Bishop, 2018).

Understanding where the data comes from or how to acquire it should not be the initial primary focus. These source and acquisition problems can eventually be solved. But, without input from the business on what is most important to them, the impact of what gets created will be marginal at best.

Having been in these kinds of discussions in many different contexts, I came up with five important characteristics that not only ensure you'll have great KPIs, but *killer* indicators. Killer performance indicators are relevant, informative, research-based, actionable, and predictive.

These characteristics are not intended to be *steps* to creating them; refer to Bishop, 2018 for those details. Also, these characteristics are not presented in any special order. The more these characteristics are integrated into your KPI solutions, the more effective they will be.

1. *Relevant*: KPIs should be based on business needs first.

It all starts with the business. Development of good BI is a management problem, not a technical one.

Any conversation regarding BI development begins with executive management. What problem(s) are you trying to solve? What kind of intelligence would make a significant difference in your decision making? What questions do you wish you had answers to?

KPI development is often mismanaged in the same way agile adoption is, being driven from the bottom up by developers or project managers instead of from the top down by executive leadership and the business. Strategic business relevancy requires top management vision and insight. A technical expert, such as a developer, IT manager, or software architect, is not necessarily a business expert; expecting such to evoke relevant KPIs from the depths of large magnitudes of available data will likely bring lackluster results.

Another problem in relation to this is the temptation to pick out easy-to-obtain metrics that are readily available. Focus on what the business needs and then work out the way to obtain the data and calculate the metric. Don't worry so much in the beginning about how the metric data will be obtained. This is considered top-down design, instead of working from the bottom up, and it is a much more effective method of problem solving. Failure to do so will create a tendency towards a *business-as-usual* mindset and a narrow set of measures.

2. *Informative*: Killer KPIs are informative indicators that tell you something about your business that you don't already know.

At one job long ago, I was asked to take over *Phase Three* of the development plan for the company's BI solution. I quickly realized that the contractors who had been working for the past three years had done little more than port data over from several existing systems into one location, along with some nice visuals. It saved the user time by providing one central location to find their data, but provided little else.

KPIs are part of an overall BI solution that is usually based on an extract, transform, and load (ETL) approach. All too often, the *transform* aspect of ETL is left out, with most KPIs being nothing more than porting data over from some antiquated system into a fancy dashboard.

Killer KPIs consider business needs, analyze data from multiple sources, and juxtapose them by using research-based algorithms to create *new knowledge* or insights that would otherwise be unavailable. With this approach, executive leadership now has special knowledge that they didn't have before, and perhaps even their competition doesn't have.

The KPI solution is transformed from a mere data aggregator to *a truly informative and transformative business tool* that provides *competitive advantage*.

In the previously mentioned example, I revamped *Phase Three* into a whole new BI strategy that followed this ideal. The results put the business at a major competitive advantage compared to their industry peers. The company continues to reap the benefits to this day.

3. *Research-based*: The composition of killer KPIs should be based on research and engaged scholarship.

Although the needs of the business should drive KPI development, such development should be based on research principles to ensure validity, accuracy, and relevance. Approaches based on anecdotal evidence, trial and error, or tribal knowledge can be error prone or inaccurate. They can also be subject to human emotion and bias. Research principles are particularly important when building complex, transformative KPIs that provide new knowledge based on computation and analysis rather than simply porting data from one system to another.

Research-based characteristics require good algorithms. An algorithm is a process or series of steps for performing a calculation, processing data, or solving a problem. For example, let's say an airline executive wants a KPI that measures the profitability of each trip. There are many inputs necessary for calculating that profit—fuel, personnel, aircraft maintenance, passengers serviced, and cost of meals, to name a few. The calculation can become even more exact by determining when the flight attendants and pilots log on and off the plane along with the various types of seats being sold and how much money is made on each. Something that may seem straightforward could become complicated to create. This is a simple example. Algorithms can become even more challenging if they include esoteric and intangible data, such as employee morale, customer satisfaction, or market pressures. These algorithms need to be based on research, instead of opinions or supposition, to ensure validity and build trust. Most important, what use are your KPIs if your decision makers second guess them or feel like they have to double check them before making decisions?

4. *Actionable*: Killer KPIs can be broken down into components or *controls*.

A good KPI is not only informative, it is *actionable*. A killer KPI can be broken down into components or *gauges and dials* so that users actually have tools to facilitate decision making and actuate change. These components could be smaller, more narrowly defined metrics or *gauges*, but could also be something that could be tuned like a *dial*, such as resource allocation.

As an example, a KPI may show that a company is losing money—but where or how? The user needs to be able to *slice and dice* the indicator or break it down in such a way as to identify where the greatest loss is occurring, and preferably, why. Your executive management should be able to use the KPI to clearly identify the problem and determine a plan of action without needless queries or verification.

5. *Predictive*: Killer KPIs are predictive, allowing leadership to visualize tomorrow, as well as today.

These days, BI has transformed into business analytics. Such solutions not only provide information on the current state of the business, but also the ability to perform predictive analysis.

High rates of technological change are resulting in increasingly turbulent and dynamic markets. This disruption has created the need for tools that inform leadership decisions on how to reduce risk, adapt quickly to changing conditions, and above all, garner the greatest market share in quickly evolving markets.

The good news is that the typical enterprise has more available data to mine than ever before. The challenge is how to leverage such big data analytics into a comprehensive BI and business analytics solution.

Unfortunately, the bad news is that our capacity to create data has vastly exceeded our ability to make sense of it. Many companies are still struggling with making sense of all of the data being gathered. Following the aforementioned *five important characteristics* will help you navigate the rough waters of these unknowns; emerging from the other side of the data swamp with a high-value BI solution.

Examples of Tools

After all of this discussion of tools, it is only fitting to show some examples. As mentioned, program and project management tools often have the complexity of an airplane cockpit, resulting in information overload. The following figures are examples of Metagility-based dashboards. Figure 9.1 is a project-level dashboard and Figure 9.2 is a program-level dashboard. These examples have the following key characteristics:

1. *Multi-track display*: The dashboards are based on a circular pattern, reflecting the *whirlpool* concept that was described in Chapter 4. This allows for easy visualization of multi-track development. Each ring within the circle aligns with a software, firmware, and hardware development track as it does in the whirlpool thought experiment. Such a dashboard could be easily customized with fewer, or more development tracks, with their placement based on the speed at which they are running.

2. *Agile triangle based*: The circle or *whirlpool* is divided into three sections, representing the agile triangle. Each section of the pie includes a development track as well, so that every domain (software, firmware, and hardware, or a combination) has a section for value, quality, and constraints. More tracks could conceivably be added to the diagram as needed, depending on the size of the organization.

3. *Top level roll-up*: The intention for the diagram is that a user could click on any section of the *pie* and drill down to a series of individual metrics. These metrics all roll up to the section displayed on the main screen, which can change color based on the cumulative status of the metrics that compose it.

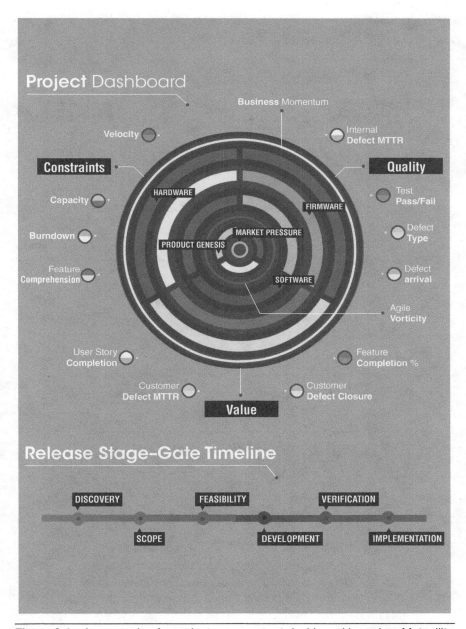

Figure 9.1   An example of a project management dashboard based on Metagility

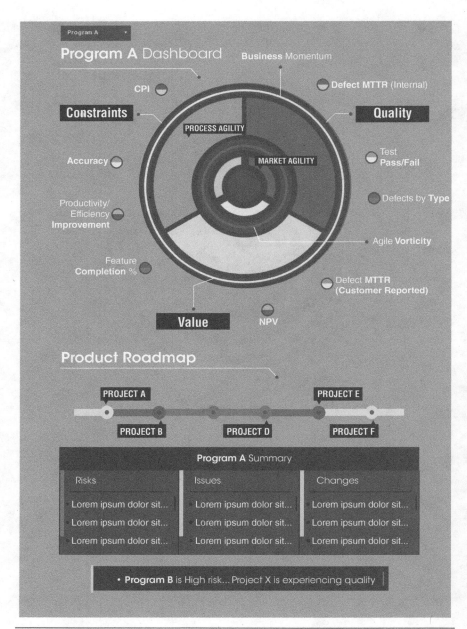

Figure 9.2   An example of a program management dashboard based on Metagility

4. *Immediate status*: Traditionally, most project managers are familiar with having a *green, yellow, or red* status for their projects, or some aspect of the project. Each section of the *pie* could be colored accordingly—in red, green, or yellow—reflecting this classic *project status*. For example, if software constraints are in trouble, the constraints section of the software ring could be colored yellow or red, thereby notifying the user of a possible issue. The user could then click on that section and drill down to more specific metrics that identify the problem. The point here is that immediate status is provided upon first glance of the dashboard. When asked, a project manager knows right away if his or her project is red, yellow, or green, and can provide this status to executives and drill down quickly for more detailed indicators.

5. *Hot-button or short metrics*: Although each section could be composed of several metrics, there may be special *hot-button* or *short* metrics for constraints, value, or quality that leaders want to know about right away. These metrics can be displayed as buttons surrounding the *whirlpool* in their respective sections, as displayed.

6. *Stage-gate alignment*: Our diagram for the project or *release* screen also includes a stage-gate timeline as described in previous chapters. This allows the user to visualize where the project is in a hybrid agile environment where stage gating is employed.

7. *Trending*: In our project diagram, the *hot buttons* include small arrows next to them that point up or down; these can indicate *trends* of movement for these particular metrics, letting the user know that the status they are seeing reflects significant and recent change. The sections of the pie can also be made to flash or be colored in *hot* or *cool* hues to indicate the same kind of trending. Again, this provides a sort of predictive intelligence in one shot for the executive.

The project screen in our example provides an information rich status all in one shot, via an elegant and simple diagram. Once the idea of the agile triangle and hybrid agile implementations are understood, the user can usually go straight to work using a tool of this type without extensive training or coaching.

Similar, to the project screen, the program screen provides the same kind of pie or *whirlpool* color-coded diagram. Since projects typically roll up into programs, the screen is a little different. The different sections of the *pie* link to metrics with a broader scope that apply across all projects within a program. Instead of a *stage-gate* line at the bottom, the program screen has a product roadmap that reflects the different planned releases with a high-level summary of each that can be selected by the cursor. At the bottom of the program screen is a summary of the selected program, which includes risks, issues, and changes. These three items are typically of particular importance to executives when evaluating programs. And below that summary is a sort of ticker tape that provides real-time updates on issues of importance. Users can select between programs and projects using menus at the top.

This is just one way of developing a dashboard for a program and portfolio management solution that meets the requirements discussed in this chapter. There are other ways of designing such a tool, but these examples attempt to prioritize simplicity and agility above other ideals.

Communication

We have seen how tools can be leveraged as a way to communicate both upward to executives and downward to team leaders and individual contributors.

When Things Go Awry Despite Your Best Efforts

Things can go wrong in any development environment, whether waterfall, agile, or hybrid. However, the failure points of each can be different. In an agile or hybrid agile environment, our case studies brought forth certain problems that were unique to these environments, and when they remained unaddressed, they ballooned into significant problems.

1. *Waterfall-style requirements decomposition*: We discussed this in a previous chapter. Business analysts are often transformed into product owners when a waterfall organization adopts agile. These business analysts are typically used to taking requirements from product managers or customers and *brainstorming* additional feature functionality that they think will be needed. This is based on the waterfall concept of attempting to anticipate every possible requirement beforehand and work it into the release so that the customer isn't disappointed later when things change. However, this results in a number of problems:
   a. Features that are rarely or never used
   b. Lost capacity due to the rarely or never-used features
   c. High or inaccurate estimates
   d. Blurry prioritization—release scopes can end up being bloated and packed to the hilt, making prioritization even more difficult than it already is
   e. Lost business—high estimates can result in losing bids to more nimble competitors

2. *Failure to use top-down design*: This applies to the item in number one, but also to development teams as well. Whether decomposing requirements or building an initial design, work should start at the top with a requirement, and then be broken down into smaller and smaller chunks that all roll back up into one. This ensures that what is being built is needed and prevents the temptation to manage things from *the ground up*. A trap that developers and analysts can run into is trying to provide a solution for a problem or requirement that is not yet well understood.

3. *Story-point inflation*: Teams provide estimates in story points that are fed into sprint planning to make commitments. When the work is completed, the sum is referred to as the velocity. This is an indicator of how fast the team was able to work. However, in some cases, leaders tend to focus on this metric—betting on the idea that teams will be able to accomplish the same number of points every time without considering the different kind of work that may be coming down the pike. If teams are measured too closely to this metric, teams may start providing larger estimates, resulting in story-point inflation, which reduces the effectiveness of the metric and makes teams more difficult to assess. Velocity should not be used as a device for competition or a yardstick for *good* or *bad* performance. It is what it is—and it can depend on many factors, not just how good your team is. Similar problems can result if executives or leaders have tunnel vision with regard to a specific metric.

4. *Failure to understand and adhere to value*: Everyone in the organization needs to understand what business value is, and that producing it is of chief importance. It's not what *you* think is most valuable—it's what the business needs. Some people have a very hard time with this concept. Business value is an executive decision that is based on the strategy, roadmap, and capabilities of the organization; and what that value is needs to flow from the top down—from the people who have access to all of the information necessary to make the right decisions.

THE NUMBER ONE SECRET INGREDIENT TO BECOMING AND REMAINING AGILE

Organizations are made up of people. You've heard it before: *your employees are your greatest asset*. It may sound tired and corny, but it is truer in today's hybrid agile development that it ever has been. For any organization to be agile, it must be made up of agile teams, and these teams must be composed of agile people. Agile people have the following characteristics, which I refer to as the *agile mindset*:

1. *They are proactive*: Agile people don't wait to be told what to do.
2. *They are go-getters*: Agile people are motivated to make a difference.
3. *They speak up*: Agile people willingly communicate status and are not afraid to make suggestions for improvement.
4. *They are not limited*: Agile people are not only good at suggesting improvements to their own area of specialization or team, but also process improvement and other aspects as well.
5. *They have a positive outlook*: Agile people have a positive attitude when it comes to the product they are developing, the organization they work in, and the company they work for.

Indeed, the number one secret ingredient to becoming and staying agile is a highly motivated and competent workforce, particularly when it comes to your development and testing teams.

In one of our case studies, a successful organization was bought out by a larger company with an emphasis on hiring less expensive people. New engineering management was gradually put in place that hired and promoted people based on social agendas. Much of the research and development department was reorganized to combine lower performing regions with higher performing ones. Leadership selections and promotions were based on politics. As a result of these changes, many high performers from all ranks left the company, and those who remained became unmotivated and disillusioned. Instead of being *proactive*, the teams began pushing back on work unless it was already broken down to the nth degree. They had no interest in development solutions or making suggestions; they wanted product owners and managers to spell out to them exactly what they wanted done—just as in a waterfall environment. Managers also began pushing back to protect their teams because they knew the capability was no longer there. Estimates became bloated, costs soared, and cycle times increased dramatically. Innovation became based on vapor-ware and existed only in marketing swag and trade shows with little real technology or development behind it. Due to its high estimates, the company began to lose business to its more agile and motivated competitors. Although the high business momentum that it had developed through years of agile management helped it to remain a market leader, growth slowed to a halt. It should be noted that this case study also reflected a phenomenon of the agile vortex. As the market for the flagship product became saturated in some of the largest regions, market pressure weakened, and so did the market agility and process agility that was driven by it. Just like our whirlpool example, as the center driver begins to weaken, the entire whirlpool slows and may eventually disappear if companies fail to create new markets. In our case study, the company's leadership maintained a laser focus on its networking technology, which was beset by competition and innovation threats from all sides. The company had acquired several smaller companies with software products in other markets, but due to politics at the top, it failed to adequately invest and grow them. It remains to be seen how long the business momentum that the company has built up over so many years will continue to drive it before profitability becomes an issue.

When confronted about the aforementioned situation, many people dismissed the challenges as *culture* or *company cultural issues*, which is a favorite term of weak leaders. Strong, effective leaders can change company culture. It may take some disruptive change in the short term, but the long-term results will be enriching. Sadly, leaders often do not make such changes unless their back is against the wall, and unfortunately, at that point it can be too late to recover. Cultivating an agile workforce with an agile mindset results in an agile culture and organization—and that is the surest way of achieving agile vorticity and becoming number one in your market!

10

THE FUTURE OF AGILE METHODS

The purpose of this book was to determine how agile processes are orchestrated in an embedded systems context. The result was an empirical analysis of a hybrid agile implementation involving high innovation within a turbulent marketplace. We now discuss *fluidity* and how this concept links together hybrid agility, embedded systems, continuous releases, and innovation within the context of our *fluid* whirlpool metaphor.

AN INQUIRY INTO HYBRID AGILITY

As our vortex metaphor implies, a hybrid agile implementation is a complex one—subject to powerful forces of market and innovation, thereby making the management of it particularly challenging. So how does the organization in such an environment organically adapt to these forces, and can they actually be controlled? Based on the results of our study, hybrid agility is a delicate balance of agile methodologies and stage-gate processes. While the agile aspects of this balance allow for higher degrees of market response, the stage-gate characteristics function largely as the *boundary conditions*. They serve as the checks and balances against agility. This is due, in large part, to the embedded systems context and the constraints that such technology places on an engineering firm. Embedded systems environments include not one, but multiple development domains that operate independently, yet are forever linked. While the business as a whole considers itself agile, each domain within the embedded context has adopted agility in very different ways.

Software, the most nimble of the domains, has adopted agile Scrum methods almost entirely. As a result of this high level of adoption, they serve as the *early responders* of the engineering team. In contrast, the slowest of the domains—hardware—has not adopted any agile methods at all and remains largely stage gate managed. Despite this fact though, our study found that hardware does employ lean concepts of rapid prototyping and a *fast-track* stage-gate pathway that it uses to maintain rhythm with the rest of the company. In the middle is the firmware domain, which has employed some aspects of agile and Scrum in terms of requirements management and stand-up meetings, yet stays away from the rigidity of two-week development sprints. Due to the shared resource nature of firmware, its complexity and the specialized expertise that is required to develop it, breaking up work into small, rigid iterative sprints is not very feasible.

In this way, the nature of the different domains places boundaries on the level of agility that each can accept. Additionally, since hardware is the slowest domain and the primary profit center for the company, the stage-gate process that is used to manage it is also used to keep the other domains grounded. Regardless of their level of agile adoption, stakeholders from each of the three domains must check in at the various gates within this waterfall process. In this way, the boundary conditions of hybrid agility are largely provided for by this stage-gate process.

Why has the engineering organization in our study adopted agility in this way? As explored earlier, causal factors for organizing development in ways such as this have been found to be:

- A desperate need to rush to market,
- A new and unique market environment, and
- A lack of experience developing under the conditions imposed by the environment (Baskerville et al., 2003; Lyytinen and Rose, 2005).

As mentioned previously, the nature of many markets in the Internet of Things has created a *gold rush* situation. This is definitely in line with the first two causal factors. Second, although some components of the business being studied have been around for years, the current combination of merged organizations has only been in place for a relatively short time. Adoption of agile methodologies within the business was started only a few years ago. Such adoption occurred fluidly and organically over time because no one involved had much prior experience when it came to implementing agile in a complex embedded systems environment with such high market turbulence.

FLUIDITY AND CONTINUOUS RELEASES: THE CAUSE FOR LEANER METHODOLOGIES

The implementation and orchestration of hybrid agility can be at least partially explained by a fluid view of agile methodology. Allowing agile implementations to be tailored provides for better accommodation of change, especially when frequent releases are necessary (Baskerville et al., 2003; Lyytinen and Rose,

2005). This can be further enhanced with parallel development, which allows developers to correct problems as they occur. As with the different domains within embedded systems, it has been shown that different methodologies can be isolated for different releases (Baskerville et al., 2003). Further, this fluid view of development methodology provides a framework that can contain the behavior of system components that have been developed with different approaches, such as software developed with agile and hardware created with waterfall.

Methodological flexibility allows different teams to find their ideal working style given the mix of the group such as firmware teams versus software teams (Baskerville et al., 2003). It also allows developers to vary their approaches when environmental constraints change, such as the examples of *C-Level* and *hero-model* approaches in our study (Vidgen, 2009). All of these *fluid methodology* characteristics are in line with our findings of hybrid agility. Although the literature shows that boundaries are needed on process innovation, we can see these boundaries in our study with the adoption level of each embedded domain and the decision points provided by stage gating.

This fluid approach to process innovation is likely to continue to influence the subject of our study as well as the industry at large. Recent studies have noted a movement from agile methods to more lean practices in software development (Wang, Conboy, and Cawley, 2012). Kanban is a good example (Sjøberg, Johnsen, and Solberg, 2012). When one examines the agile business vortex, it is easy to see that as business momentum increases and the point of vorticity becomes more challenging to achieve, the organization may be required to move from the time-boxed iteration style of Scrum to the more *fluid* process of Kanban. This strategy combines both event and time pacing into more of a *flow*. Such a strategy can better accommodate more continuous releases with less lead time (Sjøberg, Johnsen, and Solberg, 2012). Indeed, in some ways, the subject of our study has already expressed some tendencies toward this end. Even though time-boxed iterations are used within the company's agile process, *event pacing* is employed when necessary with such techniques as the aforementioned *hero model*. This allows the development organization to get things done *on the fly*, thereby allowing the business to be more reactionary when needed.

HYBRID AGILE IMPLEMENTATIONS: WHIRLPOOLS WITHIN A *RIVER OF INNOVATION*

Innovation has also been characterized as a sort of *flow* (Rogers, 2003). Innovation takes place when a technology is created and more innovation occurs as that technology is transferred to others (Rogers, 2003). In other words, when one event happens upstream it triggers other events downstream, just like a river.

These events can be influenced by market dynamics and technology turbulence. With respect to our agile business vortex, agile is accelerating the response to increasing market pressures, which in turn, is creating these whirlpools within a river of innovation. This increased agile response, and the resulting whirlpool, place higher demands on the organization. As implied earlier, this demand may force an organization to supersede the time-boxed agile iteration with a Kanban type of flow just to keep up.

In his book, *Diffusion of Innovations*, Rogers notes the following research opportunities with respect to innovation development processes (Rogers, 2003):

- How are user's needs and problems communicated to development teams?
- To what extent are technological innovations developed by *lead* users instead of research and development experts? Is the creation of innovations by end users a general pattern?
- What are the key linkages and interrelationships among the various organizations involved in the innovation development process?

In the context of embedded systems development and hybrid agility, this book provides answers to these questions. It shows how user's needs are communicated in a hybrid agile environment. This process begins with product genesis, the continuous activity of requirements comprehension and refinement. Expectations with customers are then actively managed and negotiated by the engineering organization as the product is iteratively developed. Finally, different modes of acceptance are negotiated with the customers, which typically includes intense customer involvement in the testing process.

Customers who are willing to accept a *less-than-perfect* product in exchange for added influence in product direction, enhanced service levels, and the chance to be an *early adopter* could well be considered *lead users*, as Rogers describes them. When it comes to highly innovative products or technologies, requirements comprehension within product genesis can only get so far due to gaps in knowledge. *Lead users*, in the context of hybrid agile embedded systems, are critical to bridging this gap. This gap bridging is an element of *customer acceptance* within agile orchestration. It is one way in which the designated point of agile vorticity is reached. To further answer Rogers's query, it is indeed a general pattern with respect to our context.

Finally, the results of the study explicate in detail the linkages and interrelationships among the embedded systems development organization (including software, firmware, and hardware domains), the business, and how these are *orchestrated*.

Implications for Research

Our study discovered that hybrid agility can include a mix of agile, stage-gate, and even lean concepts, depending on the domain, project, and development context. The optimum mix for this hybrid approach is often actively tailored to the needs of the organization. Additionally, our theory of agility orchestration in the vortex of embedded systems provides a deeper understanding of how hybrid agile is adopted in embedded systems, how it is managed, and the enablers or inhibitors that are specific to this context. Most important, our inquiry into the orchestration of agility revealed new insights on some very interesting processes and behaviors, such as product genesis, customer appetite, business momentum, and agile vorticity. As there are not many studies involving agility in embedded systems development, or in combining agile with stage-gate processes, we believe our study is an important addition to both of these branches of research.

One of the primary drivers for adopting agile methodologies (and indeed, a key tenet of the *Agile Manifesto*) has been stated as the need for a higher level of customer responsiveness (Alliance, 2001). Our research shows that in particularly turbulent markets with high technical innovation, whirlpools or *agile business vortices* can result. Agile innovation creates the whirlpools due to its high responsiveness to market demands or pressures. Despite the existence of such whirlpools, these forces do not run amok. We found that the organization uses agility to manipulate as well as respond. Product genesis combined with different modes of customer acceptance and customer appetite for innovation all place limitations on *how high the vortex can be revved*. Interestingly, the literature of agile methodologies is relatively silent with respect to such limitations.

Beyond customer responsiveness and technical innovation, the delineation of a clear goal or *end game* with respect to agility is also seemingly absent in the literature. The subject of our study was found to actively seek out a *sweet spot* that it can *back itself into* when it needs to conduct an enterprise-wide systems release. Doing so required the creation of some very elegant techniques for project management, systems engineering, and customer management across the enterprise. How this *agile vorticity* occurs in embedded systems is particularly important because of the different levels of agile and stage-gate integration in each domain.

In addition to these learnings in hybrid agility and embedded systems, our work contributes to agile process innovation as well. The current state of agile methodology literature has been said to be in a largely *post-agile* mode where the chief concerns have shifted from agile versus plan driven and workflow to simply creating agility in a variety of ways in all aspects of development (Baskerville, Pries-Heje, and Madsen, 2011). This process innovation of agility is focused on proactively creating fast responses to changing requirements and frequent releases using concepts from other methods such as stage gate and Kanban. Our study shows that this process innovation was impacted by the desire to reach a point of agile vorticity, a desire shared by release development and product management. The results of our research show that lean methods of rapid prototyping and *event pacing* or *hero models* were often used in place of time-boxed iterations. Elements from stage-gate models were used as *decision points* or boundaries against pure agile implementations. These are all examples of process innovation. Although these boundaries were largely influenced by the various embedded systems domains, the desire to reach a point of agile vorticity was the driving factor. This same desire for agile vorticity also impacted requirements comprehension and the linkages and interrelationships used to manage the hybrid process. Using these interconnections, *lead users* were employed extensively to bridge the gap between product knowledge within the organization and innovation. Out of all this activity, the central theory of agile vortices proved to be the common denominator.

Implications for Practice

In industry, agile methods are seldom seen in clean form. A practical implication of our study is that it shows in detail a framework for combining agile and stage-gate methods. As our research implies, process innovation is tailored to its respective environments. Each organization must focus on its own development context, projects, and limitations. In developing an approach to process innovation, the concepts of agile and stage gate, and what these methods bring to the table should always be considered. The framework brought forth in this book can be used as a *playbook* for similar organizations to manage a hybrid approach of their own.

Practical recommendations could include the introduction of more lean methods into the current hybrid mix. A move from iterative agile development to methods such as Kanban may reduce the amount of work in progress and allow for better process flow between embedded domains. This move would be in line with other research findings as more organizations with mature agile adoptions are beginning to move in this direction (Wang, Conboy, and Cawley, 2012).

Kanban has been shown to be well suited to situations where great uncertainty and high amounts of change occur more frequently than that allowed by agile iterations (Wang, Conboy, and Cawley, 2012). The use of *hero models* and C-Level projects may indicate that the subject of our study is experiencing such conditions. The literature has explicated that development teams will often resort to such methods if the existing process seems to be falling short (Vidgen, 2009). Many of the organizations studied have been working with a hybrid agile environment for a few years now, and the current implementation is considered relatively mature. Based on the literature, this indicates that embedded systems organizations may consider moving to leaner methods (Wang, Conboy, and Cawley, 2012). Another indicator for a need to move to leaner methods could be difficulty or failure to achieve a point of agile vorticity. Very high responsiveness to market pressures can continue to increase to a level that demands replacing the time-boxed agile iteration with more of a Kanban flow. Organizations considered mature in their adoption of agile or hybrid approaches should be mindful of their agile vorticity. This may indicate that it is time to change the approach to continuous process innovation in their business.

TRENDS: LOOKING AHEAD

In Chapter 1 we discussed how the *Agile Manifesto* has changed since its inception—at least in practice, if not officially. Not only have the agile concepts themselves changed, but also the enablers of it. Just like a perfect storm, certain conditions must exist for the tenets described previously to be effective.

What follows is a discussion of trends that will continue to shape agile concepts and the companies that adopt and implement them.

Data Science Along with Advanced Tooling Will Drive Decisions

As mentioned previously, there are possible pitfalls around basing decisions on one or two measures. However, there should be no illusions about the fact that artificial intelligence is slowly coming into its own. It is not inconceivable that agile management applications and program and portfolio management solutions could advance to a level as to make decisions about resource allocation, business value, and program portfolio mix. The amount of *big data* available has greatly outpaced our ability to make sense of it, but algorithms capable of doing so are quickly catching up. Your program and portfolio solution may not be running your business for you anytime soon, but it may certainly be able to make intelligent recommendations on what products to drop, changes to make in your teams, and yes, how to reach agile vorticity for your company. Adoption of agile-based program and portfolio management and product roadmapping should be an integral component of any agile transformation strategy today.

Approaches to Communication Methods Must Be Continually Re-evaluated

Communication is a critical and often overlooked component of agile success. Even though it is explicitly called out in the *Agile Manifesto*, few organizations have placed specifics around *interactions*. Metagility addresses this by breaking down interactions into six distinct classes, each of which is managed in a certain way to achieve success. As agile tools become more sophisticated, their usage will become more prevalent and critical to making these interactions happen and getting the most out of them. A clear process for supporting and implementing the interactions in Metagility and the right tooling for documenting and disseminating the knowledge gleaned from them should be integrated into any agile transformation effort.

Agile Organizations Require Agile Individuals

In the last chapter we talked about the importance of agile people and how critical they are to making—or breaking—agile organizations. When it comes to motivating employees to become and stay agile in order to maintain a level of high engagement and participation and to take advantage of all of the available brain power that their team has to offer, many managers assume this is based on compensation or prestige (as in being a team lead, Scrum Master, or architect). However, this is only part of the equation, and in fact, may not play as big a role as you may think. The following list includes three tenets that will help when it comes to cultivating agile individuals:

- Teams must understand not only the what and how, but the why as well.
  - In a waterfall environment, it was common for product managers and architects to create a design for a solution, and then throw it over the wall for developers and testers to build. To have agile teams, these sorts of walls must be torn down. Developers can do a much better job if they understand *why* something is requested the way it is, as opposed to just the *what* and *how*. Only by understanding the *why* behind a requirement or user story are they going to be able to provide suggestions for improvement. With that said, a user story should always have, among other things, a statement that describes the what, how, and why. The typical sentence included in these stories goes along the lines of: "as a system user, I need to do *x*, so I can accomplish *y*."

- Visibility into product genesis and development should be available to every level—from the executive down to the individual contributor.
  - This does not mean that product managers, product owners, and other stakeholders intimately involved in the product genesis process must communicate to the whole world, nor does it mean that developers should be constantly burdened with providing status or documentation. What this does mean is that there should be access to and from every level to see what is going on with the product development at each stage. Traditionally, this has been very difficult to accomplish without consuming a lot of people's time, but the right supporting tools or applications can provide this visibility.
- Ideas and opinions should be allowed to flow freely without hindrance or fear of ridicule.
  - All team members need to feel valued and nothing accomplishes this more effectively than providing a forum in which they can be heard, listened to, and appreciated. Everyone has valuable input to offer, and the more employees feel like they have a voice, the more engaged they will become. This cultivates a sense that everyone has a *stake in the game* or to put it more succinctly, a *stake in the company's success*. Create this and you will have to worry very little about employee apathy. Estimates will not inflate, cycle times will stabilize, and in short, your company will become more nimble and win more business as a result.

Agile Companies Require Agile Leaders

As has been discussed, executive support and sponsorship is absolutely critical to any agile transformation effort, yet it is one of the most cited *missing items* when surveying agile experts. All too often, agile is considered by executives to be a *developer process* or *something for the project managers to worry about*. Today, it's no longer just about agile teams, it's about agile businesses. It takes agile leaders to not only support the transformation and execution of any agile initiative, but to express the kind of leadership that can change cultures and attitudes. In the future, companies will be looking for and requiring *agile leaders*.

Agile Is Becoming Integral to Strategic Planning

For an entire business to be agile, agility needs to find its way into strategic planning. Agile-based portfolio management and program/project management combined with continuous delivery and product roadmapping are required for the whole system to be successful. By focusing on putting the proper feedback loops into place using Metagility, agile vorticity can be achieved—not once or twice, but regularly through agile strategic planning.

A Caution Regarding *Agile Frameworks*

Today, a number of *agile frameworks* abound and are being readily adopted. Some of the most well-known are scaled agile framework for the enterprise (SAFe), disciplined agile framework (DA), and large-scale Scrum (LeSS) just to name a few. These frameworks purport to accomplish many things, the most significant of which is the ability to solve the problem of *managing agile at scale* or *scaling agile*. This is based on the idea that the *Agile Manifesto* was written mostly by people from small companies who were used to working with small teams. These frameworks were developed in large part as a way to compensate for this and allow agile to be adopted in larger enterprises. These frameworks are not necessarily bad, but there are a few things to keep in mind when evaluating such frameworks and selecting one for adoption.

Earlier, we discussed the work of an agility researcher, Kieran Conboy. He developed a taxonomy for evaluating agile methodologies and practices, and one of the important tenets he found was that any agile methodology or approach should never detract from (Conboy, 2009):

1. Economy
2. Quality
3. Simplicity

If such a methodology is indeed found to detract from any of these three elements, then it cannot be called agile. Upon close examination, many of the so-called agile frameworks do not meet these criteria. The one tenet that is most commonly missed is *simplicity*. Agile is all about simplicity and if a framework makes it into a convoluted mess of a process, then that is not an agile framework, it's something else entirely. When examining the diagrams or *maps* of some of these frameworks, they are so complicated that it requires hours of training to understand them and even more to implement. One common failing these frameworks have is the idea that agility must be integrated into every facet of the company—so much so that even the janitors must have a Scrum meeting to decide which bathrooms to clean. That's a facetious statement, but in a sense, it is not far from reality. When researching these frameworks, many of them are so bloated and process heavy it almost appears that someone took agile and tried to make it into an enterprise waterfall process. Metagility certainly supports the concept of an agile business—from strategic planning and executive management all the way down to the agile teams—but the difference is that it focuses on *the product engine*. The product engine is created by market and process agility to meet agile vorticity at a certain point with a systems release or product that is beyond the competition in terms of customer satisfaction and technological innovation. Air conditioning and leather seats are nice, but if you are trying to have the fastest car to win the race, it's the drivetrain that counts. Many of the frameworks lose sight of the simplicity, economy, and quality focus that agility is—failing to enhance the product creation engine, while spending too much time on extra gauges, power windows, and sound systems. Not that those aren't good things, but in the context of our metaphor, they detract from the purpose and lose sight of the goal post.

Be cautious about jumping on the bandwagon of any *agile framework*; and before doing so, ask yourself if it truly meets Conboy's requirements for quality, economy, and simplicity. Remember that as agile as the framework may sound and as popular as it may be, if it doesn't meet these criteria, it should be approached with caution.

Agile Evolution and Natural Selection

Studies show that companies and industries are increasingly adopting agile concepts. Those that do will garner higher market share over time—slowly but surely edging out companies that are not agile, or not as much so. Organizations that are continually resistant to agile due to *cultural* or other concerns will be slowly eclipsed by their competitors. Similarly, individuals who are resistant to agile will be supplanted by more agile ones. In short, people, organizations, companies, and even industries that fail to change may find themselves endangered and as extinct as a sabre-toothed tiger—relegated to becoming a discussion point for business school students on how to avoid failure.

New Markets Must Be Continually Sought Out

The agile vortex can be visualized as a whirlpool, or even a galaxy, driven by the central pull of market pressure for a certain product line. As the pressure for that product line begins to weaken for any reason, the vortex as a whole—including the market agility, process agility, and product engine that compose it—will weaken as well. In one of our case studies, the company failed to invest in other markets as demand for its primary product began to wane. They made a number of acquisitions for products in other markets, but invested very little to grow them and internally even stopped selling them in many cases. The organization fell victim to internal politics as executives and other stakeholders became afraid of losing power and influence to managers of the other product lines. Executive leadership began to have the idea that their current product lineup was a *winning recipe* that was not to be tampered with, and so other promising product lines were starved for attention, support, and investment, even though the company continued to use them as a *feather in the cap* when producing sales literature or attending trade shows. Since the company built up significant business momentum over time, the system kept running for a while even though the company was continually losing new business to its more nimble and innovative competitors. Slowly but surely, the company began to lay off employees and close offices. Although it continued to survive, its spot as a number one innovator in its market was slowly lost.

Companies must continually seek out new markets. An agile vortex can, in a sense, be viewed as a market iteration as a company moves from one market to the other. Some markets last for decades and some for only a few years, but either way, it is critical to seek out *new galaxies* to participate in—no matter how successful the primary one may be. Again, agile businesses require agile people, and that means people who will change with the technology just like the companies they work for. If markets for certain hardware products are becoming saturated, and innovative competitors are focusing more on their software to differentiate themselves, then stakeholders within the company need to change their focus as well. All too often, people try to force the company—and by extension the market—to fit their own needs and desires, and an agile culture means exactly the opposite.

Agility Will Continue to Evolve

Changing agility has been a continuing theme of this book. Agile concepts will continue to morph as the markets that their proponents play in continue to change at an increasing pace. Hybrid agility will continue to grow and become a more dominant force as not only processes like waterfall and agile, but the development of software, firmware, and hardware evolve as one.

REFERENCES

Abrahamsson, Pekka, Kieran Conboy, and Xiaofeng Wang. (2009). 'Lots done, more to do': the current state of agile systems development research. Editorial, *European Journal of Information Systems*, pp. 281–284. Retrieved from http://ezproxy.gsu.edu:2048/login?url=http://search.ebscohost.com/login .aspx?direct=true&db=bth&AN=44385902&site=bsi-live.

Alliance, The Agile. (2001). *Manifesto for Agile Software Development*. Retrieved August 12, 2014, from http://www.agilemanifesto.org.

Arteta, B.M. and R.E. Giachetti. (2004). A measure of agility as the complexity of the enterprise system. *Robotics and Computer-Integrated Manufacturing, 20*(6), 495–503. doi: http://dx.doi.org/10.1016/j.rcim.2004.05.008.

Bae, Jung Ho, Heung-Seok Chae, and Carl K. Chang. (2013). A metric towards evaluating understandability of state machines: An empirical study. *Information and Software Technology, 55*(12), 2172.

Barlow, Jordan B., Mark Jeffrey Keith, David W. Wilson, Ryan M. Schuetzler, Paul Benjamin Lowry, Anthony Vance, and Justin Scott Giboney. (2011). Overview and Guidance on Agile Development in Large Organizations. *Communications of AIS, 29*, 25–4.

Baskerville, Richard and Jan Pries-Heje. (2004). Short cycle time systems development. *Information Systems Journal, 14*(3), 237–264. doi: 10.1111/j.1365-2575 .2004.00171.x.

Baskerville, Richard, Jan Pries-Heje, and Sabine Madsen. (2011). Post-agility: What follows a decade of agility? *Information and Software Technology, 53*(5), 543–555. doi: 10.1016/j.infsof.2010.10.010.

Baskerville, Richard, Balasubramaniam Ramesh, Linda Levine, Jan Pries-Heje, and Sandra Slaughter. (2003). Is Internet-Speed Software Development Different? *IEEE Software, 20*(6), 70–77.

Bavani, Raja. (2012). Distributed Agile, Agile Testing, and Technical Debt. *IEEE Software, 29*(6), 28–33. doi: 10.1109/MS.2012.155.

Bishop, D.A. (2018). Key Performance Indicators: Ideation to Creation. *IEEE Engineering Management Review, 46*(1), 13–15.

Boehm, B. (2002). Get Ready for Agile Methods, with Care. *Computer, 35*(1), 64–69. doi: 10.1109/2.976920.

Boehm, Barry and Richard Turner. (2005). Management Challenges to Implementing Agile Processes in Traditional Development Organizations. *IEEE Software, 22*(5), 30–39.

Broadus, William. (2013). The Challenges of Being Agile in DOD. *Defense AT&L, 42*(1), 4–9.

Cao, Lan, Kannan Mohan, Xu Peng, and Balasubramaniam Ramesh. (2009). A framework for adapting agile development methodologies. *European Journal of Information Systems, 18*(4), 332–343. doi: 10.1057/ejis.2009.26.

Caswell, N.S. and A. Nigam, "Agility = change + coordination," Seventh IEEE International Conference on E-Commerce Technology Workshops, Munich, Germany, 2005, pp. 131–139. doi: 10.1109/CECW.2005.3.

Christian, I., H. Ismail, J. Mooney, S. Snowden, M. Toward, and D. Zhang. (2001). Agile manufacturing transitional strategies. In Proceedings of the Fourth SMESME International Conference, Aalborg, Denmark, pp. 69–77.

Conboy, Kieran. (2009). Agility from First Principles: Reconstructing the Concept of Agility in Information Systems Development. *Information Systems Research, 20*(3), 329–354.

Conboy, Kieran, Sharon Coyle, Xiaofeng Wang, and Minna Pikkarainen. (2011). People over Process: Key Challenges in Agile Development. *IEEE Software, 28*(4), 48–57. doi: 10.1109/MS.2010.132.

Conboy, Kieran and Lorraine Morgan. (2011). Beyond the customer: Opening the agile systems development process. *Information and Software Technology, 53*(5), 535–542. doi: 10.1016/j.infsof.2010.10.007.

Dingsøyr, Torgeir, Sridhar Nerur, VenuGopal Balijepally, and Nils Brede Moe. (2012). A decade of agile methodologies: Towards explaining agile software development. Editorial, *Journal of Systems and Software*, pp. 1213–1221. Retrieved from http://ezproxy.gsu.edu:2048/login?url=http://search.ebscohost.com/login.aspx?direct=true&db=bth&AN=74095428&site=bsi-live.

Douglass, Bruce Powel. (2004). *Real Time Agility.* Upper Saddle River, NJ: Addison-Wesley.

Dove, R. (1994). Tools for analyzing and constructing agility. In Proceedings of the Third Annual Agility Forum Conference/Workshop, Austin, TX.

Dove, R. (2002). *Response Ability: The Language, Structure, and Culture of the Agile Enterprise.* John Wiley and Sons, Hoboken, NJ.

Drury, Meghann, Kieran Conboy, and Ken Power. (2012). Obstacles to decision making in Agile software development teams. *Journal of Systems and Software, 85*(6), 1239–1254. doi: 10.1016/j.jss.2012.01.058.

Dybå, Tore and Torgeir Dingsøyr. (2008). Empirical studies of agile software development: A systematic review. *Information and Software Technology, 50*(9–10), 833–859. doi: http://dx.doi.org/10.1016/j.infsof.2008.01.006.

Eisenhardt, Kathleen M. and Shona L. Brown. (1998). Time Pacing: Competing in Markets that Won't Stand Still. (cover story). *Harvard Business Review, 76*(2), 59–69.

Fitzgerald, Brian, Gerard Hartnett, and Kieran Conboy. (2006). Customising agile methods to software practices at Intel Shannon. *European Journal of Information Systems, 15*(2), 200–213. doi: 10.1057/palgrave.ejis.3000605.

Floyd, Christiane. (1992). *Software Development and Reality Construction.* Springer.

Galliers, R.D. (1991). *Choosing Information Systems Research Approaches in Information Systems Research*: Alfred Waller.

Giachetti, Ronald E., Luis D. Martinez, Oscar A. Sáenz, and Chin-Sheng Chen. (2003). Analysis of the structural measures of flexibility and agility using a measurement theoretical framework. *International Journal of Production Economics, 86*(1), 47–62. doi: http://dx.doi.org/10.1016/S0925-5273(03)00004-5.

Goldman, S.L., R.N. Nagel, and K. Preiss, (1995). *Agile Competitors and Virtual Organizations: Strategies for Enriching the Customer* (Vol. 8). Van Nostrand Reinhold, NY.

Goranson, H. (2000). *The Agile Virtual Enterprise, Cases, Metrics, and Tools.* Quorum Books, Westport, CT.

Greer, D. and G. Ruhe. (2004). Software release planning: an evolutionary and iterative approach. *Information and Software Technology, 46*(4), 243. doi: 10.1016/j.infsof.2003.07.002.

Haeckel, Stephan H. (1999). Adaptive Enterprise: Creating and Leading Sense-And-Respond Organizations. 10.1016/S0024-6301(00)00018-2.

Highsmith, J. (2010). *Agile Project Management* (2nd ed.). Pearson Education, Inc., Boston, MA.

Highsmith, J. and A. Cockburn. (2001). Agile software development: the business of innovation. *Computer, 34*(9), 120–127. doi: 10.1109/2.947100.

Iivari, Juhani and Netta Iivari. (2011). The relationship between organizational culture and the deployment of agile methods. *Information and Software Technology, 53*(5), 509–520. doi: 10.1016/j.infsof.2010.10.008.

Ismail, H.S. and H. Sharifi. (2006). A balanced approach to building agile supply chains, *International Journal of Physical Distribution & Logistics Management, 36*(6), 431–444.

Janson, Marius A. and L. Douglas Smith. (1985). Prototyping for Systems Development: A Critical Appraisal. *MIS Quarterly, 9*(4), 305–316.

Karlstrom, Daniel and Per Runeson. (2005). Combining Agile Methods with Stage-Gate Project Management. *IEEE Software, 22*(3), 43–49.

Kettunen, Petri and Maarit Laanti. (2005). How to steer an embedded software project: tactics for selecting the software process model. *Information and Software Technology, 47*(9), 587–608. doi: 10.1016/j.infsof.2004.11.001.

Kidd, P.T. (1995). *Agile Manufacturing: Forging New Frontiers.* Addison-Wesley Longman Publishing Co., Inc., New York, NY.

Klein, Heinz K. and Michael D. Myers. (1999). A Set of Principles for Conducting and Evaluating Interpretive Field Studies in Information Systems. *MIS Quarterly, 23*(1), 67–93.

Kong, Sue, Julie E. Kendall, and Kenneth E. Kendall. (2012). Project contexts and use of agile software development methodology in practice: a case study. *Journal of the Academy of Business and Economics, 12*(2), 1–15.

Kumar, A. and J. Motwani. (1995). A methodology for assessing time-based competitive advantage of manufacturing firms, *International Journal of Operations & Production Management, 15*(2), 36–53. https://doi.org/10.1108/01443579510080409.

Kurian, T. (2006). Agility metrics: a quantitative fuzzy based approach for measuring agility of a software process. In ISAM-Proceedings of International Conference on Agile Manufacturing (Volume 6).

Laanti, Maarit, Outi Salo, and Pekka Abrahamsson. (2011). Agile methods rapidly replacing traditional methods at Nokia: A survey of opinions on agile transformation. *Information and Software Technology, 53*(3), 276–290. doi: 10.1016/j.infsof.2010.11.010.

Lomas, C.D.W., J. Wilkinson, P.G. Maropoulos, and P.C. Matthews. (2006). Measuring design process agility for the single company product development process. *International Journal of Agile Manufacturing, 9*(2), 105–112.

Lyytinen, Kalle and Gregory M. Rose. (2005). How Agile is Agile Enough? Toward a Theory of Agility in Software Development. *Business Agility and Information Technology Diffusion*, pp. 203–225: Springer.

Malmbrandt, Malin and Pär Åhlström. (2013). An instrument for assessing lean service adoption. *International Journal of Operations & Production Management, 33*(9), 1131–1165. doi: 10.1108/IJOPM-05-2011-0175.

Maruping, Likoebe M., Viswanath Venkatesh, and Ritu Agarwal. (2009). A Control Theory Perspective on Agile Methodology Use and Changing User Requirements. *Information Systems Research, 20*(3), 377–399.

Mathiassen, Lars and Jan Pries-Heje. (2006). Business agility and diffusion of information technology. *European Journal of Information Systems, 15*(2), 116–119. doi: 10.1057/palgrave.ejis.3000610.

McAvoy, John, Tadhg Nagle, and David Sammon. (2013). Using mindfulness to examine ISD agility. *Information Systems Journal, 23*(2), 155–172. doi: 10.1111/j.1365-2575.2012.00405.x.

McHugh, Orla, Kieran Conboy, and Michael Lang. (2012). Agile Practices: The Impact on Trust in Software Project Teams. *IEEE Software, 29*, 71–76. doi: 10.1109/MS.2011.118.

Metes, G., J. Gundry, and P. Bradish. (1998). *Agile Networking: Competing Through the Internet and Intranet.* Prentice-Hall, Inc., Upper Saddle River, NJ.

Mohan, Kannan, Balasubramaniam Ramesh, and Vijayan Sugumaran. (2010). Integrating Software Product Line Engineering and Agile Development. *IEEE Software, 27*(3), 48–55.

Morlok, Edward K. and David J. Chang. (2004). Measuring capacity flexibility of a transportation system. *Transportation Research Part A: Policy and Practice, 38*(6), 405–420.

Muthitacharoen, Achita and Khawaja A. Saeed. (2009). Examining User Involvement in Continuous Software Development (A case of error reporting system). *Communications of the ACM, 52*(9), 113–117.

Nagel, R. and R. Dove. (1991). *21st Century Manufacturing. Enterprise Strategy.* 1991, Iacocca Institute, Lehigh University, Bethlehem, PA.

Orr, Ken. (2004). Agile requirements: Opportunity or oxymoron? *IEEE Software, 21*(3), 71–73.

Persson, John Stouby, Lars Mathiassen, and Ivan Aaen. (2012). Agile distributed software development: enacting control through media and context. *Information Systems Journal, 22*(6), 411–433. doi: 10.1111/j.1365-2575 .2011.00390.x.

Port, Daniel and Tung Bui. (2009). Simulating mixed agile and plan-based requirements prioritization strategies: proof-of-concept and practical implications. *Eur J Inf Syst, 18*(4), 317–331.

Pozzebon, Marlei, Maira Petrini, Rodrigo Bandeira de Mello, and Lionel Garreau. (2011). Unpacking researchers' creativity and imagination in grounded theorizing: An exemplar from IS research. *Information and Organization, 21*(4), 177–193. doi: http://dx.doi.org/10.1016/j.infoandorg.2011.09.001.

Qumer, A. and B. Henderson-Sellers. (2008). A framework to support the evaluation, adoption, and improvement of agile methods in practice. *Journal of Systems and Software, 81*(11), 1899–1919. doi: http://dx.doi.org/10.1016/ j.jss.2007.12.806.

Qureshi, M. Rizwan Jameel. (2012). Agile software development methodology for medium and large projects. *IET Software, 6*(4), 358–363. doi: 10.1049/ iet-sen.2011.0110.

Ramesh, Balasubramaniam, Lan Cao, Kannan Mohan, and Xu Peng. (2006). Can Distributed Software Development Be Agile? *Communications of the ACM, 49*(10), 41–46.

Ramesh, Balasubramaniam, Lan Cao, and Richard Baskerville. (2010). Agile requirements engineering practices and challenges: an empirical study. *Information Systems Journal, 20*(5), 449–480. doi: 10.1111/j.1365-2575 .2007.00259.x.

Ramesh, Balasubramaniam, Kannan Mohan, and Lan Cao. (2012). Ambidexterity in Agile Distributed Development: An Empirical Investigation. *Information Systems Research, 23*, 323–339. doi: 10.1287/isre.1110.0351.

Ramesh, G. and S.R. Devadasan. (2007). Literature Review on the Agile Manufacturing Criteria, *Journal of Manufacturing Technology Management, 18* (2), 182–201. https://doi.org/10.1108/17410380710722890.

Rogers, Everett M. (2003). *Diffusion of Innovations* (5th ed.). New York: Free Press, NY.

Ronkainen, Jussi and Pekka Abrahamsson. (2003). Software Development under Stringent Hardware Constraints: Do Agile Methods Have a Chance? In Michele Marchesi and Giancarlo Succi (Editors), *Extreme Programming and Agile Processes in Software Engineering 2675*, 73–79. Springer Berlin Heidelberg.

Royce, Winston W. (1970). *Managing the development of large software systems.* Paper presented at the proceedings of IEEE WESCON.

Salo, O. and P. Abrahamsson. (2008). Agile methods in European embedded software development organisations: a survey on the actual use and usefulness of Extreme Programming and Scrum. *IET Software, 2*(1), 58–64. doi: 10.1049/iet-sen:20070038.

Schatz, Bob and Ibrahim Abdelshafi. (2005). Primavera Gets Agile: A Successful Transition to Agile Development. *IEEE Software, 22*(3), 36–42.

Sharifi, H. and Z. Zhang. (1999). A methodology for achieving agility in manufacturing organisations: An introduction, *International Journal of Production Economics, 62*(1–2), 7–22.

Sharifi, H. and Z. Zhang. (2001). Agile manufacturing in practice—Application of a methodology, *International Journal of Operations & Production Management, 21*(5–6), 772–794. https://doi.org/10.1108/01443570110390462.

Sheffield, Jim and Julien Lemétayer. (2013). Factors associated with the software development agility of successful projects. *International Journal of Project Management, 31*(3), 459–472. doi: 10.1016/j.ijproman.2012.09.011.

Sieger, D.B., A.B. Badiru, and M. Milatovic. (2000). A metric for agility measurement in product development. *IIE Transactions, 32*(7), 637–645.

Sjøberg, Dag I.K., Anders Johnsen, and Jørgen Solberg. (2012). Quantifying the Effect of Using Kanban versus Scrum: A Case Study. *IEEE Software, 29*(5), 47–53. doi: 10.1109/MS.2012.110.

Skaistis, Bruce. (2008). Measuring IT agility. *Enterprise Innovation, 4*(1), 40.

Sliger, M. and S. Broderick. (2009). "Selling agile: how to get buy-in from your team, customers, and managers", Presentation, PMI Global Congress North America 2009.

Smith, Michael, James Miller, Lily Huang, and Albert Tran. (2009). A More Agile Approach to Embedded System Development. *IEEE Software, 26*(3), 50–57.

Ståhl, Daniel and Jan Bosch. (2014). Modeling continuous integration practice differences in industry software development. *Journal of Systems and Software, 87*, 48–59. doi: 10.1016/j.jss.2013.08.032.

Stankovic, John A. (1996). Strategic directions in real-time and embedded systems. *ACM Comput. Surv., 28*(4), 751–763. doi: 10.1145/242223.242291.

Strauss, Anselm and Juliet Corbin. (1990). *Basics of Qualitative Research: Grounded Theory Procedures and Techniques.* Sage, Newbury Park, CA.

Sugimori, Y., K. Kusunoki, F. Cho, and S. Uchikawa. (1977). Toyota production system and Kanban system Materialization of just-in-time and respect-for-human system. *International Journal of Production Research, 15*(6), 553–564. doi: 10.1080/00207547708943149.

Svahnberg, Mikael, Tony Gorschek, Robert Feldt, Richard Torkar, Saad Bin Saleem, and Muhammad Usman Shafique. (2010). A systematic review on strategic release planning models. *Information and Software Technology, 52*(3), 237–248. doi: http://dx.doi.org/10.1016/j.infsof.2009.11.006.

Tedre, Matti and Erkki Sutinen. (2008). Three traditions of computing: what educators should know. *Computer Science Education, 18*(3), 153–170. doi: 10.1080/08993400802332332.

Toward, M., H. Ismail, I. Christian, and S. Snowden. (2003). The application of agility. In Advances in Manufacturing Technology Conference *17*, 443–448. Taylor & Francis, Ltd.

Van de Ven, A. (2007). *Engaged Scholarship: A Guide for Organizational and Social Research.* Oxford University Press, New York, NY.

Van Horenbeek, Adriaan and Liliane Pintelon. (2014). Development of a maintenance performance measurement framework—using the analytic network process (ANP) for maintenance performance indicator selection. *Omega, 42*(1), 33–46. doi: 10.1016/j.omega.2013.02.006.

Vidgen, Richard. (2009). Coevolving Systems and the Organization of Agile Software Development. *Information Systems Research, 20*(3), 355–376.

Vinekar, Vishnu, Craig W. Slinkman, and Sridhar Nerur. (2006). Can Agile and Traditional Systems Development Approaches Coexist? An Ambidextrous View. *Information Systems Management, 23*(3), 31–42.

Vlaanderen, Kevin, Slinger Jansen, Sjaak Brinkkemper, and Erik Jaspers. (2011). The agile requirements refinery: Applying SCRUM principles to software product management. *Information and Software Technology, 53*(1), 58–70. doi: http://dx.doi.org/10.1016/j.infsof.2010.08.004.

Wang, Xiaofeng, Kieran Conboy, and Oisin Cawley. (2012). "Leagile" software development: An experience report analysis of the application of lean approaches in agile software development. *Journal of Systems and Software,* 85(6), 1287–1299. doi: 10.1016/j.jss.2012.01.061.

Wang, Xiaofeng, Kieran Conboy, and Minna Pikkarainen. (2012). Assimilation of agile practices in use. *Information Systems Journal,* 22(6), 435–455. doi: 10.1111/j.1365-2575.2011.00393.x.

Yauch, Charlene. (2011). Measuring agility as a performance outcome. *Journal of Manufacturing Technology Management,* 22(3), 384–404.

Yin, Robert K. (2003). *Case Study Research Design and Methods.* Sage, Thousand Oaks, CA.

Zhang, Z. and H. Sharifi. (2000). A methodology for achieving agility in manufacturing organisations, *International Journal of Operations & Production Management,* 20(4), 496–513.

INDEX

Note: Page numbers followed by "f" indicate figures and those followed by "t" indicate tables.